# THE PROMISE

# THE PROMISE

## EXPERIENCING GOD'S GREATEST GIFT THE HOLY SPIRIT

## TONY EVANS

Renaissance Productions

**MOODY PRESS**

CHICAGO

ISBN: 0-8024-3921-7

*This book is gratefully dedicated to
my good friend and colleague
Ramesh Richard,
whose spiritual life, theological astuteness,
and personal camaraderie
have done more for me than words can ever express.*

*"I thank my God in all my remembrance of you."
(Philippians 1:3)*

# CONTENTS

# WITH GRATITUDE

Once again I am extremely grateful to the Moody Press family for their partnership with me in the development of this project. Special thanks go to Greg Thornton, whose vision has made this book possible; to Bill Thrasher, who oversees the marketing of this work; to Cheryl Dunlop, whose editorial skills helped produce a quality finished product; and to my close friend Philip Rawley, who organizes my ideas and words into a sharp, clear literary style.

# INTRODUCTION

**L**et me set a scene for you. This is hypothetical, so give me a little theatrical license here.

You have just been to the store and seen the most incredible refrigerator you can imagine. The thing is huge. It not only has all the bells and whistles you expect, it has some you've never seen before. This refrigerator will do everything but turn the lights off, put the dog out, and lock up at night. It costs thousands more than a normal refrigerator, but you buy it anyway because it is unbelievable.

The store delivers your new refrigerator to your home. In your excitement, you shop for all the goodies you want to store in it. You stock that refrigerator with everything you can think of, then retire for the evening.

The next morning you run into the kitchen excitedly, only to discover that the milk is spoiled, the ice cream is running out the bottom of the freezer compartment, and the vegetables are changing color. Your new refrigerator is not working.

You call the store to give the people there a piece of your Christian mind. The man says, "I don't understand it. Open the door and see if the light comes on." You open the door. No light.

"Put your ear up close to the refrigerator and tell me if you can hear the hum of the motor." You do, and there's no hum.

He then says, "There's a cord at the back of your refrigerator. Please check to see whether it has been plugged in." Lo and behold, you go to the back of your new refrigerator and there it is. The cord has not been plugged in.

You come back to the telephone and say, "You're right. The cord was not plugged in. But for the kind of money I paid for this refrigerator, that shouldn't matter. This thing should work anyway."

I told you this was pretend, so stay with me. If you were to say this, at this point you would probably receive a brief lesson in how appliances work.

The man would proceed to say to you, "No, no, you don't understand. Appliances are dependent in nature. Although your refrigerator has all the parts and Freon® necessary to cool all the food you put in it, it was manufactured in such a way that it will not operate without an invisible power source called electricity. Unless you plug in that cord, your food will continue to spoil."

Now that's a long way around to state an obvious truth. No matter how much you paid for it, your refrigerator won't work the way it was designed to work unless it is plugged in to electric power. Neither will your spiritual life work unless it is plugged in to Holy Ghost power.

When God saved us, He gave us all the component parts necessary for spiritual life and victory. But we are dependent creatures. We have not been designed to work on our own. Only as we are empowered by the indwelling Holy Spirit will we produce what our lives are supposed to produce. If you don't rely on that power, don't be surprised if the milk of your life turns sour and the ice cream begins to melt.

God never intended us to live the Christian life on our own. The Holy Spirit is His supernatural gift to make the new being we have become alive and real. In the pages that follow I will seek to demonstrate from Scripture and illustrate from real life the importance of the Person and work of the Holy Spirit.

Our study will seek to avoid the extreme of many in the fundamentalist community who allow the doctrine of the Holy Spirit to be a smokescreen which keeps them from experiencing His reality, resulting in a dead orthodoxy and truth without experience. On the other hand, we want to avoid the extreme of many in the charismatic community who seek an experience at the expense of doctrine, which results in an empty, emotional fanaticism.

It is my contention that this wonderful yet mysterious member of the Trinity is not some esoteric Being or irrelevant theological truth unrelated to time, space, and our day-to-day realities. On the contrary, the Holy Spirit is the heart and soul of the Christian faith and the victorious Christian life, and if we don't get plugged in to Him we will continue to experience defeat after defeat. The Holy Spirit is necessary to make sure that our knowledge about God is transformed into an experience with God. He is a Person who performs, and He represents a doctrine that delivers.

Once plugged in we will experience the supernatural wonder of a life in which the "Freon" of God's grace flows through the conduits of our new nature, keeping our spiritual lives at a temperature that, like an expensive refrigerator, protects us from spoil and ruin and keeps us fresh for God and nourishing to others.

# PART ONE
# THE HOLY SPIRIT'S PRESENCE

# CHAPTER ONE

# EXPERIENCING THE SPIRIT'S PROMISE

The Holy Spirit is not merely a nice addendum to the Christian faith. He is at the heart and core of it. He is not merely a force or an influence. He is the third Person of the Trinity, God Himself.

If there is anything you and I must understand if we are going to live what is commonly called the victorious Christian life, it is the Person and ministry of the Holy Spirit. Therefore, my task in this book is to try to address in as biblical and practical a way as possible the issues surrounding this most important Person.

So we've got a huge task to undertake in these pages, for several reasons.

First, because my subject is the eternal God Himself, in the Person of God the Holy Spirit. So I've got a huge subject, and the most I can hope to do is help you understand and experience the presence and work of the Holy Spirit in a way you never have before. I could never reach the end of the subject.

Second, I'm overwhelmed by the importance of what we're going to study together. If everything in life emanates from the knowledge of God, then it's safe to say that everything in the Christian life emanates from the knowledge of the Holy Spirit.

Think about it. When He left this earth to go back to heaven, Jesus sent us the Holy Spirit to do and to be all that we would ever need to live victorious Christian lives. The age we live in—the church age—was inaugurated by the Spirit's arrival at Pentecost. And when the Holy Spirit's presence is removed from this world, we're going with Him!

Let me give you some idea of the importance of the Holy Spirit's work, beginning right at the beginning. If there were no Holy Spirit, there would be no creation. If there were no Holy Spirit, there would be no human race because we would not have the principle of life operating within us.

Without the operation of the Holy Spirit, there would have been no Virgin Birth, because Jesus was born of a virgin by the power of the Holy Spirit. There would have been no victory over Satan in the wilderness for Jesus, because it was the Spirit of God who led Him there to be tempted of the Devil.

Again, if there were no Holy Spirit, there would be no Christians, no Bible, no one to restrain sin in our world, and no expectation of the return of Christ. Without the Holy Spirit, there would be nothing.

## THE CENTRALITY OF THE HOLY SPIRIT

So the Holy Spirit is absolutely central to the Christian life. And yet, because of the mystery surrounding this third Person of the triune God, a great deal of confusion has been connected with the work of the Holy Spirit. This has led to a lot of misappropriation, as well as a lot of gross *under*appropriation, of His power and gifts.

Usually, the Holy Spirit is approached from one of two extremes. Either we know very little about Him or we try to make Him into a celebrity, someone we all think we know but don't really know at all. Neither is desirable, but we cannot let a lack of familiarity in some circles or excesses in others keep us from pursuing the knowledge of the Holy Spirit. The fact is, His role is the indispensable factor in determining whether you win or lose spiritually, whether you are a failure or a success as a Christian.

So I want to begin our study by looking at one of the foundational New Testament passages for understanding the Person and work of the Holy Spirit. I'm talking about Jesus' Upper Room Discourse, which He delivered on the night of the Last Supper and His betrayal. It was here He promised His followers that God the Father would send them "another Helper" (John 14:16).

This was not one of the greatest moments in the lives of the disciples. This was what you would call a spiritual downtime. Everything was going wrong. Judas had shown himself to be a traitor and had just left the room on his way to betray Christ. One of the Twelve was a Benedict Arnold.

What's more, Peter had just been told that within the next twenty-four hours he was going to publicly deny Christ (John 13:38). And the Jews wanted to get rid of Christ and all His followers. So the disciples had reason to be afraid.

Then came the worst blow. Jesus told them, "I am going to go away to prepare a place for you. You can't come to Me until I come for you. I am not going to tell you when I will come for you, but trust Me" (see John 14:1–3).

Thomas reacted right away. "Jesus, You have got to be kidding. We put all of our eggs in Your basket, and now You tell us You have to leave us. Jesus, we had enough problems trying to make it with You here. How in the world do You expect us to make it if You leave us?" (see v. 5).

So this was the tension-charged, late-night environment in the upper room of a second-story flat in Jerusalem, when Jesus introduced His disciples to the ministry of the third Person of the Trinity:

> I will ask the Father, and He will give you another Helper, that He may be with you forever; that is the Spirit of truth, whom the world cannot receive, because it does not behold

Him or know Him, but you know Him because He abides with you, and will be in you. (John 14:16–17)

## THE SPIRIT'S PERSON

Jesus assured His followers that even though He would leave, they would not be left alone. There would be another divine Person who would take His place in their midst. This Person would be with them as Jesus had been with them for comfort, strength, and guidance, but this Person would also be *in* them. Jesus wanted the disciples to know He was going to send them a Somebody, not a something.

### A Real Person

How do we know the Holy Spirit is a Person instead of just a force or an "it"? Because He bears all the attributes of personality: intellect, emotion, and will.

The Spirit's intellect is demonstrated by the fact that there are things He knows with His mind (Romans 8:27; 1 Corinthians 2:10–11). His emotions or feelings are seen in the fact that He can be grieved (Ephesians 4:30). His will is seen in the fact that He acts with intentionality or purpose (1 Corinthians 12:11). Only persons intend to do things.

In addition, the Bible uses personal pronouns for the Holy Spirit. Jesus referred to the Spirit as "He" (John 15:26; 16:13). The Spirit refers to Himself in the first person and also speaks His thoughts intelligibly to others, something only a person can do (Acts 13:2).

When God saves us, then, He calls us into a personal relationship with the Holy Spirit. In fact, God wants us to enter into intimate communion with the Spirit's Person (John 14:17). It is for this reason we are not to sin against the Holy Spirit (Matthew 12:31; Acts 5:3).

One of our fundamental problems is that we look for the wrong thing first when it comes to the Holy Spirit. People talk about their need for Holy Ghost power. Now make no mistake about it, we do need Holy Ghost power. But only after we have met Holy Ghost *Person*.

When you start dealing with the Holy Spirit as a power first, then you are always looking for the power and you may just miss the Person. But you cannot deal with a person without dealing with relationships.

What many Christians want are power surges to live the Christian life. They want a boost to take them to the next spiritual level. Many people come to church on Sunday morning looking for a Holy Ghost "oomph" to get them rolling and carry them through the week. They leave church all fired up.

But if you leave with momentary Holy Ghost power without a relationship with the Holy Ghost as a Person, as God, you will wind up with a Holy Ghost deficit in your spiritual life. The Holy Spirit is a Person we can know and relate to, not just a force or power to be used.

## A Divine Person

The Holy Spirit is God, the third member of the Trinity. The word *trinity* refers to the reality that God is one in essence, yet plural in personality. There is one God composed of three distinct Persons. The Father is not the Son, and the Son is not the Spirit, yet each is equally and fully God.

In theological terms, the Father, the Son, and the Holy Spirit are *homoousios*, "of the same essence or substance," not *homoiousios*, "of like or similar essence or substance." That extra Greek letter *i* in the second term makes a world of difference!

While the doctrine of the Trinity is a paradox and difficult to understand, it is not a contradiction, because the doctrine says that God is different in essence (one) than He is in person (three). Now since essence is different from person, there is no contradiction. This is a simple distinction that is hard to grasp with our finite minds.

For that reason, no picture of the Trinity is really adequate. But the one that helps me is to picture it as a pretzel. The way a pretzel interlocks, often you will see three holes in it. One hole represents the Father, one represents the Son, and one the Spirit. They are distinct holes, but they intertwine to make one pretzel. Don't try to figure it out. Just enjoy it while you chew on it!

The thing I want you to see here is that the Holy Spirit is God. This truth is in abundant evidence in Scripture. He possesses the attributes of deity. The Spirit is omniscient or all-knowing (Isaiah 40:13; 1 Corinthians 2:2), omnipresent or in all places at once (Psalm 139:7), and omnipotent or all-powerful (Job 33:4; Psalm 104:30).

The Spirit is also equally associated with the other members of the Trinity in the writing of Scripture (Isaiah 6:9; cf. Acts 28:25; Jeremiah 31:31–34; cf. Hebrews 10:15–17). To lie to the Holy Spirit is the same as lying to God (Acts 5:3–4). Matthew 28:19 is especially crucial here because the singular "name" is used with the Father, Son, and Holy Spirit.

So to talk about a relationship with the Holy Spirit is at the same time to talk about a relationship with the Father and the Son. Yet, because the Spirit is a distinct Person in the Godhead with a distinct ministry, we also benefit from His unique ministry.

### A Unique Person

Jesus called this Helper "the Spirit of truth" in John 14:17. In verse 26, Jesus called Him "the Holy Spirit." There is a lot in that second name.

The Spirit is holy because He is God, totally separate from all that is unlike who and what God is. This title also focuses attention on His primary work in the life of believers: to progressively conform us to the image of Christ, the process we call sanctification (1 Peter 3:15).

The Holy Spirit is spirit because He is nonmaterial, intangible, and invisible. Both the Hebrew and Greek words for *spirit* mean "wind, breath." The Holy Spirit is the very breath or wind of God. And like the wind, He wields great power even though He is invisible. So you can't relate to Him simply by trying to use your five senses.

Now I'm not talking about Casper the friendly ghost. I mean the invisible reality of almighty God. So the Holy Spirit is not simply a power. Trying to explain an invisible reality is difficult, because it's like trying to explain electricity.

You know electricity is there. You know it is powerful. You know you need it. You know you can benefit from it. But trying to explain electricity can be tough. The same is true about the Holy Spirit, but Jesus made clear in John 14:17 that the Holy Spirit is knowable. We who know Christ can know the Holy Spirit.

Why doesn't the world know the Holy Spirit (v. 17)? For the same reason you cannot pick up radio stations if you don't have a radio. It has nothing to do with whether or not radio waves are going through the air. It has everything to do with not having anything with which to receive the signals.

The world does not have a spiritual receiver. But Jesus Christ has implanted a receiver within those who know Him that picks up heaven's signals so the believer can tune in to the heavenlies, to the very voice of God. So in the midst of discouragement, fear, loneliness, insecurity, or even sin, a believer can tune in to the Holy Spirit.

Therefore, to talk about the Holy Spirit is not to talk about a doctrinal formula that is unrelated to day-to-day living. The Holy Spirit is part of day-to-day living because He is a Person who lives within us.

## THE SPIRIT'S ENABLING

A second truth about the Holy Spirit we find in the text is this: The Spirit is the Helper, the Enabler. When He indwells the believer, He enables that believer to be and to do what God wants that person to be and to do.

Jesus was about to tell the disciples something very crucial: "Apart from Me you can do nothing" (John 15:5). This blanket statement of inability without divine enabling made what Jesus was saying in John 14 even more critical. There would be no effective ministry or life that pleased the Lord by mere human effort.

Many of us have discovered that. No matter how many times we say to ourselves, "I'm going to do it this time," we find that we really are unable to be what God wants us to be on our own.

If you have discovered your own spiritual insufficiency, you are a good candidate for the ministry of the Holy Spirit. If you have not discovered that yet, you are a good candidate for spiritual disaster.

## An Internal Helper

Because the disciples' need was complete, Jesus promised them that "another Helper" would come after He left (John 14:16). The Greek word for "helper" is *paraclete*, translated differently in various Bible versions because it is a pregnant term. Some versions translate it "counselor." One version translates it "advocate," because the word literally means "one called alongside to help," that is, to enable.

Jesus knew that after His resurrection, the disciples would need supernatural power to pull off what He wanted them to do. And He knew where they were going to get that power: from the enabling, internal presence of the Holy Spirit. Now this is very important because whenever the disciples needed help, Jesus was always there.

When they were lonely and needed a friend, Jesus was a faithful friend. When they were discouraged and needed encouragement, Jesus was there to encourage them and give them joy. When they were defeated and needed to be picked up, Jesus was there to pick them up. When they were afraid out on the sea and wondering how they were going to make it, Jesus could walk on the water and calm their fear.

Whatever these men needed, Jesus was there to provide. So when they heard that Jesus was leaving, the question on the floor was "Who is going to help us?" That is, "Jesus, if we are going to keep on, who is going to help us when we are down and encourage us when we are discouraged? Who is going to strengthen us when we are weak? Who is going to lead us when we are confused? You did all that for us."

One of my tasks when I first met my wife, Lois, was to let her know that if she had me, she did not need her father any more. One thing that I could always do was talk. I was a rapper par excellence. I said a lot of things I could not back up, but the person I was talking to never knew it because I could camouflage all that with my rap.

Basically, I told Lois that everything provided to her by her father would be obsolete when she came to me. The best he could provide for her belonged to the Ice Age compared to what I would provide if she came over to me.

Guess what? She came over to me. So to some degree, my rap worked. Now, in our more than twenty-five years of marriage I have fallen short of my guarantees from time to time, but that's not part of this discussion.

## A Helper Like Jesus

Jesus' task on this night was to convince His fearful, confused followers that the Helper He was sending was just like Him, only this Helper would be able to do even more for them.

So Jesus told them, "I am going to leave you now. But I am going to send you Someone who is always going to be there for you. No matter what your problem, no matter what your circumstance, no matter what your trial, frustration, or irritation may be, no matter what you come up against, this Helper will be with you."

We call this the indwelling ministry of the Spirit of God. When a believing sinner comes to Jesus Christ, the Holy Spirit takes up residence in that person's life and becomes his Helper.

Now I need to explain something critical here. If you are a believer, the best help you have for whatever problem you face is inside you, not outside you.

See, if you had a problem and Jesus Christ were physically here, who would you go to with your problem, Jesus or your pastor? Don't come to me, because I am going to be over there with Jesus too! I don't think there is any debate that if Jesus were here on earth and told us we could come to Him, we would go to Him first.

Well, Jesus is not here in person, but He has left you and me another Helper who is just like Him. If you are a believer, this Helper is closer to you than anybody else could ever be, because He is within you.

One fundamental reason many Christians don't get the help they need when they are afraid or lonely or needing encouragement or whatever is that they go to the wrong person first. In case you didn't know this, let me underline it. Your pastor is not the Holy Spirit. Your Christian counselor or therapist is not the Holy Spirit, and if you are more dependent on these people than you are on the Holy Spirit, you are settling for second-class help.

The Holy Spirit is in you, and that's why no matter what help you may seek, if the priority is being placed on outside helpers rather than the Person inside you, you are never going to realize the full power of God in your life.

You say, "But wait a minute. I don't want the third member of the Trinity. I want Jesus." Again, the text helps us because in John 14:16, the Greek word Jesus used for "another" is *allos*, which means "another of the same kind." He did not use *heteros*, which means "another of a different kind."

Jesus' choice of words emphasizes the unique work of the Spirit in continuing what He had begun while on earth without any loss of character, quality, power, or intimacy. Jesus could promise this because the Spirit is of equal divine essence with Jesus Himself.

In other words, Jesus was telling the disciples, "The Holy Spirit will be all to you that I was to you. You are not getting any less of Me. In fact, you are getting exactly what I would give you if I were here." So to appeal to the indwelling Spirit is to appeal to the same level of help you would get if you were standing before Jesus Christ in the flesh.

You do not get less when you get the Holy Spirit. You get all of God, for He is the third Person of the Trinity. Because many of us have not cultivated a relationship with the Holy Spirit, we are not finding the power to do what God has commanded us to do.

That's because we are not seeking the assistance of the Holy Spirit. Unfortunately, we wind up running all over the place to get help or counseling from a secondary source.

Now counseling has its place. Spirit-led people have been called to assist Christians to move forward. But they have never been called to replace the Holy Spirit in you. That is why, if your relationship with the Spirit is not cultivated, you will not have all the power you could have to deal with your need.

Without the assistance of this third member of the Trinity, trying to solve problems is like rubbing Ben-Gay® on a broken leg. It may feel good, but it doesn't help the problem at all. Many believers go to church Sunday after Sunday for a Ben-Gay rub. Going to church by itself can only make a wound feel good. It can't fix the bone, the broken spirit.

You need another kind of Helper who is just like Jesus. Someone who will be with you Monday at work, Tuesday at home, Wednesday in the neighborhood, and so on through the week. You need Someone who will be with you wherever you go. You have that Someone in the Person of the Holy Spirit.

### An Ever-Present Helper

The Spirit is not only our Helper, He is our ever-present Helper. It's very important to understand what's going on here because Jesus said later that night, "It is to your advantage that I go away; for if I do not go away, the Helper shall not come to you" (John 16:7).

Do you realize that if Jesus Christ were on earth today, we would actually be worse off as His people? If Jesus Christ were on earth today in His bodily presence, we would be a defeated, decimated people.

Why? Why did Jesus tell His disciples it was better for them that He leave and the Holy Spirit come? Because when Jesus was here on earth, He encased His deity in His humanity. Philippians 2:5–8 makes clear that Jesus Christ willingly poured the totality of His deity into the location of His humanity.

The result was that even though Jesus is God, He could only be in one place at a time. His deity was always in the same vicinity as His humanity. Jesus never traveled more than a few miles from home or preached to more than a few thousand people. That's why He said we would do greater works than He did (John 14:12).

In my years of ministry, for example, I have preached to more people than Jesus ever preached to. I have traveled many more miles than Jesus ever traveled. Now obviously, I haven't done greater works than Jesus in the sense that I have ever turned water into wine or raised the dead.

But because the Holy Spirit is ever present with me and indwells me, I can draw on the full power of deity wherever I go. When Jesus walked this earth, He limited His deity to the location of His humanity. He could only visit one village at a time. Of course, I am also limited to only one place, but the Holy Spirit who indwells me can work through many believers at the same moment.

So what's the advantage we enjoy today? Here's the illustration I used with our church people. After I give the benediction on Sunday morning, some of the people at Oak Cliff Bible Fellowship get in their cars and go to north Dallas. Others drive to south Dallas. Still others scatter throughout Oak Cliff, and a good portion of our members head to surrounding towns like DeSoto, Lancaster, and Duncanville.

Now suppose Jesus were to come to our church some Sunday morning and announce that He wanted to go home with one of us. Well, since Jesus in His humanity could only be in one place at a time, let's say that since I am the pastor, He chose to go home with me.

Now if you're in Duncanville and you need Jesus, you don't want to hear that He is tied up with me in Oak Cliff. If you are up in north Dallas and you need Jesus, you don't want to hear that He is with another saint in Lancaster and won't be coming your way for many days.

You get the idea. When you need Jesus, you need Him right now and you need His undivided attention. So guess what? In order for Jesus to meet the needs of all saints everywhere—whether it's in south Dallas or South Korea —He had to leave so that He could send the Holy Spirit, who is not limited to time and space and can go home with all of us simultaneously.

Since the Spirit is in you, He is wherever you happen to be, going wherever you happen to go. All of God that you ever want to have, if you come to Christ, is in you. You are never at any point in a situation where you have less access to Jesus Christ than the next Christian.

Why then are some Christians perpetually defeated? It is not because they have less of the Holy Spirit than victorious Christians. Jesus said in verse 26 of John 14, "The Helper, the Holy Spirit, whom the Father will send in My name, He will teach you all things, and bring to your remembrance all that I said to you."

Please notice the work of the Trinity in verse 26. The Father, in the name of the Son, sends the Holy Spirit. So we have the whole Trinity involved in the sending of the Spirit. If Christians are defeated, it is because the Holy Spirit has less of them.

When you call a major law firm with a real estate problem, it doesn't matter that some of the lawyers in that firm specialize in tax cases, others in civil cases, and still others in criminal cases. What matters is that they also have lawyers who are experts in real estate law.

So your call gets transferred to the right expert, and your real estate problem gets taken care of. You may only be dealing with one person in that firm, but you have the power and influence of the entire firm behind you.

There is a law firm in glory called the Godhead. There are three on staff—God, God, and God. Each one has a sphere of responsibility. The Father oversees the plan. The Son delivers the plan. The Holy Ghost implements the plan in your life. When you call you get the right Expert, and your need gets handled.

## THE SPIRIT'S PURPOSE

Here's a third truth I want you to see about the work of the Holy Spirit:

But when He, the Spirit of truth, comes, He will guide you into all the truth; for He will not speak on His own initiative, but whatever He hears, He will speak; and He will disclose to you what is to come. He shall glorify Me; for He shall take of Mine, and shall disclose it to you. (John 16:13–14)

## Glorifying Christ

The Holy Spirit has one overarching goal. If you want to sum up what the Holy Spirit is about, He is about glorifying Christ. What do I mean by glorifying Christ? The Spirit advertises Christ. He puts Jesus Christ on display.

The Spirit does not put Himself on display. He does not even speak on His own initiative. His job is to glorify Christ. So whenever you have anything that transcends the priority of Jesus Christ, it is not the Holy Spirit's doing. Anytime there is an emphasis on the Spirit that supersedes the centrality and priority of Jesus Christ, it is not the Holy Spirit doing it.

The Holy Spirit is not here to advertise Himself. His goal is to advertise Christ, to make us God's advertising agency by working in our hearts in such a way that our lives magnify the Person of Christ. The Spirit is busy making Jesus preeminent.

## No Glory, No Help

In fact, 1 John 4:2–3 says anything that diminishes Jesus Christ's glory is "the spirit of the antichrist." He is to be preeminent. Now this is very important because this means if your passion is not to glorify Christ, then you are not going to get help from the Holy Spirit.

You see this in 1 Corinthians 6:18–20 in a passage where Paul is talking about sexual immorality:

> Flee immorality. Every other sin that a man commits is outside the body, but the immoral man sins against his own body. Or do you not know that your body is a temple of the Holy Spirit who is in you, whom you have from God, and that you are not your own? For you have been bought with a price: therefore, glorify God in your body.

The Holy Spirit is in you that you may glorify God in everything you say and do. That's why Jesus said, "He [the Spirit] shall glorify Me" (John 16:14). So if you want the help of the Holy Spirit in whatever you are facing, then your priority in life must be to glorify, to advertise Jesus Christ.

## THE SPIRIT'S BENEFITS

When you read John 16:7, where Jesus told His disciples, "It is to your advantage that I go away; for if I do not go away, the Helper shall not come to you," you know you're in for something good. Jesus doesn't make promises lightly.

In my wallet, I have an Advantage Club card from the airline I use when I travel. Every month, the airline writes me a personal letter to let me know the benefits I have as an Advantage member.

You see, over the last ten years I have established a very intimate relationship with this airline. It has been very close to my pocketbook, because over the last ten years I have flown more than a million miles. In the eyes of this airline, that makes me a preferred customer.

Because I am an Advantage cardholder, I get certain rights and privileges the occasional flyer does not have. Advantage members are invited to board first, so I get to go on the plane earlier. I also get certain ticketing benefits. I don't have to stand in certain lines because I have an Advantage Club card.

But the part I like best is that if there are empty seats in first class, one is made available to me even though I have not purchased a first-class ticket. Why? Because I have made a commitment to fly this airline consistently. I have a relationship with this company, and therefore certain benefits accrue to me when it comes to flying.

Jesus says that, because of your relationship to Him, He is going to make you an Advantage cardholder. He is going to enroll you in the "Holy Ghost Club." If you will keep flying Jesus, He will make sure you stay in the club and accrue the Spirit's benefits.

A lot of people have joined the Advantage Club program with this airline, but a lot of others have not, even though it is available to them. Any Christian can join the Holy Ghost Club when it comes to taking full advantage of the benefits He offers. But a lot of Christians don't, even though the Advantage card is available.

Let's talk about a few of the Spirit's benefits.

### Guidance

First of all, Jesus said the Spirit will "guide you into all the truth" (John 16:13). Isn't guidance something you need? Are there decisions you need to make that you wish somebody would advise you on? Don't you wish there was somebody who understood your situation perfectly and could guide you? You have that Person in the Holy Spirit. Now for the apostles Jesus was talking to, this promise of guidance had a special application because the Holy Spirit guided several of them in the writing of Scripture. The reason the Bible has no errors in it is that the Spirit guided men like Peter in recording "all the truth."

Peter knew he wasn't just writing words. He said, "No prophecy was ever made by an act of human will, but men moved by the Holy Spirit spoke from God" (2 Peter 1:21). When somebody tells you there are mistakes in the Bible because men wrote it, here is your answer.

The writers of Scripture were "borne" or "carried along" by the Holy Spirit as they wrote. The picture here is of a sailboat being moved according to the direction of a blowing wind. So they wrote what God wanted to record, not just what they wanted to write.

We aren't writing inerrant Scripture, but we can enjoy the Spirit's guidance today in the decisions of life. His guidance will be always be tied to the truth, so we have an advantage because we have the completed revelation of God's truth in the Bible. So if you're seeking guidance from the Spirit, you can be sure it will align with Scripture and will glorify Christ.

The Holy Spirit stands ready to guide us even in the little things of life. Not long ago, I was on my way to a speaking engagement, and time was tight. I despise being late because I believe it abuses other people's time, so I was in a hurry. But when I got ready to leave, I couldn't find my car keys.

I looked everywhere. First, I searched sort of helter-skelter. Then I did an organized, room-by-room search. Next, I did my "exegetical" search, looking in every crevice, under the bed, wherever. But no keys.

I started to panic, but then I remembered that I had another Helper. I sat down on the couch and prayed, "Lord, You know that I need to leave now for this engagement, and You know where my keys are. So that I might glorify Your name, I am asking You right now to direct my mind to where my keys are."

As I reached out to get up off the couch, my hand slipped between the pillows—and there were my keys. Now you can call that luck if you want to, but I believe the Holy Spirit guided me to those keys, for He is interested in guiding us in all truth.

My good friend Ramesh Richard, to whom this book is dedicated and who ministers around the world, told me of an occasion when he and his son were overseas and had transportation problems. They went to a corner of the airport and prayed for direction. Then a friend from halfway across the world bumped into them and provided the help they needed. We have another Helper to guide us.

## Remembrance

Jesus also said the Holy Spirit would "bring to your remembrance all that I said to you" (John 14:26). Jesus had taught the disciples a lot. How were they going to remember it all? How could they remember every word and every event, how many people were there, and all of that? They couldn't, but the Holy Spirit would recall these things to their minds.

How are you going to remember every sermon you've heard and every word of the Bible you've read? You can't, and you don't have to. Your responsibility is to study to show yourself approved, to hide the Word in your heart.

When you do that, the Holy Spirit is your built-in computer system to pick up the words and illustrations and everything you need to know. Then at the proper time, He can punch the button and the information will show up on your mental screen. He will bring to your remembrance the things you need to remember. That's a benefit of belonging to the Spirit's Advantage Club.

But you say, "Wait a minute. How come I don't seem to remember anything when I am in trouble? How come it does not seem to come back to me?"

Well, if you are a new Christian, you aren't going to have that much in your computer yet. Or if you're under sustained attack by Satan, the screen can get fuzzy.

But in either case, you can still be committed to glorifying Christ. And the bottom line is that this ministry of remembrance only comes to those to whom the Father wills to disclose it, and He only discloses it to those who are in concert with the Spirit on this matter of bringing glory to Christ.

So if you are not committed to glorifying Jesus Christ, your computer screen will come up blank. But if you are committed to Christ and cultivating a relationship with the Spirit, the data will be there when you need it.

## Peace

Another benefit of the Holy Spirit is peace. "Peace I leave with you; My peace I give to you; not as the world gives, do I give to you," Jesus said in John 14:27. Therefore, "Let not your heart be troubled, nor let it be fearful." Now remember the situation. Jesus is leaving. Judas has betrayed Him. The Jews want to kill Him—and the disciples are still going to have peace. The Holy Spirit is going to deliver it when He comes.

What's your situation today? Whatever it is, if you have the Holy Spirit you can have peace in the midst of it because He lives within you. It's a peace that circumstances can't shatter.

It's unfortunate that many evangelicals approach these promises with a double standard, allowing certain of these works of the Spirit to apply only to the disciples while making others available to all Christians. Such a dichotomy is unwarranted. His benefits are available to all of us in accordance with God's sovereign will. The lack of the practical experience of these benefits is related to one simple fact—a poor relationship with the Spirit.

There are many more great benefits to being in the Holy Spirit's Advantage Club: things like assurance and security, which we'll talk about in upcoming chapters. They're all part of the Spirit's promise.

# EXPERIENCING THE SPIRIT'S PROMISE

The Holy Spirit is where it all begins. As I said at the beginning, everything in the Christian life starts with the Spirit. And since this book is all about *experiencing* the Holy Spirit in your life, let me suggest some ways to experience His Person, His enabling, His purpose, and His benefits:

1. Romans 8:9 says if you don't have the Holy Spirit, you don't belong to Christ. If you don't know whether the Holy Spirit is in you, perhaps it is because you haven't come to Christ for salvation. You can experience the Person of the Spirit right now. Admit to God that you're a sinner (Romans 3:23) and cannot save yourself, believe that Christ died on the cross to pay for your sins (Romans 5:8), and receive Him by faith as your only God and Savior (John 1:12: "As many as received Him, to them He gave the right to become children of God"). When you do, the Holy Spirit will come to live within you, and He will never leave. Be sure to tell your pastor or a Christian friend about your decision.

2. Since it's true that we cannot do anything in the Christian life apart from the enabling power of the Spirit, all our self-efforts are doomed to failure. Examine your life. Is there some area of recurring failure, some place where you just can't seem to get it together? Submit that to the Holy Spirit today, and ask Him to enable you to do whatever it is you've been trying to do on your own.

3. The Spirit's purpose is to glorify Christ. Is that your purpose? One way to find out is to look at where you spend your time, abilities, and money, and ask yourself how many of these things have as their ultimate goal the exaltation of Christ in some way. The ones that don't may need to go. That's between you and the Holy Spirit.

4. Which benefit of the Holy Spirit do you need most in your life right now? If your life is lined up with His purposes as we've talked about above, be bold in asking Him to meet your need!

# CHAPTER TWO

# EXPERIENCING THE SPIRIT'S BAPTISM

I f you're an observer of the current Christian scene, you can tell by the title of this chapter that we are about to enter turbulent waters. We have a few more controversial topics coming along later in the book, but we can't allow controversy to scare us away from seeking the truth.

Baptism is an indispensable ministry of the Spirit of God, one that is critical to our Christian experience. It marks the beginning of the Spirit's indwelling presence. The fact that much of the teaching about Spirit baptism has led to confusion, misunderstanding, and disharmony within the family of God means we need all the more to understand what God is saying to us.

Part of the controversy about baptism starts with the term *en pneumati* itself. Is it the baptism "of" the Spirit, "by" the Spirit, "with" the Spirit, or "in" the Spirit? The preposition in the original can be and has been translated all of these ways, and there is a difference in the meaning based on the translation you accept. Is the Holy Spirit the primary agent of the baptism, is He Himself the baptism, or is He the means by which believers are baptized?

How you answer that will probably depend upon your theological frame of reference. That little preposition has caused a lot of confusion, so in as clear and biblical a way as possible, I want to address this area of Spirit baptism.

My purpose, however, is not simply to settle an argument, but to help you experience the fullness of the Spirit's Person and ministry in your life. The verse I want to center on for our study is 1 Corinthians 12:13, where Paul writes:

> For by one Spirit we were all baptized into one body, whether Jews or Greeks, whether slaves or free, and we were all made to drink of one Spirit.

## THE MEANING OF BAPTISM

Let's start by talking about the word itself, which is a transliteration of the Greek word *baptizō*. It means "to immerse" or "to dip." It was used to describe the process of dyeing cloth. If you wanted a piece of cloth to be purple, you would dip it in purple dye. When the cloth came out of the dye, you had a different-looking piece of cloth because it had been immersed or dipped into a colored dye.

So this process of immersion, this baptism of the cloth, was not just an act. It was a transformation because the cloth took on a whole new color. When God wanted to describe the ministry whereby His Spirit places us into a whole new environment, this is the word He chose.

Thus a redeemed sinner experiences a transformation when converted (2 Corinthians 5:17). Although this transformation varies from person to person in intensity, content, immediacy, and visible expression, it is real and therefore experiential. No transformation, no baptism.

God chose the imagery of baptism to explain the Spirit's ministry of taking sinful people who believe on the Lord Jesus Christ and immersing them into a whole new dynamic of life, an entirely new realm or environment called the body of Christ.

Much of the problem comes when people confuse the baptism of the Holy Spirit with either His indwelling or

His filling of the believer. So let's separate these three related but different works of the Spirit.

When I speak of the baptism of the Spirit or by the Spirit or with the Spirit or in the Spirit (I will clarify that in a moment), I am referring to the time when true believers become identified with Jesus Christ and placed into His body. That transaction is clearly stated in the verse I quoted above, because Paul says that by the Spirit's baptism we are immersed or dipped into one body.

The distinguishing feature of baptism is that we are placed into another realm, a new family: the body of Christ, the family of God. This baptism occurs at the moment of our conversion. It is our initiation, if you will.

The indwelling of the Spirit refers to the Spirit's taking up permanent residence in the life of the believer, which continues throughout our lives here on earth. The filling of the Holy Spirit refers to His control and empowerment in the lives of believers to enable us to live the victorious Christian life.

So when the Bible talks about the indwelling of the Spirit, it means where the Spirit is. When the Bible talks about the filling of the Spirit, it means what the Spirit empowers us to do. When the Bible talks about the baptism of the Spirit, it means the new environment in which the Spirit places us when we come into a new relationship with Jesus Christ at salvation.

In Matthew 3:11, John the Baptist says concerning Jesus Christ:

> As for me, I baptize you in water for repentance, but He who is coming after me is mightier than I, and I am not even fit to remove His sandals; He Himself will baptize you with the Holy Spirit and fire.

So John says that Jesus is actually going to do the baptizing: with the Holy Spirit for those who trust Him, and with the fire of judgment for those who reject Him. In one sense, then, everyone will get baptized by Christ— either in the realm of blessing through the Holy Spirit, or in the realm of judgment.

For our purposes here, I want to point out that Christ is the One doing the baptizing. He is the baptizer, not the Holy Spirit. The Spirit is the means by which this baptism takes place, the means by which believers enter into this new realm or environment called the body of Christ or the family of God.

So let me put the statement together. The baptism Paul refers to in 1 Corinthians 12:13 is a baptism by Christ, "by means of" the Holy Spirit, whereby we are placed into a new spiritual environment.

Why is this distinction critical? Because there are many who say that the baptism of the Holy Spirit is a work subsequent to salvation that elevates the recipient into a special, elite realm of spiritual power that only a few select people achieve. We will address these issues as we go along, but I wanted you to see the basic understanding and framework within which I will deal with the Spirit's baptism.

## THE NATURE OF SPIRIT BAPTISM

I want to make a couple of important points in this section. They're found in the opening phrase of our text, 1 Corinthians 12:13: "For by one Spirit we were all baptized into one body." Notice especially the uniqueness and the universality of the Spirit's baptism.

### It Is Unique

Nothing could be clearer than that there is only one baptism by one Spirit. Paul affirms the same thing in Ephesians 4:4–5: "There is one body and one Spirit . . . one Lord, one faith, one baptism."

What does this mean? It means you don't get a piece of Spirit baptism when you get saved and then a second helping of baptism later. God does not have baptism "halfway houses," nor does He baptize on the installment plan. There's no such thing as layaway baptism where you make a down payment up front, pay on it each month, and then after enough time as a Christian you get to take your baptism out of layaway and enjoy the whole deal.

No. All of the Holy Spirit you are ever going to get as a believer, you received when Jesus baptized you by means of the Spirit into His body at your salvation. The Holy Spirit came to take up permanent residence in your life at that time. The question in the Christian life is not, How much of the Holy Spirit do you have? but, How much of you does the Holy Spirit have?

People say, "Oh, if I could just get more of the Spirit." The Spirit is saying, "If I could just get more of you." People say, "Holy Spirit, come down." The Holy Spirit is saying, "I am already inside of you. Where do you want Me to go?"

Just as the Spirit's indwelling of us is a one-time, complete work of God's grace, so there is only one baptism by means of the Spirit. Based on Paul's absolute statement in 1 Corinthians 12:13, we could say that if the Spirit's baptism were not complete at salvation, then we would not be full members of the body of Christ at salvation. Our salvation would then be progressive. I don't know anyone who wants to defend that line.

The Spirit's baptism is a unique, completed ministry. Look how Paul puts it in Colossians 2:10: "In [Christ] you have been made complete." Nothing partial here. Then he goes on to say that we have been "buried with Him in baptism" (v. 12).

## It Is Universal

"We were all baptized into one body." The baptism by means of the Holy Spirit is not only unique, but it is also universal. It applies to every Christian.

There is a sense in which all people, including the unregenerate, know what it is to experience the Holy Spirit. There is an inseparable link between life itself and the work of the Spirit. This is not only true of human life (Job 33:4), but of all life, since it is by the Spirit that the grass grows (Psalm 104:30) and the wilderness becomes fruitful (Isaiah 32:15). Thus the Holy Spirit is the dynamic, active, life-generating power of almighty God. Although the unregenerate don't recognize or acknowledge this reality, it is still true.

Whereas all mankind has experienced the Spirit's work in the reception of biological life, all believers have experienced the Spirit's unique and universal work in the reception of spiritual life. All who have received Jesus Christ as their only God and Savior have been spiritually baptized by Him through the Spirit into the family of God. No one is excluded. Every one of us has been the beneficiary of this baptism. In fact, Romans 8:9 says anyone who does not have the Spirit is not even a Christian.

So anyone who tells you that you don't have the Spirit yet is saying you are not saved. Paul says you cannot be minus the Holy Spirit and call yourself a Christian. All Christians are Spirit-baptized.

Now it's interesting that Paul would say this to the church at Corinth because, according to 1 Corinthians 3, this was not the most spiritual church in town. It was a very carnal church, a church that lived by the flesh, a church soaked with immorality. There was litigation between members. People were choosing sides over personalities and leaving the Lord's Table drunk (chapter 11).

Yet Paul still says to them, "We were all baptized." What this shows is that baptism does not necessarily have anything to do with your present spiritual practice. It has to do with your spiritual position.

Many families have at least one member they're embarrassed by, someone who isn't living up to the family name. Unfortunately, God has some members of His family He's ashamed of. They're still family, but they aren't acting like it.

The story is told that the emperor Napoleon was once embarrassed by the behavior of one of his soldiers, who also happened to be named Napoleon. The emperor looked at his fellow Napoleon and said, "Either change your behavior or change your name."

Baptism has to do with the fact that you have been placed into the family. It is universal for believers. So not only were all the Corinthian believers baptized, but all the believers in the church at Galatia were too.

In Galatians 3:27, Paul says, "All of you who were baptized into Christ have clothed yourselves with Christ." That is, they had been placed into this new environment called Jesus Christ. They were dressed in Christ.

Let's see how spiritual the Galatians were. Paul

opened the book by telling them how amazed he was at their readiness to walk away from the faith (1:6). Later on he said the same thing in a different way (4:9). The Galatians were not a terribly spiritual group at all.

So let me say it again: Baptism has nothing necessarily to do with your spiritual practice. It places you into spiritual relationship to Christ and His body. It gives you the Spirit, but by itself it does not guarantee the results. Now the Holy Spirit is going to work on you until He gets you where He wants you. But that's a different ministry of His.

I'm making this point for an important reason. People who want to make the baptism of the Spirit a later work, often called the second work of grace or the second blessing, emphasize that you must be spiritually prepared and primed to receive it. They may tell you that you need to get the baptism of the Spirit in order to ascend to a higher plane of spiritual life.

That's not why you need the baptism of the Spirit. You need the baptism of the Holy Spirit to get you into the family so you can live the spiritual life in the first place. The baptism of the Spirit gives you access to the resources of spiritual life, all the ingredients necessary to live for Christ. Other ministries of the Spirit enable you to pull off the spiritual life. It's not your obedience, dependent on your own resources, that "qualifies" you to receive the Spirit; the Spirit empowers you to live the Christian life if you let Him. It's *His* work within you, not your own effort.

When we lose this vital distinction between the Spirit's baptism and His other ministries, great confusion abounds. And that's just what we are seeing today.

## THE RESULTS OF SPIRIT BAPTISM

If the baptism of the Spirit is for every believer, and if it's an already accomplished fact, what are its results? What does the baptism do for us, since His work is experiential in nature?

### A New Life

We've already alluded to this first result of Spirit baptism. It gives us new life in Jesus Christ. You can see this in John 3, the well-known conversation between Jesus and Nicodemus.

Nicodemus was a model man, a Pharisee, a "ruler of the Jews" (v. 1), at the top of the religious order in Israel. *Nicodemus* is a Greek name, meaning this Jewish man also had gotten the finest in Greek culture.

So Nick was powerful, religious, and cultured. Yet when he came to Jesus that night, Jesus knew he wasn't there just to compliment Him on His miracles. In verse 3, Jesus told him, "You came because you have a hole inside you so big you could drive a caravan through it. So let Me give you the bottom line so we can skip all this other stuff" (Evans paraphrase).

"Unless one is born again, he cannot see the kingdom of God" (v. 3b). Nicodemus did not understand, so Jesus clarified in verses 5–6:

> Unless one is born of water and the Spirit, he cannot enter into the kingdom of God. That which is born of the flesh is flesh, and that which is born of the Spirit is spirit.

It is the Spirit who gives us spiritual life. In fact, there is no possibility of new life without Him.

In John 7, Jesus made clear that the Holy Spirit also gives us all the supply we will ever need to maintain our spiritual lives:

> Now on the last day, the great day of the feast, Jesus stood and cried out, saying, "If any man is thirsty, let him come to Me and drink. He who believes in Me, as the Scripture said, 'From his innermost being shall flow rivers of living water.'" But this He spoke of the Spirit, whom those who believed in Him were to receive; for the Spirit was not yet given, because Jesus was not yet glorified. (vv. 37–39)

The Spirit not only gives you life, He keeps that life pumping. The reason you have access to God is that the Holy Spirit is always pumping rivers of living water through you. So the life of God is not only in you, it is always operative. The Spirit starts a river flowing in your soul.

You say, "I have the Holy Spirit. He has baptized me, yet my river is not flowing." Well, that's because you have cut off the tap. It's not because the river is not available. He has rivers of living water for each believer.

Now Jesus makes a very interesting statement here that bears on the subject of the Spirit's baptism and also has importance for the doctrine of the Spirit's deity. When Jesus said the Holy Spirit had not yet been given, He did not mean that the Spirit's existence began on the Day of Pentecost, any more than Jesus' existence began at Bethlehem.

As we have already discussed, the Holy Spirit is eternal God, without beginning or end. He was active in the Old Testament, but there was no such thing as the baptism of the Holy Spirit prior to the coming of Christ. You could be filled with the Spirit in the Old Testament, but you could never be Spirit-baptized.

That's because the baptism of the Spirit is uniquely related to the church as a new work of God, the body of Christ. You could not have the body of Christ until Christ had been glorified; that is, until He had died, risen from the dead, and ascended to heaven. When the time came for the formation of the church, which is Christ's body (Ephesians 1:22–23), the Spirit was uniquely involved in that work. And He's still adding to the church today.

### A New Identity

The second thing the baptism of the Holy Spirit gives you is a new identity. In fact, identity is a major component of baptism in the New Testament.

I like to use the example of the wife in a marriage, because we are the wife in our relationship to Christ; we are His bride. A woman undergoes an identity change when she marries. She changes her last name, taking on her husband's name. She leaves her family and goes to live with her husband.

If he has to move because of his job, the wife will most likely move with him because she is now identified with him in a special way. Of course, it works the other way too. If you are married, that identification has a mas-

sive effect on your life. Now you are responsible for someone else. Another agenda has been placed on the table
because a new identification has occurred.

Romans 6:1–5 explains the identification aspect of
the Spirit's baptism:

> What shall we say then? Are we to continue in sin that grace
> might increase? May it never be! How shall we who died to
> sin still live in it? Or do you not know that all of us who
> have been baptized into Christ Jesus have been baptized
> into His death? Therefore we have been buried with Him
> through baptism into death, in order that as Christ was
> raised from the dead through the glory of the Father, so we
> too might walk in newness of life. For if we have become
> united with Him in the likeness of His death, certainly we
> shall be also in the likeness of His resurrection.

To be identified with Christ is to be so linked with
Christ that we become like Him. We had an identity before we came to Christ, but it was nothing to brag about.
We were totally identified with Adam as the head of a
fallen, sinful race.

Let me tell you what Adam did for us. He plunged us
into sin. He separated us from the life of God. He placed
us under a curse. He made the Devil our daddy. Adam
plunged us into a kingdom called darkness and provided
for us in his will eternal separation from God in hell.

By the way, if you don't know the Lord Jesus Christ as
your Savior, you are still identified with Adam because you
have only two choices. All of us are either in Adam or in
Christ. These are the only two options. You either take your
identity from Adam or you take your identity from Christ.

You say, "If I'm in Adam, I want out of that mess."
Well, Christ has provided a means to switch families. He
has provided the way by which we can cancel our identity
with Adam and gain a new identity in Him. It's called salvation, and it's made real to us by the ministry of the
Spirit as He is given to us in baptism and lives within us.

Now this means more than just being a Christian. As
I said earlier, Jesus' baptism by means of the Spirit puts

you into a whole new environment, a whole different family. He transfers you to a new kingdom and He puts you in His will, giving you a whole new destiny: heaven instead of hell.

Imagine a coin lying loose on a table. It has no protection, no one to cover it. Anybody walking by can grab that coin. That's what it's like to be outside of Christ. Adam can't protect you because he's in trouble himself. He couldn't even deal with his own broken relationship with God, let alone do anything for you. So if you try to find protection in Adam, you are in trouble.

The Bible says that in Adam, all of us died (1 Corinthians 15:22). If your identity is still in Adam, then you inherit the destiny of Adam and his race. That was my identity and my destiny until, at the age of twelve, I heard the message of the Cross, the good news that Jesus Christ satisfied the demands of a holy God against me. When I heard that message from my father, I put my faith in Christ and became identified with Him. I was baptized into the body of Christ, and the Holy Spirit came to live within me. He gave me a new identity.

Now let's go back to that coin lying on the table. Suppose I pick it up and hold it in my hand. Then you say, "Evans, I'm going to take that coin away from you."

I will respond, "Well, that all depends on whether you're strong enough to open my hand." In John 10:28, Jesus says we are held in His hand and no one is strong enough to snatch us out of His hand. That's how strong our identity with Christ is. And it's a benefit of salvation that is made real to us by the ministry of the Spirit. Through the Spirit we experience the identity and security that are ours in Christ.

## A New Unity

The Spirit's baptism also gives us a new unity. "We were all baptized into *one* body" (1 Corinthians 12:13, italics added). We are to preserve "the unity of the Spirit" (Ephesians 4:3). It's already a reality. There is only one body of Christ, one family, one church. The whole point of our baptism is to create one new person out of a whole bunch of diverse individuals.

So if there is disunity in your home or in your other relationships, it's a spiritual issue. When your kids are fighting, one of the reasons you give as to why they have to stop is that they are family. "He's your brother. She's your sister. Why are you fighting like this? We're a family here." You are arguing that there is something bigger at stake than their personal desires.

The purpose of the Spirit's baptism is to bind us together in the community of the redeemed so that we function as family. That's why you can't have racism in the church. That's why you can't have sexism in the church. That's why you can't have division in the church. We're family now.

Let me show you from the book of Acts just how important this issue of unity is to the body of Christ. In fact, in the course of our discussion we'll find the answer to an otherwise perplexing problem: why on at least two occasions in Acts we see the baptism of the Spirit occurring some time *after* salvation rather than at the moment of salvation. That seems to contradict the doctrine we've just been studying.

Well, before we look at those two passages and one other important passage in Acts, let me remind you that Acts is not meant to be primarily doctrinal. That's why those who build their whole theology of the Holy Spirit from Acts soon get off course.

The book of Acts is not prescriptive, but descriptive. That is, it just tells what happened without trying to explain all the theological nuances. It is a history book detailing the beginning of the church. Acts is also transitional. Let me tell you, the idea of one new, unified body of believers made up not just of Jews, but of people of all races, was a shocking new concept to those first Jewish believers.

So the transition from the old covenant to the new covenant was a bumpy ride at times. A lot of Jews didn't even think Gentiles could get saved, let alone receive the gift of the Holy Spirit. It took the apostles themselves to verify what was happening and to verify that God really did intend for Jews and Gentiles to be united in one body with no distinctions.

Now stay with me, because here is where we find the answer to passages like Acts 8, where Philip the deacon goes to Samaria and revival breaks out. These non-Jews were getting saved, but they didn't receive the Spirit until Peter and John came and prayed for them (vv. 14–17). The apostles' presence was a way of validating and verifying the Samaritans' salvation, because Peter and John witnessed the outpouring of the Spirit on these people.

A similar incident happened in Acts 19:1–6, where Paul found some believers in Ephesus who had not yet received the Spirit. This really shows the transitional nature of Acts, because the new teaching about the Spirit simply hadn't gotten around to everyone yet.

Acts 10 and 11 give the clearest example of how important it was to have the apostles witness the coming of the Spirit upon Gentiles. This is the famous sermon Peter preached in the household of Cornelius:

> While Peter was still speaking these words, the Holy Spirit fell upon all those who were listening to the message. And all the circumcised believers who had come with Peter were amazed, because the gift of the Holy Spirit had been poured out upon the Gentiles also. (10:44–45)

Then in 11:15–17, Peter is explaining what happened at Cornelius's house:

> As I began to speak, the Holy Spirit fell upon them, just as He did upon us at the beginning. And I remembered the word of the Lord, how He used to say, "John baptized with water, but you shall be baptized with the Holy Spirit." If God therefore gave to them the same gift as He gave to us also after believing in the Lord Jesus Christ, who was I that I could stand in God's way?

The unity of the body of Christ is so important that in some cases God withheld the baptism of the Spirit until an apostle could be there to administer it and witness it.

That's why Paul confronted Peter in Galatians 2:11–21. Peter was enjoying pigs' feet, hog maw, and chitterlings with some Gentile brothers at the Soul Shack on the Gentile side of Antioch when some of his Jewish home boys showed up and asked him why he was fellowshiping with Gentiles.

Peter got up and left the Gentiles and went over to the Jews. He would have gotten away with it if Paul had not showed up with some neck bones too. Paul saw that Peter and his cronies were splitting the body that Jesus Christ had just brought together. So he opposed Peter to his face.

That's the answer to racism. The answer to racism is understanding the baptism by the Holy Spirit. And it doesn't take 250 years to solve it either. The problem of racism can be solved in ten minutes.

A man in our church once came to me and said he was getting a little distressed because there were too many white people at Oak Cliff Bible Fellowship. He was afraid we were going to get more and more whites and they were going to take over.

I told him he had better go and do some black evangelism then and get some more black people in here. He said he was leaving. I said, "'Bye."

I did not hold a sensitivity session or workshop. I don't mean there is not a place for sensitivity, but I mean we have a bottom line. We have the final word. The Spirit has baptized us *all* into one body. Therefore, when we allow or foster disunity, we lose God's power and presence in the process.

## A New Ability

Not only do you get a new unity, you get a new set of abilities when you are baptized by the Spirit. They are called spiritual gifts, the empowerment to serve Christ and build up His body. Earlier in 1 Corinthians 12, Paul called spiritual gifts "the manifestation[s] of the Spirit" (v. 7). The gifts are His to distribute "as He wills" (v. 11).

Many Christians have gifts they have never used. Like Christmas gifts, they are under the tree but not opened yet. We will talk much more about this when we get to spiritual gifts. But the Spirit's baptism gives you a new enablement to serve Christ.

### A New Nature

That's another deal you get with the baptism of the Spirit. You also get a new nature. "If any man is in Christ, he is a new creature; the old things passed away; behold, new things have come" (2 Corinthians 5:17). You get a brand-new inner you.

The Bible says you are to put on Christ. You are to clothe yourself with Christ. When you trust Christ and are baptized into His body, you are given a whole new wardrobe.

My wife recently took me to the store and bought me two sport coats. (Most days when I am looking good, it's because she has gone into the closet and taken out what I should wear that day.) Now I own the coats. They are no longer in the store. They are in my house and they belong to me. But until I put them on, they are only moth food.

God has purchased you a new wardrobe. Get dressed. Stop walking around with torn clothes when you have a brand-new pair of slacks. Stop walking around with a ragged jacket when He has purchased you a brand-new life by His precious blood. Stop talking about what you can't do and start talking about what the Holy Spirit can do in and through you. You have been made brand-new. You have a new nature now.

The federal government has a witness protection program. When you testify against certain criminals, the government places you under its protection and gives you a new identity. It gives you a new name, new address, new Social Security number, and everything else.

Why? Because the government wants to move you out of a dangerous environment to a protected environment. In order to pull that off, it has to change who you are. Nobody knows you by who you used to be. Nobody knows you by your name, your Social Security number, or your credit cards. All of those things have been changed. In the federal witness protection program, you get baptized into a new identity.

Now, you look the same. You talk the same. You still have all the same features and characteristics, but as far as your identity is concerned, you are a brand-new person. That is what Christ does by the Holy Spirit.

He moves you from the kingdom of darkness to the kingdom of light. He changes your sentence of death to one of eternal life. He gives you hope when you didn't have hope, meaning when you didn't have meaning, purpose when you didn't have purpose. He gives you rivers of living water. He places you in His spiritual witness protection program because you are now under the protection of God rather than under the tyranny of Satan. You are under God's care. You belong to Him.

## BAPTISM AND SPEAKING IN TONGUES

Now there's still a fundamental question I need to answer, because a lot of Christians are still trying to answer it in their own lives. The question is, What is the indispensable and visible experiential proof that the baptism of the Spirit has taken place in a person's life?

Many in the charismatic and neo-pentecostal movements teach that the indispensable proof of the Spirit's baptism is speaking in tongues (called "glossalalia," after the Greek word for language, *glōssa*). They argue from events in Acts (2:1–4; 8:14–17; 10:44–46; 19:1–6) that baptism is a work of the Spirit subsequent to salvation and related to a special endowment of His power.

According to this position, then, a person may be saved and indwelt by the Spirit, but not baptized until sometime later when he is lifted to a new level of spiritual power and vitality. This event is validated by speaking in tongues.

There are a number of problems with this interpretation. First, not all Christians speak in tongues; not even all spiritually mature Christians do so. If speaking in tongues is necessary to prove the Spirit's power and fellowship in a believer's life, we have a problem. Why? Because it is possible to identify many believers from the beginning of the church to today who are being used powerfully by the Spirit, but who never spoke in tongues.

Second, Paul clearly stated that not all Christians speak in tongues (1 Corinthians 12:30). So to expect all Christians to do so contradicts Paul's expectations. It's interesting, though, that Paul did expect all Christians to be spiritual (Colossians 1:28).

The third argument that makes this position untenable is that nowhere does the Scripture teach that speaking in tongues is a necessary sign of the Spirit's baptism or that there has to be a time lapse between conversion and Spirit baptism.

Then how should we interpret the relationship between Spirit baptism and speaking in tongues in Acts? The answer lies in understanding the Old Testament prophecy that is the basis of the New Testament phenomenon.

In Numbers 11:16–17, God spoke to Moses about the leadership burden he was under:

> Gather for Me seventy men from the elders of Israel . . . and bring them to the tent of meeting. . . . Then I will come down and speak with you there, and I will take of the Spirit who is upon you, and will put Him upon them.

So God promised to expand the distribution of the Holy Spirit to these seventy men for a collective manifestation of His power. Now this happened, and the men prophesied when the Spirit rested on them (vv. 24–25). But two other men who were not there also received the Spirit and began to prophesy (v. 26).

Someone ran and told Moses, and Joshua asked Moses to restrain the men (vv. 27–28). But notice Moses' response: "Would that all the Lord's people were prophets, that the Lord would put His Spirit upon them!" (v. 29).

Now it gets interesting, so stay with me. The prophet Joel said it was in fact God's intention to put His Spirit upon all His people. Joel prophesied, "And it will come about after this that I will pour out My Spirit on all mankind" (2:28).

The Day of Pentecost was the fulfillment of Moses' prayer and Joel's prophecy. Peter mentioned the fulfillment of Joel's prophecy in his sermon (Acts 2:16). He even quoted Joel directly. Pentecost was the fulfillment of this Old Testament expectation that God would expand the outpouring of His Spirit from some to all of His people.

Now this happened initially only in Jerusalem and only to Jewish believers. But the rest of the book of Acts chronicles the spread of the fulfillment of this promise from Jerusalem to Judea to Samaria and ultimately to the Gentile world (Acts 1:8).

Thus all believers in every group and every place received the gift of the Spirit. Peter revealed the significance of this event when he was in Cornelius's house and the Holy Spirit suddenly fell upon his Gentile listeners (Acts 10:44–48). Peter asked, "Surely no one can refuse the water for these to be baptized who have received the Spirit just as we did, can he?" (v. 47).

The point then is that all converts in Acts received full membership in the church, even though word of the fulfillment of the promise took some time to get around. There were no believers in Acts relegated to the back of the spiritual bus. There were no second-class Christians then, and there are none today. That this emphasis on unity is the primary concern of the baptism of the Spirit is explicitly stated by the apostle Paul when he writes:

> For all of you who were baptized into Christ have clothed yourselves with Christ. There is neither Jew nor Greek, there is neither slave nor free man, there is neither male nor female; for you are all one in Christ Jesus. (Galatians 3:27–28)

So what was the significance of tongues? It became the outward, tangible sign that the Holy Spirit had descended as promised. The fact that the tongues experience in Acts was verbal in nature reflects the experience of Numbers 11, for we just saw that when the Spirit came, Moses' elders began prophesying.

What can we conclude, then? The reality of Spirit baptism is to be demonstrated by the common public confession and proclamation of the Person and work of Christ (Romans 10:9–10). This confession may be in previously unknown languages (tongues) or known languages (prophecy). It is made visible by the inclusion of people who are racially, culturally, and socially different as equal members in the body of Christ (Acts 15:7–11) and who maintain the same confession of faith.

In this way, the baptism of the Spirit is in fact experiential. It affects our public confession and our personal relationship to the body.

## A WORD ABOUT WATER BAPTISM

Water baptism is to salvation what a wedding ring is to a marriage. It is a visible symbol of a deeper reality. In Scripture, water baptism followed quickly on the heels of Spirit baptism (Acts 2:41; 8:34–38). Why? To give visible and experiential witness to the spiritual transaction that had occurred.

In addition, water baptism is designed to issue into visible participation in a local church, since water baptism is a picture of spiritual baptism. Spiritual baptism identifies the believer with the universal church, whereas water baptism identifies the believer with the local church (Acts 2:37–47; 1 Corinthians 12:7–14). This is because Spirit baptism places the believer into the universal body of Christ, which is given visible expression in the local church.

Water baptism also signifies the believer's inauguration into a life of discipleship, which is to be accomplished in the context of a local church. The failure to be baptized and become a functioning member of a local church is nothing short of spiritual treason, which automatically removes the person from the context of God's blessing and full participation in the experience of the Holy Spirit.

What I'm saying is that God's symbols have meaning, and to disregard them is also to disregard the reality that the symbols represent.

Therefore, if you are to enjoy the full experience of the Spirit's presence in your life, in addition to cultivating your personal walk with God, you must follow Christ in water baptism (the first act of obedience). Then you need to build on the significance of that act of obedience through your dynamic involvement in the life of a biblically based local church.

# EXPERIENCING THE SPIRIT'S BAPTISM

**Y**our baptism by the Holy Spirit has done all of that for you—and more. You may be saying, "That's great. How can I get the benefit of it?" Here are four ways you can measure how real the Spirit's baptism is in your daily experience:

1. Since the Spirit has given you a new identity, people who knew you before you became a Christian ought to see some differences. Imagine you have just met a friend from the old days. Write down some of the new things (attitudes, habits, etc.) you hope that person would see in you.

2. Since the Spirit has given you new abilities in the form of spiritual gifts, you should be seeing some results of that as you put your gifts to work in the body. List some ways you are using your spiritual gift(s) in Christ's service. If your list is really short, you may want to pray that God will help you make better use of the gifts He has entrusted to you.

3. Since the Spirit has given His people a new unity, we are called to treat each other as equals in the body of Christ. This is a tough one, because old attitudes are hard to root out. Search your heart, and if the Spirit points out a need or a blind spot in this area, claim His power and authority to deal with it.

4. Since the Spirit has baptized you into the body of Christ, you need to be in fellowship with other believers in a local church. If you are in a church where the Bible is taught and Christ is honored, thank God for this blessing—and pray regularly for your pastor. Otherwise, ask God to lead you to a church where you can worship Him in spirit and truth.

# CHAPTER THREE

# EXPERIENCING THE SPIRIT'S SECURITY

Many Christians are insecure about their salvation. They are insecure either because they are not sure they are saved at all or because they fear doing something that will cause them to lose their salvation.

Security is a very important component of salvation and one benefit of the Holy Spirit's presence in our lives. Therefore, it's tragic that so few believers seem to understand or experience the peace that comes from belonging to Christ forever. Even on the human level we know that the more secure you feel, the more stable you are. The more insecure you feel, the more unstable you are.

Over the centuries, two basic, opposite positions have arisen as theologians have grappled with the doctrine of the believer's security. The first is known as Arminianism, the position that even the true child of God can in fact lose his or her salvation at any point due to sin or some departure from the faith. As a whole, Arminians tend to view eternal security as an unbiblical teaching that lures Christians into complacency in their walk with Christ.

The other position is called Calvinism, which holds that once a person is truly saved, he or she can never be lost. A more extreme form of Calvinism, often called Hyper-Calvinism, says that a believer is only secure if he or she perseveres in a life of obedience.

In other words, the only way to really know you are saved is to persevere faithfully to the end. Hyper-Calvinists would say that if you don't persevere, you don't lose your salvation, because your lack of perseverance shows you were never really saved in the first place. The trouble with that is you have to wait until it's over to find out. But the Bible tells us security is a blessing we can know and enjoy today.

Now this is not the place for an extended discussion of these positions, but let me summarize them by saying that there is an element of truth in both of those teachings. What I hope to do is preserve these elements while articulating what I believe to be the clear biblical teaching on the believer's security.

Let me begin by stating my thesis: A true Christian can never lose his salvation. A true Christian can never become like Seven-Up, an "uncola." A true Christian is forever saved and is never again in jeopardy of eternal condemnation.

In light of the larger topic at hand, the indwelling presence of the Holy Spirit, let me add that the Spirit's task is to make real in the lives of true believers the comfort and joy of their security in Christ and to disturb those who are trusting anyone or anything else other than Christ for their salvation. Thus security is a very experiential issue.

But once you have come to Christ in repentance and faith and settled the issue of your salvation, you can move forward in your Christian life with the security that you never again have to worry about your eternal standing before God. We have solid biblical reasons for believing in the security of the saints. Let's get to them.

## THE GROUNDS OF YOUR SECURITY

If the doctrine of security is biblical, then there ought to be plenty of biblical evidence for it. There is, and it's this evidence I want to consider first.

By the way, it may seem that the Holy Spirit drops out of the discussion for a few pages. But don't worry, we haven't forgotten about Him. Of necessity, when we talk about the grounds of our security, we must deal in some detail with the work of Christ.

So the spotlight may shift for a while, but remember this. It is the Holy Spirit who makes the truths we're about to study come alive in your heart, because the Spirit is also the Illuminator of Scripture (we'll talk about that in chapter 5). When you read God's Word about your security in Christ and something within you says, "Amen, that's true and I believe it," that's the ministry of the Spirit.

We'll be treading some important and familiar biblical ground in this chapter, so stay with me.

### Christ's Finished Work

When you understand that Christ died on the cross in your place for your sin and rose bodily from the dead; when you respond to the truth and put your complete trust and confidence in Him; when you rest your eternal destiny on Jesus Christ alone for salvation; then the Holy Spirit comes to indwell you, you are baptized into the body of Christ, and the Spirit's presence is your guarantee of security, as we will see in a minute.

In Ephesians 1, Paul writes:

> He chose us in [Christ] before the foundation of the world, that we should be holy and blameless before Him. In love He predestined us to adoption as sons through Jesus Christ to Himself, according to the kind intention of His will, to the praise of the glory of His grace, which He freely bestowed on us in the Beloved. (vv. 4–6)

> In Him also we have obtained an inheritance, having been predestined according to His purpose who works all things after the counsel of His will, to the end that we who

were the first to hope in Christ should be to the praise of His glory. (vv. 10c–12)

Paul says that God saved us with a goal in mind: to create a family of people who are passionate for His glory and His honor. Notice that all of this is "in Christ" and "through Christ." It's all based on what He did for us on the cross.

Many people don't understand the gospel. They think they are saved because they go to church or because they are doing better this year than they did last year.

However, once you mix anything with Christ, you dilute Christ. He alone must be your absolute basis of confidence for salvation if you would be born again into the family of God. Birth into God's family comes with your commitment to Christ as your only God and Savior.

My children will forever be my children because they are my children by birth. Nobody else can lay claim to them. When you come to Jesus Christ, you are born again. God has your birth certificate, and nobody else can lay claim to you.

Now, the Evans kids don't always act like Evanses, just as your kids don't always act like they belong to you. But that has nothing to do with their birth. Once you are born, you are born. Once you are born again, you are born again, because with birth comes family identity.

## Jesus' Resurrection

Consider first Romans 5:8–10:

> But God demonstrates His own love toward us, in that while we were yet sinners, Christ died for us. Much more then, having now been justified by His blood, we shall be saved from the wrath of God through Him. For if while we were enemies, we were reconciled to God through the death of His Son, much more, having been reconciled, we shall be saved by His life.

A lot of us can quote verse 8, but we tend to stop there. However, verses 9 and 10—especially verse 10—are tremendous statements of our security in Christ. The reason you can't lose your salvation is that Jesus not only died to save you, He arose to keep you saved.

Right now, at this moment, the resurrected and glorified Jesus is keeping you and me saved. Hebrews 7:25 says He is able to save us "forever" because "He always lives to make intercession for [us]." That means your salvation will only last as long as Jesus stays alive and keeps interceding for you—which is forever!

First John 2:1 tells how Jesus keeps us saved: "If anyone sins, we have an Advocate with the Father, Jesus Christ the righteous." Jesus is our defense attorney (interestingly, the word here is *paraclete*, the same word Jesus used of the Spirit's ministry in John 14:16). So when Satan says, "God, did You see what that child of Yours did? What he thought? What he said?", Jesus steps up to the divine bench in heaven.

"Father, Daddy, that believer did what Satan said he did. But if You will look on the record, You will see that his sins have been covered by My blood." So the accuser cannot take you and me out of Christ's hands when we sin.

If sin can undo your salvation and cancel out the cleansing of Christ's blood, then you will spend more time being unsaved than saved, because we all sin every day even in ways we're not aware of. But even worse, if sin can break your saving relationship with Christ, then a doubt is cast on His sufficiency to forgive sin.

But the writer of Hebrews says plainly we are kept saved "forever" by the work of Christ. Look what Jesus Himself said in John 6:39: "This is the will of Him who sent Me, that of all that He has given Me I lose nothing, but raise it up on the last day." Guess what? Jesus is not going to lose one person given to Him by the Father.

There will not be one person truly saved of whom Jesus will say later, "Oops. Got by Me." If you belong to Christ, you never have to worry about Him saying, "Sorry, you just sinned yourself out of your salvation. I can't do anything to keep you."

## God's Keeping Power

No, Jesus will lose none of His own. Let me show you why:

> My sheep hear My voice, and I know them, and they follow Me; and I give eternal life to them, and they shall never perish; and no one shall snatch them out of My hand. My Father, who has given them to Me, is greater than all; and no one is able to snatch them out of the Father's hand. (John 10:27–29)

Here is where many sincere believers make a great mistake. They think they remain saved because they hold on to God. Thus they are secure only as long as they hold on tight. No, Jesus is clear that you are secure because God holds on to you.

I received a good reminder of this truth recently during a walk with my granddaughter, Kariss. It was slippery, so I said, "Hold on to my hand, Kariss."

She said, "No, Poppy."

I said, "Why not?"

She hit the nail on the head. "No, you hold on to *my* hand." She understood the difference. What she was saying was that if her security on that slippery surface depended on her strength and her ability to hold my hand, she was going to fall. But if I was holding her hand firmly and she slipped, I could still hold her up and keep her from falling.

Someone might ask, "Can God hold me up?" The apostle Jude believed so. He wrote: "Now to Him who is able to keep you from stumbling, and to make you stand in the presence of His glory blameless with great joy" (v. 24). You will stand because God can make you stand.

According to Hebrews 13:5, we also have God's promise that "I will never desert you, nor will I ever forsake you." This is because He has His "brand" on us, and this brand is the Holy Spirit.

So a lot of us are going to have to retune our thinking. Before you were saved, you only had AM frequency. When you got saved, you got FM. If you are still listening to your

AM frequency even though you now have FM, you are not going to hear the stereophonic voice of the Holy Spirit securing you in your salvation. You are saved not because you hang on to Christ, but because you have trusted completely in His finished work.

With that trust comes security. The security is built into the trust. You don't have to accept Christ, then get saved forever at some later date. When you got saved, when you trusted Christ, you were saved forever. That's the only kind of salvation He offers. You can know you are saved if you are looking to Christ to be your only Savior.

## THE WITNESS OF YOUR SECURITY

In verses 13–14 of Ephesians 1, Paul goes on to say that those who hear, understand, and believe the gospel receive a very special witness, the seal and pledge of the Holy Spirit. These two verses are a tremendous statement of the Holy Spirit's role in making our security real to us:

> In Him, you also, after listening to the message of truth, the gospel of your salvation—having also believed, you were sealed in Him with the Holy Spirit of promise, who is given as a pledge of our inheritance, with a view to the redemption of God's own possession, to the praise of His glory.

### Your Seal

One ministry of the Holy Spirit when He comes to indwell you at salvation is to be your seal, the guarantee of your salvation. The word *seal* is very interesting because it meant to stamp ownership on something, sort of like branding cattle to identify the owner. When you come to Jesus Christ, He sets His seal on you by sending the Holy Spirit to indwell you. The Spirit is the seal that locks you into the family of God. I'm sure you've had the experience of trying and failing to open a jar because it was sealed too tightly. Your ability to break a seal is directly related to the one who sealed it. If something isn't sealed very tightly, you can unscrew the lid.

Well, you were sealed with the Holy Spirit at the moment of your salvation. In order for you or anyone else to "unseal" you, the person would have to be stronger than the sealer.

Who is the sealer? Christ Himself, who came from the Father. And what is His seal? The Holy Spirit. So you would have to outdo the holy Trinity in order to lose your salvation. You would have to be more powerful than the Godhead to screw the cap of salvation off your life. When God saved you, He saved you with an eternal purpose and He sealed you with an eternal seal.

The experiential reality of this is obvious. Since the Holy Spirit is our seal, it is His job to constantly be bringing us back in line with our salvation when we are tempted to stray away. He does this by convicting our consciences of sin, bringing people and circumstances into our lives to convict us, and disciplining us when we rebel. The Spirit keeps us within the boundaries of our salvation so that we are not judged with the world (1 Corinthians 11:32).

### Your Down Payment

In addition to the seal, the Holy Spirit is also called your "pledge," or down payment. The Greek word here, *arrabōn*, means basically the same thing as a down payment in our culture. It's a first installment.

Many of us have put things on layaway at one time or another, especially around Christmas. You put the item aside and make a down payment on it with the purpose of paying it off and redeeming it at the proper time. Now, that down payment wasn't the end; it was only the beginning. The fact of the down payment says there are more payments to come.

When you trust Christ alone for salvation, what God does is give you a down payment—the Holy Spirit—which means there is much more to come. The Spirit is your down payment or deposit on the life God is going to give you throughout eternity. The Spirit's abiding presence in your life is a promise that the transaction begun at salvation is someday going to be completed.

When a down payment is made, there is only one question left. Will the purchaser have the rest of the money necessary to redeem the merchandise? You say, "Wait a

minute! I may not be able to keep up with the payments."
Many people fear they will lose their salvation because
they don't think they can keep this thing going.

But you are not the one paying off this layaway. Since
when have you heard of a dress on layaway paying for its
own redemption? How many cars do you know of that
have made the rest of their own payments?

In other words, the question here is, Can God afford
to redeem what He has put on layaway: you and me? Absolutely! He is not expecting us to pay off the rest of our
salvation. Why not? Because on the cross Jesus said, "It is
finished!" (John 19:30).

That's one word in the original, *tetelestai*, meaning
"paid in full." All the funds necessary to pay for our total
redemption were put up by Jesus Christ on the cross. In
fact, this is much better than our idea of a down payment,
because there are no more payments to be made on our
salvation. The Holy Spirit is our guarantee of that.

If you want to shout right now, it's OK. You want to
do that when the Spirit makes all this good stuff real in
your heart.

You say, "Suppose I mess up." Well, if you recall, you
were messed up when you came to Christ. So it's not a
matter of you messing up. You entered this deal messed
up. The issue is, can Jesus afford the bill for your eternal
destiny? He most certainly can!

## THE FOCUS OF YOUR SECURITY

Why does God want you to know that you are secure
in Him? Why does the Holy Spirit want to help you experience the truth of your security? Well, one reason is that
if you are not sure you are saved, Satan will stay busy
doing everything he can to keep your spiritual equilib-
rium upset and keep you from moving forward in terms of
your growth in Christ.

Imagine, for example, how unsteady you would feel if
you weren't really sure your spouse loved you. Such ap-
prehension would keep you off balance and insecure in
your marriage. You would constantly be wondering if your
next misstep would cause your mate to disappear, or if

your attempts to show love and devotion would backfire or be met with indifference and even hostility.

Security is so important that the apostle John writes, "These things I have written to you who believe in the name of the Son of God, in order that you may know that you have eternal life" (1 John 5:13).

## Pleasing Christ

If you have eternal life abiding in you and that life is lost, it can't be eternal. Now the first objection you usually hear to the doctrine of the believer's eternal security is this: If you teach people that they cannot lose their salvation no matter what they do, they will just go out and live any old way they want because they are guaranteed salvation.

But that's like a person saying, "Now that I have health insurance, I think I'll go out and deliberately have an accident so I can take advantage of my new insurance policy."

That's not how it works. Only a fool, a criminal trying to cheat the insurance company, or somebody whose elevator doesn't go all the way up would get insurance and then go out and do the very thing he insured himself against.

Yes, God has secured us with His insurance policy, the Holy Spirit. But God does not cover us eternally so we can go out and abuse His grace. Paul dismissed that nonsense idea in no uncertain terms in Romans 6:1–2, when he asked, "Are we to continue in sin that grace might increase? May it never be!"

If all you want to do is use salvation as a cover for your sin, then you either don't have Holy Spirit salvation, or you are a Christian living in spiritual rebellion and therefore a prime candidate for the Spirit's judgment. The Scripture is clear that sometimes true Christians can abuse God's grace (Galatians 5:1–2; Hebrews 12:15; 2 Peter 3:17).

Instead, if you really know Christ, you will be eternally grateful for His eternal grace. You will be saying thank You to Him throughout eternity.

## Moving On to Maturity

Another blessing of security is that it allows us to move on from "the elementary teaching about the Christ" and "press on to maturity" (Hebrews 6:1).

This is a serious issue, not just a point to argue about. The writer of Hebrews specifically tells us not to keep on laying "a foundation of repentance from dead works and of faith toward God" (6:1b). That's salvation. Why are we to leave the basics and move on? Because the foundation is already laid. It's solid. Get on with the building.

See, a lot of Christians are so busy worrying about whether they're still saved that they never get around to being spiritual. What they do is spend all their time and effort trying to make sure they keep themselves saved. The result is that they often start doing things in the flesh to make themselves feel more sure about their salvation.

But Paul says in Galatians 3:3 that you can't begin in the Spirit and then get sanctified in the flesh. He says it's foolish to try. But you say, "I don't feel saved." That's because you are looking in the wrong direction.

## Looking to Jesus

Your feelings are not your Savior. Some believers are constantly looking within themselves to make sure they are saved. But the problem with that is if you are messed up inside, you are going to get mixed signals.

When the Holy Spirit is living in you, He will constantly turn your focus away from yourself or anything else and put it on Christ. You do not experience the joy and peace of security by looking inside, but by looking to Jesus. Let me show you what I mean from John 3, where Jesus Himself used an illustration from the Old Testament.

In John 3:14–15, Jesus said, "As Moses lifted up the serpent in the wilderness, even so must the Son of Man be lifted up; that whoever believes may in Him have eternal life." The incident He refers to happened in Numbers 21. The people of Israel complained against Moses and God, and God sent fiery serpents among them as a judgment.

The people called on God, who told Moses to make a bronze snake and put it on a pole. Then God said, "And it shall come about, that everyone who is bitten, when he looks at it, he shall live" (v. 8).

Now suppose I have been bitten by one of those snakes and I want to be healed. So I get real introspective and say to myself, "Self, are you really looking at the serpent on the pole?" Well, I am going to die, because the command of God was not to look to myself, but to the bronze serpent on the pole. It took an act of faith for the Israelites to look up at the pole, but the result was life.

The Bible says that Jesus was hung on a pole, a cross. Anybody who looks to Him in faith is granted eternal life. So the issue is not whether you feel saved, but who you are looking to for salvation. If you are looking to Jesus Christ alone as the only hope for your salvation, you are saved because Jesus is the Savior. And by the way, if you have the Holy Spirit you have help here, because His job is to keep pointing you to Jesus.

Now I am not divorcing feelings totally from this. But Hebrews 11:1 says that the assurance and conviction of faith is found in things hoped for, things you cannot see. If your confidence is in Christ and Christ alone, then you can have the assurance that you are secure in Him.

This is so because the Holy Spirit will confirm to your human spirit the security of your salvation as you look at Christ. The inner experience of security (assurance) is gained only as you look to Christ. It does not come from looking inwardly for assurance.

## THE BENEFITS OF YOUR SECURITY

If the security of the believer is a biblical doctrine, if it is part of the redemption purchased for us on the cross of Christ, then it ought to have some real benefits and experiences that the Holy Spirit brings into our lives. And it does.

For example, the preserving work of the Spirit goes all the way back to the dawn of creation (Genesis 1:2). The purpose of the Spirit's "moving" over the waters was to preserve God's created material and prepare it for the further creative activity of God so that the world would become well ordered as God's work continued to unfold. The picture here is similar to an eagle hovering over its young to protect and preserve them (Deuteronomy 32:11).

One of the Spirit's primary roles, then, is to preserve and protect what the Father brings into being. His presence removes chaos and confusion and brings instead structure, unity, and order.

In the same way, the Spirit hovers over and in God's children to preserve what God has redeemed. The Spirit's preserving work is not static or passive, however. Just as in Creation, it is filling up emptiness, taking the barren wasteland and giving it life. Even so with us, the Spirit does not demonstrate His protective power just to make the enemy stay put, but also to produce righteousness within; transforming the desert of our lives into an oasis of holiness.

Let me show you more of the Spirit's benefits in Romans 8, a chapter we seem to keep coming back to no matter what the topic.

I want to set the stage for this section by pointing you to verses 29–30. I won't take the space to quote them here, but notice that the process of your salvation began in eternity past when God "foreknew" and "predestined" you (v. 29), and it continues into eternity future with your glorification (v. 30).

The word *glorified* here is in the past tense. You are already glorified in the mind and plan of God. He has already fitted you for heaven. You are as good as there. Do you think God would foreknow and predestine and call and justify you, then drop the ball when it came to finishing the job and getting you into heaven? There is no possible way.

When Lois gave birth to our three children (all I did was fan her), in our minds they were already guaranteed adulthood. Our decision to have children included certain commitments on our part.

For example, we guaranteed that they would eat and be clothed, no matter what it cost. And so, in those early days I loaded buses, not because I was into loading buses or got a spiritual high from it, but because my kids had to eat and be clothed.

Their eating and being clothed was unrelated to their behavior. It was unrelated to the fact that they had to be spanked at times. It was unrelated to the fact that they did not always listen and still don't listen sometimes. As much as it was within my power to do so, my kids were guaranteed adulthood because they are mine by birth.

Of course, I can't guarantee that something won't happen to them, since I am not God. But when God says you are His by birth, nothing can change that. He may have to spank you, but He is still going to be your Father.

### No Opposition

So Paul comes out of the promises of verses 29 and 30 of Romans 8 with this question: "What then shall we say to these things? If God is for us, who is against us?" (v. 31). Now that is a heavy question. If God has made you His child, who can unmake you? Answer: nobody, because nobody can overrule God.

If God the Father didn't spare Jesus, but gave Him up for us (Romans 8:32), then giving us eternal security as part of our salvation is no big deal. In fact, there are a whole bunch of other good things that come with Him.

### No Condemnation

"Who will bring a charge against God's elect? God is the one who justifies; who is the one who condemns?" (Romans 8:33–34a). When you become a Christian, you become one of God's elect, His chosen. Who is going to "unjustify" you? We've already seen that Christ Jesus died and rose again for you and is in heaven today keeping you saved.

So who is going to condemn you when God has already told you that you are free? See, we spend too much time listening to the wrong folk. Enough people tell you that you are nothing, and you begin to believe it. Then it controls your life because you buy into it. So you begin to live like you are nothing.

But God says, "You need to change who you are listening to. I have said that you are something now. You are somebody. You are going somewhere. Who are you going to believe?"

## No Separation

The final benefit I want to deal with is found in Romans 8:35: "Who shall separate us from the love of Christ?" Love by its nature is experiential. We know when someone loves us. Christ will continuously demonstrate His love for us in tangible ways, thus validating our security in Him. This demonstration will be most clearly seen whenever Satan, sin, self, or circumstances try to interfere with or separate us from Christ's love.

You say, "But I don't feel like I love Christ all the time." No, you misread the question. It's not who is going to separate us from our love for Christ, but who is going to separate us from Christ's love for us.

Sometimes our love for Christ gets cold, but His love for us stays hot. Good thing too, because the rest of the verse is full of the hard stuff that life hits us with. Are you going through a rough time? That's not going to take away your salvation. Is your world collapsing? That has got nothing to do with Christ's love for you. Neither do persecution and all that other stuff.

On the contrary, "in all these things we overwhelmingly conquer through Him who loved us" (Romans 8:37). Then Paul concludes by stating his conviction that nothing can separate us from Christ's love (vv. 38–39). Notice that one of the things on the list is angels.

Who was created as the most glorious angel before he went bad? Lucifer, who became Satan. See, we give Satan too much credit for messing things up. But even angels can't separate you from the love of Christ. Not "principalities" or demons either. Cultivating our relationship with the Holy Spirit will keep the experience of God's love alive and fresh in spite of attempts by outside forces to remove it.

Also on the list is "things to come." God has already covered the future. But you say, "I may sin on my death-bed." That's a thing to come. You say, "I may backslide." There is nothing in the future that can take away your security in Jesus Christ.

You say, "But I might decide to leave Christ. What if I decide not to be saved anymore?" Read the last item on the list: "any other created thing" (Romans 8:39). That includes you. You can't take yourself out of Christ's hands because, as we saw above, Christ is holding on to you.

Now the Bible does say there is a "sin leading to death" (1 John 5:16). Some believers die before their time. God is going to have to drag some of us into glory. But He still has hold of us, because nothing can separate us from Him. To put it simply, the only way you can lose your salvation is if you are more powerful than God! Any more questions?

## EXPERIENCING YOUR SECURITY

I said earlier that when the Holy Spirit makes the truth of your security real to you, you may want to shout. That's what I mean by experiencing your security in Christ.

But you say, "Tony, I don't seem to have that internal sense of security. I know I have assurance based on the truth of Scripture and my faith in Christ. But how do I get that internal sense of assurance?" This is important because the internal is where the Spirit lives.

### Grieving the Spirit

If the Spirit is not ministering the peace and joy of your security to you, it could be that He is grieved. Ephesians 4:30 says, "Do not grieve the Holy Spirit of God, by whom you were sealed for the day of redemption."

Notice first that even in this context, Paul still goes back to his earlier word of certainty in Ephesians 1:13 that you are sealed by the Spirit. So let's get it straight right here that if you are trusting Christ as your only God and Savior, the issue is not your salvation. In fact, you can't grieve the Holy Spirit unless He is in you and is your seal.

But whereas you can't lose the Holy Spirit, you can sadden or grieve Him. If you are an unhappy Christian, it is because living inside of you is an unhappy Spirit. It's pretty hard to feel secure when you know you've made the Spirit unhappy. See, when He is happy you have joy, because joy is not dependent upon external circumstances but upon the indwelling Spirit.

The Holy Spirit is grieved by sin. One of the ways you know you have the Holy Spirit is by your reaction to sin. Now you may sin the same sin you used to sin when you were a sinner, but you can't sin the same sin the same way as you did when you were a sinner.

Here's what I mean. When you were a sinner, you could sin and love it, wallow in it, rejoice in it. But when the Holy Spirit comes to live in your spirit, He gets upset at sin, and you know He's upset. Your sensitivity to sin is a tremendous confirmation of the reality of His presence in your life.

## Abiding in Christ

The experience of security (not security itself) can also be lost by a failure to focus on Christ (Hebrews 12:1–2). The epistle of 1 John is written to teach us to abide in Christ. It's about fellowship. In 2:27 the apostle writes:

And as for you, the anointing which you received from Him abides in you, and you have no need for anyone to teach you; but as His anointing teaches you about all things, and is true and is not a lie, and just as it has taught you, you abide in Him.

Now John says you have the Holy Spirit, the anointing. But the question is, Does the Spirit have you? He is abiding in you, but are you abiding in Christ? See, you can lose the internal validation and enjoyment of your security when you are not developing an intimate walk with Jesus Christ.

In 1 John 3:24, John gives us another look at this issue: "The one who keeps His commandments abides in Him, and He in him. And we know by this that He abides in us, by the Spirit whom He has given us." When we commit ourselves to living obedient Christian lives and glorifying Christ, the Spirit validates His presence within us. When we rebel, the Spirit inside us is very quiet.

## Loving the Brethren

How we treat our Christians brothers and sisters also affects our sense or experience of security. John addresses this too:

> No one has beheld God at any time; if we love another, God abides in us, and His love is perfected in us. By this we know that we abide in Him and He in us, because He has given us of His Spirit. (1 John 4:12–13)

If you are an ornery, hateful, selfish Christian, then the Spirit will not validate His presence within you. The Spirit has made you part of the family of God, and He will make His presence felt when you are loving the members of His family the way He loves the members of His family.

## Receiving the Witness

Let me show you one final passage, 1 John 5:9–10, that bears on this issue of security:

> If we receive the witness of men, the witness of God is greater; for the witness of God is this, that He has borne witness concerning His Son. The one who believes in the Son of God has the witness in himself; the one who does not believe God has made Him a liar, because he has not believed in the witness that God has borne concerning His Son.

The witness within you is the Holy Spirit, testifying to the truth about Jesus Christ and your faith in Him. When you seek to follow and focus on Christ, you engage the Holy Spirit in your heart and your walk with Christ becomes richer and more alive. His reality is being experienced subjectively because you keep your objective focus on Jesus Christ.

There is no danger in teaching security. Anyone who would use this doctrine as a pretense to sin either doesn't possess, or doesn't understand, salvation. God has saved you and sealed you with the Holy Spirit not so you can go your own way, but to free you up to serve Him in gratitude and not because you fear He's going to dump you. That won't happen. No one can snatch you out of His hand.

# EXPERIENCING THE SPIRIT'S SECURITY

If you are married but not enjoying intimate fellowship with your spouse, you are missing out on many of the joys of marriage even though you are still married. If you are saved but not in intimate fellowship with Christ, one of the joys you miss out on is the wonderful sense of security the Holy Spirit gives. Other things can quench this witness too, so let's deal with them:

1. Perhaps you feel unworthy of salvation. Well, theologically speaking, join the crowd! None of us is worthy. But if people have made you feel worthless, write down all the ways you feel unworthy of security. Then go through the list and thank God that in Christ, these things are no longer true of you.

2. As a follow-up exercise, commit Romans 3:4 to memory: "Let God be found true, though every man be found a liar." It's not your usual memory verse, but it reinforces an important truth you need to remember.

3. You can't claim to love a Savior who guarantees your future for eternity and then not live a life that says "Thank You." What are you doing for Jesus right now that is a thank offering to Him for your salvation and security in Him?

4. Romans 8:38–39 covers the waterfront when it comes to anything that can shake you loose from Christ. If you feel uncertain about your salvation, if you struggle to feel secure, or if you think you have to hang on tight to Jesus or be lost, begin thanking God for the objective truth of His Word and asking the Holy Spirit to help you live in the confidence of it.

# CHAPTER FOUR

# EXPERIENCING THE SPIRIT'S FILLING

The Holy Spirit can be in you, and yet you can know very little of His power and influence. The issue we always have to deal with is not how much of the Holy Spirit we have, because we have all of Him. The issue is how much He has of us. In fact, we're going to get to this issue right off as we consider the filling of the Spirit.

## OUR NEED OF THE SPIRIT'S FILLING

Our text is Paul's classic treatment of this subject in Ephesians 5. I want to deal with verses 14–17 to introduce the subject:

> For this reason it says, "Awake, sleeper, and arise from the dead, and Christ will shine on you." Therefore be careful how you walk, not as unwise men, but as wise, making the most of your time, because the days are evil. So then do not be foolish, but understand what the will of the Lord is.

Paul says it is possible to be a Christian and yet be asleep; to be a Christian and yet waste your time; to be a Christian and yet be unwise; to be a Christian and yet not know what God's will is. These verses all lead up to our key verse: "And do not get drunk with wine, for that is dissipation, but be filled with the Spirit" (Ephesians 5:18).

I wonder what the response would be if we took a poll among an average group of Christians and asked how many of them could point to wasted portions of their lives, to unwise decisions, or to periods of sleepiness and sluggishness in their lives. I wonder how many would say they aren't sure whether they're in the will of God, or even if they know what God's will is for them.

Well, we would all probably have to say yes at some point. Why is that? Why do we do some of the things we do and make some of the decisions we make? I want to suggest that it is because we are not filled with the Holy Spirit. He is not the dominating influence in our lives. He is not in control.

Now, as I said above, if you are a believer the concern is never that you don't have access to the Spirit's fullness. The concern is that the Spirit be given the place in your life that He wants and deserves to have.

This is the purpose of the Spirit's filling. We'll see a little later that a synonym for filling is control. The Spirit of God wants to control our lives so that we wake up spiritually, we become wise spiritually, and we stop being foolish spiritually so that we know what God's will for us is.

It is only when these things operate in us that we can live the victorious Christian life. This is important to understand, because the more consistently you are filled with the Spirit, the faster you will grow in your faith. The less filled you are, the slower will be your growth. So the issue of filling is crucial to experiencing the Spirit's benefits.

The fastest way to get from where you are to where you are supposed to be spiritually is to learn to live a life of "Spirit-filledness." The absence of this means spiritual defeat and, ultimately, disaster. God gave us the Holy

Spirit because He knows something we tend to forget. It is impossible to live the Christian life on our own.

I cringe a little bit when I hear Christians say something like, "I'm going to stop doing that. I am going to change." Now don't misunderstand. There's nothing wrong with a determination to change. God can use that. But I fear that often behind statements like that lies a misunderstanding of the Christian life.

If you could do it, you would not need the Holy Spirit. If you could pull it off, His energy would not be necessary. But Jesus Himself said in John 15:5, "Apart from Me you can do nothing." That's why knowing He would soon return to heaven, He sent us "another Helper," the precious Holy Spirit.

So whenever we start talking about what we ought to do or plan to do, we need to be careful, because whatever it is, we will not be able to sustain it without our Helper. When Jesus Christ saved us, He gave us Someone to lean on who has the strength to hold us up. He gave us the Spirit because He knows the number sin has done on us.

We've been through this before, but allow me a few lines of review. When you got saved, you did not lose your fleshly desires. If you've been a Christian very long, you are probably thinking, "Don't I know it!"

Your old flesh got dragged kicking and screaming into your new life, but your flesh has no intention of letting you go without a fight. That's why so many of us have so many of the same old propensities we had before we got saved.

See, your flesh is as corrupt today as it was when you were lost. There is nothing in your flesh that is going to help you live the Christian life (Romans 7:18). This means that in your own strength, your attempts at self-improvement won't be any more successful today than they were in your unconverted state. The only remedy for the flesh is crucifixion with Christ.

If the Christian life is a supernatural life, then we need supernatural help to live it. The only thing that makes you more powerful now than you were before is "He who is in you" (1 John 4:4). It's not a matter of doing your best and letting the Holy Spirit make up the difference.

Have you ever gritted your teeth after committing a sin for the umpteenth time and said, "I am never going to do that again"? Have you ever lied to yourself like that? Tell the truth and shame the Devil. We all have.

If it were just a matter of being sincere, we might make it. But sincerity is not our problem; the power to change is. God has given us the Holy Spirit to provide us the enablement we need to overcome. Our challenge is to "be filled with the Spirit."

## FOUR OBSERVATIONS
## ABOUT THE SPIRIT'S FILLING

Every word in this brief phrase—"be filled with the Spirit"—is packed with meaning, so let me make four observations about this phrase that will help us understand what God is saying to us.

### God's Command

The first thing we need to note is that this is a command, not a suggestion. God is not saying, "If you want to, it would be nice if you were filled with the Spirit." God is not into suggestions. He is only into commands. Therefore, if we are going to experience the benefit of being wise, making the most of our time, and discovering the will of God, we need to be filled with the Spirit.

Interestingly, there is no command in the Bible to be baptized by the Spirit or indwelt by the Spirit. Those are blessings we receive automatically when we come to Christ. But we are commanded to be filled with the Holy Spirit, because, as we will see, this relates to our daily experience of His influence.

### For Every Believer

A second observation may not be readily apparent from the English text, but it is very important. The command of Ephesians 5:18 is plural in the Greek text. It applies to every believer.

That means the Spirit's fullness is not reserved for an elite group of Christians. You look at some Christians and say, "Oh, they are so spiritual. They love Jesus so, and they walk with Him so closely. The Spirit's power is so evident in their lives. Why can't I be like that?"

Well, it's hard to say what the difference is in individual cases. But it may simply be that you are seeing what happens when people allow the Holy Spirit to fill and control them.

The Spirit's filling is for every believer, including you and me. And I know we have to appropriate or claim it, because it is not automatic. Every Christian has been baptized by the Spirit into the body of Christ, and every believer is indwelt by the Spirit. But not every Christian is filled with the Spirit. If we were, a command to be filled would be needless.

## God Does It

Here's a third important observation about this command that you might have noticed if you remember your English grammar. That is, the command is passive. You are to "be filled," not fill yourself. Somebody else provides the action. You are the object of that action, the one acted upon. The content of the filling, of course, is the Spirit Himself. And you can resist the filling, but you cannot fill yourself.

You can't fill anything, including the human soul, that is already filled up with something else. If you are not filled with the Holy Spirit, anything else that may be filling your life is going to be very *un*filling. It's going to leave you empty, just like I can eat Chinese food and be hungry again a couple of hours later.

Too many Christians are trying to fill themselves with things that will never provide long-term satisfaction because they weren't designed for long-term satisfaction. God has no provision for filling and satisfying us and giving us His power other than the filling of the Holy Spirit. So don't expect anyone or anything else to do the job.

## *Keep It Up*

A fourth and final observation I want you to see is that this plural, passive command is also in the present tense. Now in Greek this means it is to be a continuous process. An accurate way of translating it would be, "Keep on being filled with the Spirit." In other words, don't get filled with the Spirit today and expect the filling to cover you from here on out.

You may eat a big Sunday dinner, but that does you no good on Monday or Tuesday. The filling is depleted. The same thing happens when you fill your car with gas. Because you must leave the gas station and drive around, you begin to run low on fuel. So no matter how full of the Spirit you are when you leave church, what you received in that service will not last all week.

In fact, some husbands and wives won't make it out of the parking lot after church without losing their sanctification! Why? Because we live in a world that depletes the experience of filling. Sin depletes it. People deplete it. They can take your attention away from the Spirit.

I want to make a crucial distinction between the Spirit's filling and illustrations like food and gasoline. When your stomach or gas tank gets depleted it is empty. The food or gas you put there is gone, and you have to replace the loss with another round of fuel.

But even though the filling of the Holy Spirit is an experiential concept, don't ever think that if you are not filled with the Spirit, He leaves you empty. He doesn't leave you, period. The depletion of the Spirit's filling that I'm talking about is the loss of the experience and enjoyment of His full benefits in your daily experience.

Anybody who knows me can tell you that I drive on gasoline fumes. My wife, Lois, is always after me about putting gas in the car because my car is always on empty. But I have gotten away with running on empty so long that it's hard to change.

Well, one time when Lois was in the car with me, it started choking and wheezing. I was out of gas, but I was at an exit that was going downhill. At the bottom of the hill was a gas station. So I took the exit and coasted downhill into the gas station. Feeling triumphant, I told Lois, "See what happens, honey, when you know Jesus!"

But she just said, "Oh, you are going to get it one day." And I did. One day I ran out of gas on one of our dangerous Dallas freeways while rushing to an appointment. I had to pull over to the side of the road and suffer the embarrassment of having some church members go by and wave at me.

What I'm saying is that the experience of filling is not perpetual. You must keep putting a tiger in your tank, or you will run low. You may have gotten away with it for a long time like I did, but one day you will get caught.

## WHAT IT MEANS TO BE FILLED

In order to understand what Spirit-filled people should look, act, and think like, I want to talk about the Greek word *plērousthe*, translated "filled" in Ephesians 5:18. This word occurs throughout the New Testament, and it has a lot to teach us.

In Luke 4:28, for example, the Bible says the people of Nazareth were "filled with rage" at Jesus when He challenged them for their unbelief. Now notice in verses 29–30 that they didn't just get filled with anger and walk away. They tried to push Jesus off a cliff. Their rage took possession of them.

In Acts 13:45, the Jews in Pisidian Antioch became "filled with jealousy" at the success of Paul and Barnabas. They began to attack the two men verbally and even to blaspheme. Now ordinarily, no good Jew would commit blasphemy. But their anger took over and made them do things they would not ordinarily do.

### A Matter of Control

These two examples, and others I could cite, give you the idea behind the word for filling. It means control. When you are filled in the New Testament sense, it means that somebody or something has taken over command in your life and is pulling the strings. You are no longer in control of yourself because this person or thing has over-whelmed you and taken over.

If you have ever been so angry that your anger over-whelms you, you know what I'm talking about. That's when you hear people say, "I couldn't help myself. I did it before I knew what I was doing." What they're saying is that the anger was in control.

The purpose of the Spirit's filling is that He might control our lives. We know from Scripture and from experience that Satan also wants to control us. He wants to rule our emotions and our passions. He wants to set the agenda for our attitudes and actions.

So we have to replace the wrong control with the right control. That's why sincerity alone isn't enough. If the wrong person is in control, how sincere you are about wanting to live an effective Christian life is really irrelevant. It's not about sincerity, it's about control.

Unless your sincerity leads you to the right kind of control, you will not have any kind of power. So let's talk about what we mean by the control of the Holy Spirit. To do that, we need to back up to the beginning of Ephesians 5:18 and pick up the opening phrase, "Do not get drunk with wine, for that is dissipation," or degradation.

## Controlled by Another

There's the picture we need right there. Even if you don't know what it means to be filled with the Spirit, you do know what it means for someone to be drunk. You know that a drunken man doesn't get that way by looking at advertisements for liquor. He gets drunk by drinking. And the more he drinks, the drunker he gets. The drunker he gets, the more completely the alcohol inside him is controlling him.

When a man becomes drunk, another power takes over his life. We say he is under the influence of alcohol. This substance transforms him into someone he was not before. One minute he is nice and quiet. But when the juice takes over, he becomes loud and boisterous. He becomes aggressive. He thinks he is Pavarotti, and he starts to sing.

When a police officer stops someone who is driving under the influence of alcohol and tells him to walk a straight line, he can't do it. Something else controls his legs. No matter what the officer tells him to do, he can't do what he used to do the way he used to do it because something else is running the show.

What alcohol is to the body negatively, the Holy Spirit is to the spirit positively. He makes you walk in ways you would not normally walk and talk in ways you wouldn't normally talk.

When the Spirit takes over, a lot of our excuses are nullified. We say, "Well, that's my personality." But the Spirit can change our personalities. "But this is how I was raised." Well, when the Spirit takes over, He can change the way you were raised into the way you ought to be. "I've always been like this." That's because you have not always been under the control of the Spirit of God.

The Spirit transforms us supernaturally. That's why I say rather than spending our time, energy, and effort trying to change, we need to spend our time getting filled. A sober man doesn't have to try to stagger. All he has to do is get drunk. The alcohol will take care of the staggering. He doesn't have to try to change his personality. He just has to get drunk.

Now you can see why Paul drew the analogy between someone who is drunk and someone who is under the Spirit's control. Actually, he wasn't the first person to make that connection. The Jews in Jerusalem on the Day of Pentecost accused the newly Spirit-filled believers of being "full of sweet wine" (Acts 2:13).

Peter and his pals were speaking in languages they had never learned. There was such a vitality and enthusiasm that the Jews said, "These people are drunk." It doesn't mean they were acting wild. It was just obvious that they were under the influence of some unseen power. Since the bystanders couldn't figure out what was going on, the best explanation they could come up with was public drunkenness.

But Peter stood up and answered that accusation. The believers weren't drunk, he said, and he proceeded to tell them what was going on (Acts 2:14–21). My point is, the filling of the Spirit of God will energize you with such a supernatural overflow that people will be hard put to explain you away.

## New Power

When you are filled with the Spirit, you will start hearing things like, "What in the world has happened to you?" Now don't get me wrong. People won't be asking this because you are acting weird or doing spectacular things. I'm saying that when the Spirit takes control, you will start loving people you used to hate.

When people become intoxicated with the Spirit, men who used to hit their wives when they got angry will find the ability to tame their temper. When the Spirit takes control, people who had no control over their passion will be able to say no to immorality.

So, rather than saying, "I am not going to do that anymore," what we need to do is get intoxicated, get filled, with the Spirit. When we yield control to Him, He takes care of the transformation. When we are filled with the Spirit, He releases His power and influence in our lives.

When you get indigestion, you may open a little packet containing two tablets and drop them in water. Those tablets start to fizz because they are releasing power to solve your problem.

But the power is in concentrated form. In order for that power to be released, you drop those two tablets in water and an explosion occurs. It's the power of the tablets being released in the water, so that the water is not plain water anymore. Now when you drink that water, you get the power to fix your upset stomach.

When you were indwelt by the Holy Spirit, you received "Holy Ghost concentrate." The Spirit was placed in you in concentrated form. But when His power is released by your submission and willingness to be filled, He cures your spiritual indigestion and empowers you to pull off great things. It's not business as usual anymore, and when this happens you have experienced the benefits of the Spirit's presence in your life.

Let me say one more thing before we move on to the process by which we are filled with the Spirit. If you are using anything other than the Holy Spirit as your crutch, your support system, then you really do not know what the filling of the Spirit is.

See, some people use cigarettes or drink as a crutch. "I need a smoke!" "A drink before dinner settles my nerves." Others lean on coffee (careful, Tony, you're meddling!). Some people use relationships as a crutch. If others don't affirm them, they are wrecks. But if you understand the filling of the Spirit, you will understand that He wants you to lean on Him and stop depending on Holy Spirit substitute.

## THE PROCESS OF BEING FILLED

How are we filled with the Holy Spirit? That's obviously a crucial question, and I disagree with many of my teachers on this point. There's a lot of confusion about the relationship between Ephesians 5:18 and verses 19–21 that follow. The issue is this: are these things the *result* of being filled with the Spirit, or are they the *means* to His fullness?

There are good people on both sides of the question, and it obviously doesn't involve any non-negotiable point of doctrine. But still it's important to understand what Paul is saying to us, so let's quote the verses and then I'll explain how I see them relating to being Spirit-filled:

> Speaking to one another in psalms and hymns and spiritual songs, singing and making melody with your heart to the Lord; always giving thanks for all things in the name of our Lord Jesus Christ to God, even the Father; and be subject to one another in the fear of Christ. (vv. 19–21)

### The Means of the Filling

Now let's answer the question, Are these verses describing the *how* of being Spirit-filled, or its *result*? Although many Bible teachers believe these things are the result of the Spirit's filling, I want to suggest instead that they are the means to His filling.

Paul's concern here is not just to command you to be filled, but to tell you how to be filled. He does not skip the process to get to the results. Let me summarize how I see this unfolding and then show you how I arrived at this conclusion. I think Paul is saying that the way to be filled with the Holy Spirit is to make worship a lifestyle.

## Making Worship a Lifestyle

Stay with me on this for a few minutes. Remember those wonderful times when you left church Sunday morning on "cloud nine"? You were spiritually full. What filled you when you came to church that Sunday? I'll tell you what filled you: being in the environment of the redeemed, worshiping God in the holy environment of the family of God.

What did you do in that environment? You got filled up on God's Word. You got filled and inspired and lifted up by the music. You poured out your heart to God and you were filled with a sense of His holy presence as you communed with Him in the quietness and celebration of that hour.

All those things add up to a worship service. For one or two hours every Sunday, God's people gather in a worship service where we minister to one another and to Him. We hear His Word and we talk to Him. We worship and adore Him.

Well, who said that had to end at noon on Sunday? The way you learn to live a Spirit-filled life is to learn to do Monday through Saturday what you did on Sunday. The way you get filled with the Spirit as a day-by-day experience is to make worship a way of life.

Isn't this what Paul is saying in Romans 12:1? "I urge you therefore, brethren, by the mercies of God, to present your bodies a living and holy sacrifice, acceptable to God, which is your spiritual service of worship." He is calling us to hold our own private worship services.

### Taking Sunday Home

Here's the way it works. You leave church full of the Spirit because you were in God's presence with God's people, communicating with God's Person. But when you go out on Monday and start jostling with people in a sin-soaked, sick world, your experience of the Spirit's filling can get depleted in a hurry. If He is going to continue ministering to and through you, you are going to need to refuel.

What Paul is saying in Ephesians 5:19–21 is that when worship becomes a way of life for you, when you begin to live in a spiritual environment on a day-by-day basis, you are going to be full of the Holy Spirit. And as the Spirit fills you, you will begin to experience His control.

Now lest it sound like the only way you can pull this off is to enter a monastery, let me say I'm talking about living this right where you are. The great thing about making worship a way of life is that you can worship anywhere and anytime you want.

### Four Ways to Get Filled

Paul gives us four specific ways we make worship a way of life, resulting in the ongoing filling of the Spirit. He says first that we are to communicate with one another. Paul says with the opening phrase of 19: "Speaking to one another. . . ." Do you know why more believers aren't experiencing the Holy Spirit's fullness in their daily lives? Because our mouths and our ears and our hearts are so full of other stuff we don't have anything to say on the subject of the Spirit's work in us.

May I get personal? I'm talking about the radio station you fill your mind and heart with all day long and on the way home; the cable TV channels you "surf" through with your remote all evening; the input that gets you so filled up with secular and ungodly stuff that the Spirit has nothing holy to draw on. There is no room for Him, so we have nothing to speak to one another about except sports, business, and the weather. Christians should regularly be reinforcing others and being reinforced by others in order that their spiritual focus might be kept on track.

How? With psalms, the Word of God set to music; hymns, having to do with the expression of spiritual truth in song; and spiritual songs, having to do with our testimony, our experience with the Spirit.

Second, we are to communicate with the Lord by making melody in our hearts. Here I am, meddling again! Maybe you can tell I get worked up about this. See, people in Dallas get "filled" with a certain football team every fall. Lord have mercy, those Cowboys sure know how to throw a "worship service"! And it works. People all over town are wearing Cowboy clothes and talking Cowboy talk and squirming in the pew on Sunday so they can get home by kickoff. No wonder we get messed up. Look what's filling us. If your heart is on the Cowboys, you become a Cowboys fan, but if your heart is on Jesus, you become a Jesus fan.

Third, we are to give thanks for everything in Jesus' name (Ephesians 5:20). That means talking to God from a point of gratitude, not grumbling. If you are a grumbler, I guarantee that you will not be filled with the Spirit.

If the only time God hears from you is when you want something, you won't be filled with the Spirit. If you can't come to God and say, "Lord, everything is wrong, but I just want to thank You I am alive to know it," then you will not know what it is to pray out of the Holy Spirit's fullness. My mind goes back to 1 Thessalonians 5:17, which says that in every circumstance you can find something to give God thanks for.

And fourth, when worship is a way of life, being subject to one another (Ephesians 5:21) won't be the kind of demeaning, subservient thing it is made out to be today. It will simply be an act of worship from a Spirit-filled heart to serve others, starting with our families. Servanthood reflects the spirit of Christ, so it is no wonder the Holy Spirit fills us as we reflect His attitude toward others.

## GETTING THIRSTY

I guess you know by now that I love John 7:37–39. It's such a beautiful picture of the Holy Spirit's fullness. I especially love Jesus' invitation to the thirsty to come and drink freely.

That really nails what I have been trying to get across. Alcoholics don't just talk about drinking, they don't just dream about it. They drink, long and deep. Why? Because they are thirsty. They have developed an overpowering thirst that they will sacrifice almost anything to quench.

But many of us say, "Well, yes, I need to spend time with God every day." The next year we say, "I haven't gotten around to it yet, but I know it's important." Our problem is we are not yet thirsty enough. We are not yet tired of trying to pull off the Christian life with a maximum of our power and a minimum of Holy Ghost power. We don't see how empty we are, so we don't come to the Spirit to get filled.

So many Christians find personal devotions boring. That's because our devotions are not worship services. We're not singing in our hearts to the Lord. We're not reading the Word like God's love letter to us.

I've made this suggestion before, but it bears repeating here. Every morning when you get up, start with this agenda. Get down by your bed and say, "Lord, for the next twenty-four hours, I'm Yours. You can do with me whatever You want and take me wherever You want, because the only thing that matters today is Your will for me. Fill me with Your Spirit this day."

Begin your day entrusting your life to the Lord. Add a song and some Scripture, and after a while you are going to start being late for work because the worship was so good. Worship went overtime. That's what God does when you are full of Him.

Do you ever meet people who are full of themselves? They let you know what they think about themselves. Everything revolves around them. Well, replace self in that equation with the Holy Spirit, and you've got the idea.

When you're full of the Spirit, you don't mind who knows it. You sing His praises instead of your own. Everything revolves around Him, and you bring His influence to bear on your life all day long. I believe that the proof of His filling is in your prayer life.

When you are Spirit-filled in your daily experience, you are calling on Him all day long about everything. It's as natural as breathing, because you are living in an environment of worship. It doesn't matter whether the prayer is five seconds or five minutes, you're in vital touch with the Spirit.

Another way of developing spiritual thirst is to hang around others who are set on becoming spiritually drunk so that you can get drunk together. Feed on each other's passion for the Spirit. Hang around those who have learned the art of spiritual drinking—not in a fake, contrived method as in many extreme emphases today, such as "laughing in the Spirit," but letting the Holy Spirit take over control of your life as alcohol takes over a drunk.

The first place we are to apply the Spirit's filling is in the family. We have a lot of marriages and families in trouble today. The problem in marriage is not that the two people are different personalities. That's the beauty of marriage. If you were both alike, one of you would be unnecessary.

So differences are not the problem in our marriages. The problem is that either one or both partners have not yet gotten drunk on the Holy Spirit. Am I telling you that the filling of the Spirit is going to change your problems? No. I am telling you that the filling of the Spirit will change *you*. Then it really won't matter as much whether your problems change or not.

The next time you get really thirsty, don't turn to a bottle or a glass or any other substance. Allow the Spirit to fill you!

# EXPERIENCING THE SPIRIT'S FILLING

When you really get a handle on the reality of the Spirit-filled life, you'll wonder how you were able to make it at all without the Spirit's fullness. This is not a blessing you have to beg the Spirit for. He's waiting to fill you with Himself. I hope these ideas will help you open your heart to Him:

1. Dr. Bill Bright, founder of Campus Crusade for Christ, has helped many Christians appropriate the Spirit's fullness with his concept called "spiritual breathing." First you exhale the bad air. That's confession of sin. Then you inhale, claiming the Spirit's fullness as yours. It's a great concept—and, like physical breathing, you can do it as often as necessary.

2. One thing about those Pentecost Christians: They were doing things that couldn't be accounted for on merely human terms. Take a long look at your life and ask if that's true of you. If it isn't, ask the Spirit to do a new work in you.

3. I hope you have a good hymnbook next to your Bible in your place of devotions. Don't take one from the church pew—pastors don't like that! Many churches have extra hymnals for sale, and any Christian bookstore will have some. Make singing a regular part of your worship. It will add a dimension of joy to your worship you never imagined possible.

4. For the next twenty-four hours, try to keep a record of what you fill your mind and heart with. Include your listening, viewing, reading, daydreaming, conversations—anything that affects your mind. Your list should tell you what you're giving the Spirit to work with and where you may need to adjust.

# CHAPTER FIVE

# EXPERIENCING THE SPIRIT'S RELEASE

We're talking about the Holy Spirit's presence in our lives, how He manifests Himself to us and makes the things of God real in our experience.

Things are going to get a little gritty in this chapter, because I want to talk about the release of the Spirit. You may say, "What do you mean, gritty? This sounds great. Doesn't release mean freedom and all that good stuff?"

Well, yes it does, and experiencing the release of the Spirit is a wonderful thing. But the process the Spirit uses to bring us to that point may not always seem so wonderful, because the Holy Spirit has to break us before He can release us. And I don't know anyone who enjoys being broken.

By brokenness, I mean the work of the Holy Spirit that strips away our self-sufficiency. Many of us experience perpetual spiritual defeat because we are too self-sufficient. We can make it on our own. Although we may go through the spiritual motions, we really don't need God.

In fact, some of us who stand most in need of being broken don't even realize it. We try to cover our need by doing other things, like seeking an emotional experience. We go to church and get filled with all the good things, only to discover that when the emotion is gone, the awareness of the Spirit's presence goes with it.

Many of us read our Bibles and pray, and for those moments that we are in the Word or on our knees, we have a sense of the Spirit's presence. But when we stop reading and praying, something happens to that reality. I want to suggest that one reason this is true is that the Spirit's primary way of revealing Himself, and releasing the experience of His presence and power in and through us, is by means of brokenness.

Now let me clarify something right here. Brokenness does not necessarily mean that everything goes wrong in our lives or that God takes everything away from us. As we'll see later, it does mean that God will deal with us in a way that cracks open the hard shell of our sin-scarred souls to release our spirits to live under the control of His Spirit.

Peruse your Bible and you will hardly find a man or woman God used who didn't get broken first. Moses had to be sent to a desert before God could use him. It wasn't until after Peter's failure and rebellion that Jesus could tell him, "Feed My sheep." Mark wasn't qualified to be a fellow worker of Paul's and a writer of Scripture until he had washed out in the ministry. It wasn't until Paul himself broke through the struggle of the flesh that he began to realize the awesome power of the Holy Spirit.

So what I want to propose and demonstrate in this chapter is that we need the discipline of the Spirit as He shapes and molds us—breaks us, if you will—to make of us the men and women He wants us to be.

I can hear someone asking, "Hey, Tony, can't I just do this the easy way by yielding myself to the Spirit and letting Him release my spirit without all this talk about being broken?" Well, it's true that some of us are more spiritually sensitive than others. And it's true that the more pliable and cooperative we are with the Spirit, the less He has to break us.

But we all need this ministry of the Spirit because of our makeup as sinful human beings. Let me show you what I mean, because until you see how we are put together, you won't understand the need for brokenness.

## THE NEED FOR BROKENNESS

First Thessalonians 5:23 says, "May your spirit and soul and body be preserved complete, without blame at the coming of our Lord Jesus Christ." We are both material and immaterial beings. Our material or physical part, the body, is that which allows us to interact with the physical world through our five senses. The immaterial is the invisible part of us, the soul and spirit.

The order in which Paul lists these elements is all-important. We are spirit, soul, and body—not body, soul, and spirit. Many people try to reverse the order as they live their lives, and they do so to disaster. If we look at ourselves as bodies first, we will work toward sanctification from the wrong direction: from the outside in, rather than from the inside out.

### Our Makeup

When God formed Adam out of the dust of the ground, Adam was made a physical being. Then God breathed into Adam the "breath of life," and man became a living soul (Genesis 2:7). When man became alive, his being became fully integrated.

First of all, man developed God-consciousness because he has a spirit. This is what makes you different from an animal. You are created in God's image because you have a spirit, for God is spirit (John 4:24).

Man also developed self-consciousness because he has a soul. Animals have instinct, but not self-consciousness. That is, there is no eternal dimension to an animal because it has no soul and certainly no spirit.

Finally, man developed what you could call environmental or world consciousness because he has a body. We are aware of the world around us and can exist in it because we have bodies. Life is the ability to relate to these different levels of consciousness: the spirit to God, the soul to self, and the body to the outside world. This is how we are made up.

## A Dead Spirit

But the day Adam sinned, something went wrong. His spirit died. He lost his God-consciousness. This is what God meant in Genesis 2:17 when he told Adam and Eve, "in the day that you eat from [the tree of the knowledge of good and evil] you shall surely die." Adam and Eve did not drop dead physically that day, but their spirits died. They were removed from the presence of God.

We saw in chapter 2 that in Adam all of us have died (1 Corinthians 15:22). Because Adam sinned, we are all stillborn spiritually. We have no capacity to commune with God. We are dead in our sins (Ephesians 2:1). That's why we need to be born again. When you come to Jesus Christ, the Spirit of God brings your spirit alive. He connects you to God's "Internet." You are now linked up so that you can communicate with God and He can communicate with you. There is still a problem, however, because in saving you, God did not kill off your sin-scarred soul and give you a brand-new one. Your newly alive spirit is still surrounded by your soul.

## A Scarred Soul

The soul is the self-conscious part of your being. It is your personhood. The reason people have different personalities is that they have different souls. Your soul has to do with your mind. It's the seat of your will and emotions, your choices and decisions. All Christians have the same Holy Spirit, but it's through our souls that we express our distinct personalities.

When you die, your soul goes into eternity. If you are a non-Christian, you have a spiritless soul that goes into hell. If you are a Christian, you have a spirit-fed soul that goes to heaven. But your soul will live for eternity.

Now please stay with me. The theological and biblical foundation I'm laying here is crucial to understand if you're going to see why even as believers, we need the Spirit's ministry of brokenness leading to the release of our spirits.

When Adam sinned, his spirit died and he lost his ability to communicate with God, but he kept his soul. He was still a person (soul) even though he was spiritually dead.

The problem is, due to Adam's sin a negative component was added to his soul: what the Bible calls the "old man" or the sin nature. Theologians call it the Adamic nature. This sin nature affected both Adam's personhood and his personality.

Since Adam passed his sin nature on to the rest of us, we inherited his problems. We are born *without* the God-quickened spirit we should have, and we are born *with* a soul scarred and contaminated by sin. So we are sinners by birth and sinners by choice.

The sin nature is the part of our soul that, like a magnet, gravitates to everything that is against God. Since we ourselves and those around us obey the sin nature so often, we get scarred by sin and build up scar tissue around our souls. Many of us have been badly scarred by the sins of others, as well as by our own sins.

Some people seem to have deep personality problems. What many really have is a deep layer of scar tissue around their souls. Now remember, we as believers are still scarred in our souls even though the Holy Spirit has made us spiritually alive and indwells us. The process of spiritual growth is peeling the scar tissue from around the soul.

Now let me make a statement you probably aren't used to hearing. I believe that if you are a Christian, your spirit is perfect. Why? Because your spirit is infused by the Holy Spirit, and God the Holy Spirit is perfect.

When you come to Christ, He gives you a brand-new spirit that is alive to God and under the control of the Holy Spirit. So there is no improvement for your spirit in the expression and demonstration of holiness. Your newly alive spirit is perfect and therefore cannot sin (1 John 3:9). Which is why Paul says that when we become believers we are already complete in Christ (Colossians 2:10). In the process of spiritual growth, the Holy Spirit is outworking our internal completeness.

The reason you need to grow spiritually is that your soul has been scarred and that scar tissue needs to be removed. To change the imagery, the reason you need the Spirit's ministry of brokenness is that the hard shell of your soul needs to be broken.

### Breaking the Shell

The spirit has a casing around it called the soul. The soul has a casing around it called the body. The spirit expresses itself through the soul, and the soul through the body. Your soul is what needs fixing, but you can't fix your soul just by fixing your body, because the body only does what your soul tells it to do.

That's why we need to deny our bodies the fulfillment of their sinful appetites (1 Corinthians 9:25–27), so that we can cooperate with the Spirit's program of soul transformation. Once the soul departs the body at death, the body has nothing more to do.

In order to fix the soul, we have to release or unleash our spirit by the ministry of the indwelling Holy Spirit. The spirit affects the soul. The soul affects the body. So if you want to live the way God wants you to live and become everything He wants you to become, His Spirit must do surgery on your soul. That's the message of Hebrews 4:12–13:

> The word of God is living and active and sharper than any two-edged sword, and piercing as far as the division of soul and spirit, of both joints and marrow, and able to judge the thoughts and intentions of the heart. And there is no creature hidden from His sight, but all things are open and laid bare to the eyes of Him with whom we have to do.

We'll unfold this critical passage in detail later, but the point I want to make is that the goal of God's Word is not to make your body feel better. If that's all that happens, you have made no spiritual progress. The goal of the

Word is not even to make your soul feel better, but to divide soul and spirit, to open up the soul and release the spirit.

My wife, Lois, loves to roast and eat peanuts. But to get at the peanut itself, she has to crack the shell. If Lois never gets around to cracking the shell, if she never gets below the surface, she will never get to the nut.

Now imagine what would happen if Lois started admiring those peanut shells, washing them and polishing them and all that. That's not what peanuts were made for. Many of us are so enamored with our shell, the body, that we never get around to fixing the part that is really worth getting to, the soul.

In fact, Satan has so rearranged our priorities that we spend much more time prettying up the shell than we do getting to the nut. Think about the time and energy you spend fixing yourself up, making yourself look good, shopping for things to pretty up your shell. It is this concern that prompted Peter to exhort Christian women to put more focus on "the hidden person of the heart" than on physical beauty (1 Peter 3:3–4).

See, going shopping will never correct the scar on your soul. If you want to get to the core, you must get beyond the shell. Once you break the shell on a peanut, there is still another covering, the skin around it. In our analogy, we can liken that to the soul. The skin of the peanut also has to be broken to release the "innermost being" of that peanut, which is the meat itself. That's the goal of cracking open a peanut.

But the analogy breaks down here because unlike the process of cracking peanuts, spiritual brokenness occurs from the inside out rather than from the outside in. That is, it does not happen from the body inward to the spirit, but from the spirit outward to the body.

It is more like the process of release that the butterfly experiences as it breaks forth from the cocoon of the caterpillar. When that breaking occurs, the beauty, power, and wonder of what was developing on the inside is revealed. If there were no breaking, the beauty of the butterfly would never be manifested. Therefore, if we want to see improvement in our external behavior, the process must begin with and center on the spirit.

Now it's here that a lot of secular psychology, and much that goes under the banner of Christian psychology, makes its greatest error. Any attempt to correct the actions of the body and the perspective of the soul without starting with the life of the spirit is not Holy Spirit–orchestrated transformation. At best, it is psychological programming that camouflages the problems rather than transforming the person.

But God is after much, much more. Authentic Christian counseling, while clarifying the problem, always focuses on the power of the Spirit and seeks His release in the believer's life so the soul is transformed and not merely reprogrammed.

Unless you get beyond the body to the soul and the soul is broken and transformed by the release of the spirit, you will never get to the core of who you are and you will never realize the Holy Spirit's power that can fix who you are. This is why the Word of God is so important. It alone can penetrate to divide the soul and spirit (Hebrews 4:12).

In 2 Corinthians 4:6, Paul paraphrased Genesis 1:3 by saying that God said, "Light shall shine out of darkness." Many of us have dark souls. That is, there are things hidden well below the surface, like a wicked heart and a depraved mind.

We have been scarred by sin, some more than others, based on our sin and the effects on us of the sins of others (child abuse, disease, war, crime, etc.). When you became a Christian, the scar tissue did not drop off. Your soul is still in need of Spirit surgery. God wants to grow you into the person He wants you to be, the process we identified earlier as sanctification.

But to do that, He has to remove the scar tissue from your soul. The way He does that is through the release of your spirit under the ministry of the Holy Spirit.

## THE AGENT OF BROKENNESS

Paul writes in Galatians 2:20:

> I have been crucified with Christ; and it is no longer I who
> live, but Christ lives in me; and the life which I now live in
> the flesh I live by faith in the Son of God, who loved me, and
> delivered Himself up for me.

In other words, Paul made a trade. He traded his soul life
for his spirit life. He allowed the Holy Spirit to break his
soul and bring forth his spirit life in such a way that it
took over and began to dominate his existence. When it
did, Paul became a transformed man.

### The Revealer

Too many of us are trying to fix our souls ourselves. We
can cover it and try to hide the scars, but the only way to fix
the soul is to crack it open so that the spirit comes forth.
Then, as we saw above, light will shine in the darkness.

There is only one way to fix darkness. You have got to
penetrate it with light. Once you turn on the light, you
have addressed the darkness. Many of us are trying to address the dark spots in our lives by trying to come up with
a darkness remedy. But the only darkness remedy is light.

Now I want to consider a familiar passage in 1 Corinthians 2:9–12:

> Things which eye has not seen and ear has not heard, and
> which have not entered the heart of man, all that God has
> prepared for those who love Him. For to us God revealed
> them through the Spirit; for the Spirit searches all things,
> even the depths of God. For who among men knows the
> thoughts of a man except the spirit of the man, which is in
> him? Even so the thoughts of God no one knows except the
> Spirit of God. Now we have received, not the spirit of the
> world, but the Spirit who is from God, that we might know
> the things freely given to us by God.

The Holy Spirit knows things we can't even imagine.
Now don't miss the point of what Paul is saying. He is not
just talking about heaven. He is talking about now. When
you don't see a solution to your problem, the Spirit can
reveal to you things you've never seen before.

You say, "Nobody has given me a real answer to my dilemma." Guess what the Spirit reveals? Things your ears have not heard.

You say, "I can't think of anything good that can come out of this mess." But the Spirit can reveal things that have never entered into your heart.

But you say, "Wait a minute. If the Holy Spirit wants to freely give me things that I can't see or hear or even think, how come I am not seeing them, hearing them, or thinking them?"

It is because you have too much scar tissue around your soul. The Spirit must break open your soul. Since the soul is the seat of the self, what gets in the way of the Spirit's supernatural work in our lives is ourselves. We are so self-oriented, so self-saturated. We want to live for self, please self, satisfy self.

But this is exactly the part of us that Christ wants us to put to death. Not our legitimate self, our identity. Christ calls us to put to death what the Bible calls the flesh, that part of self that seeks to live for its own sinful agenda. To do that He must do some breaking, and the agent is the Holy Spirit.

Many of us have tried to accomplish this in other ways, like the power of positive thinking or New Year's resolutions. We are like lion tamers trying to whip the flesh into shape. It's not that we don't mean well. The problem is we are appealing to the problem to fix the problem.

We say, "Body, don't touch that. You know better than that." We spank our bodies, but it doesn't work. The body is doing it because there is scar tissue on the soul. If we do something long enough, it becomes a habit. The answer is to remove the scar tissue, and only the Holy Spirit can do that.

### The Divine Surgeon

So it is the Spirit's job to break open the soul by cutting into it. That is not fun, but you need to begin looking at your trials as the Spirit cutting away the scar tissue of your soul.

God has been working to break many of us for years. But like strong-willed children, we refuse to be broken. Do you have a child like that? You spank him and he gets harder. "I'm not going to cry!" Many of us have increased our soulishness even though God is trying to break it by the various circumstances He brings our way. That's why God will even let your life collapse if that is what it takes to break your soul.

With some of us, God has to constantly hammer and hammer until we finally say, "I am broken." Sometimes He has to bring us to the end of ourselves because our stubborn wills refuse to yield to His control.

Why does Paul say, "I serve [God] in my spirit" (Romans 1:9) and "Walk by the Spirit, and you will not carry out the desire of the flesh" (Galatians 5:16)? Because the Holy Spirit operates through the vehicle of the human spirit. The human spirit is the wire upon which the current of the Holy Spirit's power runs.

It's interesting that Bible translators are often confused as to how to handle the word *spirit*. In many contexts it is not completely clear whether the word should be capitalized, meaning the Holy Spirit, or put in lowercase, referring to our human spirits. In many cases this problem exists because the two are so intermingled in the believer that it's hard to tell them apart.

Remember, there is only one part of you that is like God: your spirit. God is pure spirit (John 4:24). Your soul has been contaminated by sin, but the spirit is pure. It is totally under the control of the Holy Spirit.

Some people have bad personalities because they are scarred by sin. They are irritable, grouchy, and messed up. They try to do better. They try to reform, to turn themselves around. And they do. Instead of being miserable and depressed, they turn around and become depressed and miserable.

People say they can't change. They are absolutely right. They can't. But Paul says that when the Spirit penetrates the soul, the personality can be changed. When you walk by the Spirit, you get self-control. You get joy and peace and patience and all the other fruit of the Spirit that follow in Galatians 5.

That's why Paul said he could do all things through Christ who strengthened him (Philippians 4:13). In the Person of the Holy Spirit, God removes the scar tissue on your soul. He invades your soul and changes it. Your personality becomes what God wants it to be.

When you came to Christ, the Scripture says that you received the Holy Spirit. If you want your soul to benefit from this, a breaking must occur. But so many of us say, "I don't want to be broken."

Then, like an unbroken peanut, you will stay in your shell and never produce anything worth tasting. Like an unbroken seed, you will fail to bring forth new spiritual life. And like a bottle of expensive perfume whose seal is unbroken, the wonderful fragrance of the Spirit's life will never be released in you.

Do you realize what would happen if God ever broke open your soul? Do you know what would happen if you experienced the Spirit's release? You would grow spiritually more than you ever thought you could, and you would become more than you ever thought you could be. You would find your personality changing because the Spirit broke you and released Himself in you through your spirit.

## THE PROCESS OF BROKENNESS

So the Holy Spirit's job is to break us of our self-will so that we might reflect Christ. Let's go back to Hebrews 4:12–13 as we look at how the Spirit produces in us the brokenness He wants to see, so He can release our spirits to transform our souls and give us the power to act differently with our bodies.

### The Word

The author of Hebrews says that God begins to cut through the soul by the power of His Word. Notice the picturesque language. A two-edged sword cuts you on either side. What the Word of God does is cut to your innermost being, dividing your soul and spirit. If your personhood is going to be fixed, there must be a division of soul and spirit, because your soul can keep your spirit from expressing itself. See, your spirit has been constructed to possess and express the life of God.

So the Spirit of God uses the living Word of God to cut into your life and divide up your soul and spirit so that you do not drag your spirit down with the sins of your soul. God's solution is to divide the soul and spirit so that even though you have a messed-up soul, you can live based on a fixed-up spirit.

This process is a lot like what a podiatrist does. He cuts the hard calluses and dead skin from our feet so that the soft, natural tissue can be exposed again. Well, the Word of God must cut into our lives, dividing soul and spirit so that the soul no longer inhibits the soft tissue of our redeemed spirit from being exposed and expressing itself regardless of circumstances.

Notice that the Word is "living and active." For many of us, the Bible is a dead book because we have not allowed it to act on us. We do not give the Spirit permission to perform surgery with it. One reason to attend church is to be operated on by the Spirit. Church is a surgical procedure. It is the job of the Spirit to take the Word and start cutting. Every time a believer goes to church, his or her prayer should be, "Cut me, Holy Spirit." When He does, the Word will become active.

The Spirit can do this without negating your personality, just as He came upon the writers of Scripture and guided them to write perfect truth without negating their personalities or their unique experiences or writing styles. What the Spirit's intervention did was prevent the negatives of these writers' personalities from interfering with His purposes in the recording of Scripture.

In the same way, the Word is now living and active in your life so that the Spirit gives you the guidance and light of God in spite of the experiences that may have scarred your soul. How does He do that? By judging the thoughts and intentions of your heart. That's Spirit surgery.

You say, "How do I know if I have been cut?" This is how you know. You begin to see what the Spirit sees. If you can come to church and never squirm in your seat, you are not on the operating table. If you can come to church every week and sit under the Word of God and never be convicted, if you never have to take out a handkerchief because you are beginning to sweat as the Word divides your soul and spirit, then there is nothing living and active happening in your life.

You are being cut and broken when the innermost secrets of your heart are being made known and you begin to see what God sees. While everybody else is noticing how good you look, the Spirit is looking into your deepest being.

### Discipline

A second way we experience the release of the Spirit is through discipline. God's children are never punished; God's children are disciplined. Punishment is punitive; discipline is correction. There is a fundamental difference.

God brings things into our lives to reveal what is wrong so that we will make it right. Now here is where we have a major problem. We mistake the hand of God for the hand of men. Let me show you what I mean.

We say, "John did this and this to me"; "My wife is not treating me right"; "My boss is messing me over." Listen, that person may very well be the Spirit's instrument of discipline in your life. If you mistake the hand of God for the hand of men, you will miss the Spirit's corrective discipline.

God uses circumstances and people to cut through the scars in your soul. If you don't see that, you will miss the very thing He is trying to do. When you run from this person to that person because the first person was the hand of God in your life, then God will just move from this person to that person.

If you are running from a bad marriage when God is using your mate to break through your sin-scarred soul and release your spirit, then marriage number two won't solve your problem because God is still trying to remove the scar tissue. We cannot make the mistake of attributing to people what may be the hand of God.

James 1:2–3 says it best. "Consider it all joy, my brethren, when you encounter various trials, knowing that the testing of your faith produces endurance." When God puts something in your path, He says to consider or count it all joy. Our human response is, "How can I count as joyful that which is not joyful? Am I supposed to fake joy?"

No, you missed it. The key word in this text is not joy. The key word is *consider*. This is an economic word in Greek, having to do with a financial ledger. James is saying to enter trials into the ledger of your life as occasions for joy because you know God is using them to mature you. Now James is not talking about trials you create by your own sin, but trials you encounter, the things God brings into your life.

A financial ledger is based on the facts. You don't have to feel that one plus one equals two. You don't have to get excited about the fact that one plus one equals two. You just have to know that one plus one equals two.

The joy comes when by an act of your will you say, "Lord, I know that You are bringing this trial into my life to correct something in my personality that needs to be fixed so the Spirit can be freed to live out Your life in me. So Lord, even though I don't like what I am going through right now, I like why You are putting me through it. I am going to put this one in my ledger under the heading, 'Opportunity for spiritual growth.'"

God cuts through the soul and releases the Spirit through the trials He brings our way. We need to know that (James 1:3) so we don't lose it when the trials come.

I had a friend who was watching the Winter Olympics back in 1980 when the United States upset Russia in a heart-stopping ice hockey game. My friend only got to see the last part of the game, but he videotaped it. So later he invited some friends over to enjoy the replay with him.

When he watched the game the first time, he was all nervous wondering whether the U.S. was going to win. But the second time he watched, he was calm, cool, and collected. Why? Because he knew something. He had already seen the end of the game. He knew who was going to win, so his emotions were controlled by what he knew. Same game, different knowledge.

When you know what the Holy Spirit is doing in your life, when you understand where God is taking you, you can take your fingernails out of your mouth and wipe your forehead because you know something. You know He is using even the negative events of life to break through your sin-scarred soul and free you up to be what He created you to be.

As long as Satan can keep your eyes on circumstances instead of on God, you will not experience the release of your spirit through the work of the Holy Spirit. Every time a crisis hits, you should be asking the question, "God, what are You doing in my life? What are You trying to show me? Where do You want me to go?" Then His Word will become living and active.

## Consecration

A third aspect of brokenness is consecration. Romans 12:1 says, "I urge you therefore, brethren, by the mercies of God, to present your bodies a living and holy sacrifice, acceptable to God, which is your spiritual service of worship."

Consecration is a yielding of yourself to whatever the Spirit is doing in your life to fix what is wrong. It's a matter of saying to God, "Yes, Lord, this is what I need. Make me what You want me to be."

## THE BENEFITS OF BROKENNESS

What happens when God breaks you and the Spirit's power has been released in your life? He puts Christ on the throne and self on its knees at His feet. That's when things start to happen.

First of all, you get a personality transformation. The fastest way to change your personality from what it is to what it ought to be is by allowing the Spirit to cut through the scar tissue of sin in your soul and release your spirit.

When a cowboy breaks a horse, what he is basically doing is changing the horse's personality. A wild stallion says, "You are not going to ride on my back. I am going to buck you off." But a seasoned rider will take whatever time is necessary to break the horse of its wildness and bring it under control. The horse doesn't lose its strength; it just surrenders control.

We've got too many unbroken stallions in the body of Christ, too many people who are saying, "God, You are not going to ride on my back. I am going to do this my way. No one is going to tell me what to do." We keep on bucking, but the Spirit keeps on riding. It may only take eight seconds to win in a rodeo, but the Spirit will stay on as long as necessary to bring us under His control.

Let me tell you another good thing that happens when God breaks you. You get to hear His voice. People say they don't hear God speak. But God does speak today. Now He doesn't speak new revelation; He speaks on the application of existing revelation. You want to know whether you should go here, work there, marry this person. Well, if the Spirit can get through the scar tissue of your soul and break it open, you will hear His guiding voice. We'll talk about guidance in detail later in the book.

Another thing the Spirit does is give you discernment. According to 1 Corinthians 2:15, the spiritual person "appraises all things." That's discernment. John 2:25 says that Jesus knew what was inside of people. He wasn't fooled by the exterior. When you experience the Spirit's release, you begin to see below the surface of things. Women would call it intuition. It's intuition that is spiritually discerned.

Why is spiritual discernment so important? Because all you usually see on the surface is people's symptoms, not what's really wrong. It's like telling the doctor you just have a bad headache when the real problem is a brain tumor. That doctor had better be able to appraise your condition correctly. We believers often can't help each other because we are not spiritual enough to see what is wrong. We are not spiritual enough to see through what folk are telling us and get down to the real stuff. But when the Spirit breaks through to you, you can appraise things. You begin to read people, to see things as they really are so you can prescribe the right medicine.

That's why the best Christian counselors are spiritual people who can appraise what's wrong and apply God's remedy. Anything less is like taking two aspirin for cancer. You may feel better for a while, but you haven't addressed the problem. If you are never broken, you will only react to outer circumstances, not to what is really going on. You won't see things for what they really are. We must allow God to break us.

## THE BLESSEDNESS OF BROKENNESS

With true brokenness comes incredible blessedness. Just ask Jacob, whose life was filled with deceit until God broke him.

By the time we catch up with Jacob in Genesis 32, he has long since tricked his brother Esau out of his birthright and fled town when Esau threatened to kill him. Now, years later, he is coming home with the family and stuff he has accumulated, but he doesn't know whether Esau is going to hug him or choke him.

You see, Jacob was not yet a broken man. He had changed somewhat, but God still needed to break him. Jacob heard that Esau was coming out to meet him. He knew his life was on the line. So he cried out to God, "Deliver me, I pray, from the hand of my brother, from the hand of Esau; for I fear him, lest he come and attack me" (Genesis 32:11). God will scare you if that is the only way He can crack you open.

Jacob was scared to death. For the first time in his life, he cried out for help. By the way, he was calling on God just as he was about to enter the Promised Land. The land of blessing was right around the corner.

So Jacob sent his family on ahead and was left alone. "And a man wrestled with him until daybreak" (Genesis 32:24). Jacob was already afraid and alone, and now he's got a fight on his hands in the middle of the night. Jacob's adrenaline must have been pumping, because the other wrestler had to cripple him to make him let go.

Now Jacob wasn't crazy. He understood that this was a spiritual wrestling match and that his opponent was not just a man. Anybody who can cripple you with the touch of a finger isn't an ordinary man. Jacob realized he was wrestling with God.

When he discovered that, Jacob wrestled harder. "I will not let you go unless you bless me," he said (Genesis 32:26). He hung on for a blessing.

Would God have to wrestle you to get your attention? Would He have to break something, or bring some tragedy in your life, to let you know He has been wrestling with you all the time? When trouble comes, don't run from God. Run to God. Wrestle Him in prayer. Hold on to Him tightly.

So God asked Jacob, "What is your name?" (Genesis 32:27). God knew Jacob's name. But his name was part of his problem, because his name, which means "trickster, supplanter," reflected his nature. He was a trickster, a self-sufficient person.

God was saying, "I can't bless you if you are going to keep your old name, if you are going to keep acting on your old nature." God wanted to change Jacob's name because it would signal the change in nature that Jacob was undergoing. So God renamed him Israel (v. 28).

Israel means "he fights with God." As Israel, he fought with God so that God could now fight for him. As Jacob, he fought against God, and God fought against him. God will resist you so He can help you. God will war against you so He can take you to where He wants you to be.

"So Jacob named the place Peniel, for he said, 'I have seen God face to face, yet my life has been preserved'" (v. 30). I wish old Jacob could walk into your house right now, because here is what you would see. You would see a man limping badly as a reminder of that fight. He wrestled with God, and he was broken. He would have a perpetual reminder that he was only in the place of blessing by the grace of God.

Sometimes God has to dislocate something in our lives to get us where He wants us to go. Don't fight against

His process of breaking you through the Spirit or you will miss a blessing.

Recently, I got a living illustration of this. One of the men who works on our TV broadcast walks with a limp. I asked him what happened. He said, "God had to get my attention. Now every step I take, I remember two things. One, He had to hurt me to stop me. And two, I am glad He stopped me because now He is using me." A modern-day Jacob!

# EXPERIENCING THE SPIRIT'S RELEASE

**I** don't know how God wants to break you, and you don't know how He wants to break me. Let's let Him break us so He can use us:

1. Maybe you're saying, "I really don't see any need to be broken. I'm OK." If that is your position, I strongly suggest that you change your position by dropping to your knees and asking God to show you yourself as you really are. Or if you say, "Tony, I see the need, but I can't honestly say I'm willing for God to do that," tell God about it. He can handle your lack of willingness. Ask Him to make you "willing to be willing."

2. Imagine a surgeon rushing through an operation because he wants to finish before the ball game starts or trying to operate the last thing before he goes to bed when he's dead sleepy. That's how a lot of us handle our Bibles. The Holy Spirit is a skilled surgeon and the Word is sharp, but it takes more than a few hurried minutes for the Word to do its searching and dividing. How much time is in your schedule for the Word?

3. I don't know anybody who is into being disciplined. But discipline is one way God breaks us and releases our spirits. Are you running from a difficult person or circumstance God is trying to use to teach you something? Better turn around, because the second round of discipline is always harder.

4. Maybe you're still dragging around something from the old life, and it's pulling you down. Go somewhere alone, shut the door, and allow the Holy Spirit to poke around the corners of your spiritual attic until you've dealt with everything that could be holding you back from the Spirit's release.

# CHAPTER SIX

# EXPERIENCING THE SPIRIT'S ILLUMINATION

**W**hen you became a Christian, God gave you a new capacity to communicate and fellowship with Him. He transformed the inner you by making your dead spirit come alive, as we saw in the previous chapter, and by giving you a new mind. All of this is possible because the Holy Spirit came to indwell you. When that happened, you began to enjoy some wonderful benefits.

One benefit of the Spirit's abiding presence that believers enjoy is His ministry of illumination. Illumination means enlightenment. When I talk about the illuminating ministry of the Holy Spirit, I am referring to that process of spiritual enlightenment whereby the Spirit enables you to grasp, experience, and apply God's truth in your daily Christian life.

This ministry is critical because the Bible makes clear that the person without Christ, the unbeliever, has a darkened mind. That is, no matter how brilliant this person may be, he or she does not have the capacity to understand —or the access to—spiritual truth.

This person may want access to spiritual truth. He may know he needs to have access, but because his mind is dark and depraved with no capacity to receive spiritual truth, he is limited to the natural realm of the five senses. He cannot relate to the invisible realm, which is the realm of the Spirit.

In His role as the Illuminator, the Spirit enlightens us so that we are able to grasp, experience, and apply God's Word to our lives. Anybody who can do that, we need to be close to. Anybody who can put us on heaven's frequency, we need to be connected to. That's why the Holy Spirit is more important than a pastor or any other human teacher or counselor, because the Spirit can connect us to the mind of God.

The Holy Spirit can put you on the frequency of God so that you will know, in the words of the late Marvin Gaye, "What's Going On"! Through the illumination of the indwelling Spirit, you can tap into the realities of the invisible realm of heaven.

The Spirit's role as Illuminator goes all the way back to Creation. As the Spirit hovered over the earth, God dispelled the darkness by saying, "Let there be light." Ever since, it has been a primary role of the Spirit to dispel darkness by introducing light.

The Spirit does for us what He did in Creation. He serves as the light of our lives, doing for us what a nightlight does for a frightened child. The Spirit enables us to see things that would otherwise be invisible or unclear and to hear clearly that which was formerly unintelligible. The result is that order replaces chaos and clarity transcends confusion, for darkness is no match for light. So rather than being afraid and insecure, we can be confident and secure as we walk by faith.

A foundational passage of Scripture for understanding the illuminating work of the Spirit is 1 Corinthians 2. If this reference sounds familiar, it should. We just finished dealing with verses 9–12 in our previous study on the release of the Spirit, so I won't quote them again here.

I want to touch on these verses again briefly, then move on in chapter 2 because this is important to the doctrine of the Spirit's illumination.

## SPIRITUAL DISCERNMENT

One way the Spirit illumines us is by giving us spiritual discernment—the ability to distinguish good from bad, right from wrong, to make sense out of what is happening. In 1 Corinthians 2, you'll remember that in verse 9 Paul talks about the great things God has for us. Then he says in verse 10 that God has revealed these things to us by His Spirit. Thus illumination is an experience because it involves our awareness.

### The Depths of God

The Spirit can do this because He searches the very depths of the heart and mind of God. In fact, He is Himself God, the third Person of the Trinity. Paul's point in verse 11 is that the Holy Spirit functions within the Trinity the way our human spirit functions within us. Our spirit is the innermost part of our being. It's where our deepest, most private thoughts reside.

To put it another way, nobody knows you better than you. The reason is that you live with you. I don't care how well your spouse knows you or how long you have been married, no one knows you like you do. No one knows your private thoughts and those deep internal struggles you keep hidden.

Because we have a spirit, we are usually our own best interpreter. That's why when two people get into an argument, one of them will often say, "Don't try to tell me what I mean. I know what I am saying."

Therefore, if you really wanted to know someone perfectly, you would have to tune in to his spirit. The Holy Spirit is tuned in to the deepest thoughts of God. He has access to the innermost workings of the Godhead. So just as no one knows the deepest thoughts of a person better than his spirit, no one knows the deepest thoughts of God better than the Holy Spirit. And He is pleased to reveal them to us (1 Corinthians 2:12).

## Our Translator

This is important for several reasons. Think for a minute about what Paul is telling us here. Through the illuminating and revealing ministry of the Holy Spirit, we have access to the very heart and mind of God. That is a staggering thought.

Let me tell another reason this truth is important. It's important because God says, "My thoughts are not your thoughts, neither are your ways My ways. . . . For as the heavens are higher than the earth, so are My ways higher than your ways, and My thoughts than your thoughts" (Isaiah 55:8–9).

See, God is speaking a language we can't interpret. We need a translator, somebody who can put God's words into words we can understand. But we don't just need a human translator like a pastor or a friend. We need a Spirit translator who can explain what it means deep down in our innermost being.

God's language is unknown to the natural mind. That's why we need a translator. I have preached in different countries to people who did not speak or understand English. So someone from that culture who knew English and also knew the language of the people had to stand beside me as I spoke.

As I preached in English, this person would follow right behind and translate what I said so that the people would get the message. The Holy Spirit is our translator who takes the things of God and reveals them to us in a language we can understand.

I like Paul's word at the end of 1 Corinthians 2:12: God has given us these things "freely." There is no charge attached to the Spirit's ministry of illumination. It has been provided to every believer so we can get God's answers to life's realities. We have the Spirit of God, who knows the innermost thoughts of God and can communicate these realities to us.

The Spirit of God knows the deep things of God. He is like a deep-sea diver who can go down into the depths and find out what's down there. That's why the Bible says that even when you don't know what is going on, the Spirit can help you because He dives down deep. He gets way down there where the action is. He goes "deep thought fishing" to connect us to the mind of God.

Now I want to go even beyond what we have been saying, because in 1 Corinthians 2:13, Paul says this all happens "not in words taught by human wisdom, but in those taught by the Spirit, combining spiritual thoughts with spiritual words."

Here's why we know we can trust the Bible. The thoughts that the authors' minds told them to record were the thoughts given to them by the Spirit. The result was truth without error.

Now we aren't guaranteed that degree of accuracy in our lives today because our flesh often muddles God's messages, but I do think Paul is talking about a process of spiritual discernment that we have available to us. In 1 Corinthians 2:14, he writes: "But a natural man does not accept the things of the Spirit of God; for they are foolishness to him, and he cannot understand them, because they are spiritually appraised."

One of the ways you know you are spiritual is that you begin to make judgments from God's point of view. And when you do, unsaved folk will think you are crazy. They won't be able to figure you out. That's because the things of God are silliness to the lost person. They don't make sense to him because he has no apparatus to receive and appraise them.

How badly do we need the Spirit to illuminate the things of God for us? How far out of our reach is the mind of God without the Spirit's illumination? Just listen to Paul again:

> Oh, the depth of the riches both of the wisdom and knowledge of God! How unsearchable are His judgments and unfathomable His ways! For who has known the mind of the Lord, or who became His counselor? (Romans 11:33–34)

Who among us could possibly know the mind of the Lord? Answer: nobody, except the Spirit. He alone knows the mind of God, so if you want to know God you must link up with the Spirit.

## The Anointing

Let's carry this one step further. In 1 John 2, the apostle writes:

> You have an anointing from the Holy One, and you all know. . . . The anointing which you received from Him abides in you, and you have no need for anyone to teach you; but as His anointing teaches you about all things, and is true and is not a lie, and just as it has taught you, you abide in Him. (vv. 20, 27)

All Christians are anointed. I know we say that about a particular preacher or musician, but if you are a Christian, you are anointed too. What is the anointing? John says it is the capacity to know God's truth.

My mother used to say to me, "Boy, you have a brain. Use it for something other than a hat rack." She was saying that I had a capacity for learning that I was not using at the moment. The problem wasn't that I didn't have a brain. The problem was that my brain was not in use.

Every Christian has the same spiritual capacity when it comes to walking with God. We all have different IQs, but in the spiritual realm we have the same capacity for intimacy with God. That means you have the capacity to hear the voice of the Spirit. Don't think that only super-Christians hear from God. You have the anointing.

I like to illustrate the anointing by pointing to something you may have in your backyard: a satellite dish. The anointing of God is like a satellite dish that points upward, pulls in a signal from the heavens, and translates the signal into a message you can see and understand. All you have to do is turn on your television to receive it.

There's a great illustration of this type of anointing in 2 Kings 6, where the prophet Elisha was surrounded by the Aramean army (v. 14). Elisha's servant was frantic when he saw the hordes, while my man Elisha was cool

(vv. 15–16). Elisha was steadfast and confident because he saw something his servant didn't see.

So the prophet asked God to open his servant's eyes (v. 17). Was the man blind? No, but he needed illumination. When that was provided, he too saw the mountain full of the Lord's chariots and horses providing protection and deliverance for His prophet. Similarly, the Holy Spirit illumines our spiritual eyes so that we begin to see our circumstances through God's perspective.

This is the anointing, the "satellite dish" that enables you to tune in to the things of God. As God transmits His message to you, the One who translates that message is the Holy Spirit. That's why your spirit needs to stay closely linked with the Holy Spirit. John calls it abiding in Christ (1 John 2:27). This illuminating or enlightening work comes to and through the human spirit, since "the spirit of man is the lamp of the Lord, searching all the innermost parts of his being" (Proverbs 20:27).

John makes a statement in verse 27 that confuses a lot of people: "You have no need for anyone to teach you." John doesn't mean that the body of Christ has no need for human teachers. Teachers are one of Christ's gifts to His church (Ephesians 4:11). If we didn't need proper teachers, John would not have had to write his book in the first place.

Let me tell you what I think John means. Since you have the satellite dish, the anointing, and since your spirit is illuminated by the Holy Spirit, you can put everything you receive through a spiritual grid. You don't need teachers who approach life from a non-Christian perspective.

Can I get real practical? You don't need horoscopes. You don't need to open the newspaper to see what your Zodiac sign is telling you today. You don't need some natural man or woman who has no spiritual sensitivity telling you about your tomorrow. You need God's Holy Spirit telling you about your tomorrow.

You also don't need Ouija boards and palm readers and non-Christian therapists. Read verses 21–26 of 1 John 2 and you'll see that John's concern is false teachers who seek to deceive and mislead God's people. Do you see the connection? The anointing will guard you from these deceivers. The Spirit of truth will keep you from the spirit of error.

If you have a smoke detector in your home, you know how sensitive that device is. You don't have to have a fire before it goes off. You just have to have smoke. Even the steam from a boiling tea kettle can set off some sensitive smoke detectors.

When the Holy Spirit has sensitized your human spirit, you know when something is not right spiritually. Your "truth alarm" goes off. You may not know exactly what it is, but you just know what you're hearing or reading isn't right.

If somebody got up in the pulpit at your church and started using all kinds of spiritual analysis to teach stuff that wasn't right, something would go off inside you. The Holy Spirit would be saying, "Watch out." When this happens, you are experiencing the Spirit. God has given this spiritual sensitivity to all believers. But if you don't know the Word and aren't in touch with the Spirit, you'll be relying on what man says.

John talks about this later in his book when he says: "It is the Spirit who bears witness, because the Spirit is the truth" (1 John 5:7). We have a Witness, Somebody who will say yea and nay. If you are a Christian and yet are not hearing the witness, it is because you are not abiding. God has given you the ability to know.

## THE POWER OF RECALL

A second aspect of the Spirit's illuminating work is what we could call the power of spiritual recall. You can see it in John 14, a text we have already visited once. In verse 26, Jesus says: "But the Helper, the Holy Spirit, whom the Father will send in My name, He will teach you all things, and bring to your remembrance all that I said to you."

That's good news, because we all tend to forget. Now this promise had a specific application to the apostles, because several of the men with Jesus that night in the Upper Room later became authors of Scripture.

### The Authors of Scripture

Some of the books in the Bible were written forty years after Jesus died. So some people wonder, How could ordinary fishermen and tax collectors and laborers remember what Jesus said and write it down exactly as Jesus wanted it written?

Because the Holy Spirit enabled these men to think things they would not normally think and remember things they would not normally remember. Jesus told them, "When the time comes for you to remember what you need to remember, My Holy Spirit has it on file and will remind you of what I said."

You say, "I try to memorize verses, but I can't remember them." Oh, but the Holy Spirit remembers them. Haven't you had an experience in which you did not know exactly where a verse was found, and you could not quote it word for word, but you knew it was in the Bible and you were able to recall enough of it to use it in a given situation? That was the Holy Spirit.

The biblical writers did this themselves. Many times when the New Testament writers quoted the Old Testament, they did not quote the passage word for word. They just sort of paraphrased it as the Holy Spirit brought that Scripture to mind. Their goal was to give the point of the passage, not necessarily look it up and quote it verbatim (see Matthew 13:14–15, where Jesus cites Isaiah 6:9–10, and Acts 15:14–18, where James uses Amos 9:11–12 to make his point about the Gentiles hearing).

### Christians Today

Now let's not get mystical or mysterious here. The Holy Spirit won't remind you of something you never bothered to learn. Kids often ask their parents, "Why do I have to study the Bible? Why do I have to go to church?" Actually, a lot of adults are wondering the same thing. Answer: It gives the Holy Spirit something to bring up, some truth to work with.

It's like praying before a test, "Holy Spirit, help me with this test. Help me to remember the things I have studied." That prayer assumes you studied. If you did not study, don't ask the Spirit for help because there is nothing for Him to draw on.

You say, "Tony, I go to church fifty-two Sundays a year. I can't remember all of my pastor's sermons." I tell the people at our church that anything in my sermons worth remembering, the Holy Spirit is going to file away. At the right time, in the right situation, He will bring it back and remind them of it, because He gives us the power of recall.

In John 16:14–15, Jesus said, "[The Holy Spirit] shall glorify Me; for He shall take of Mine, and shall disclose it to you. All things that the Father has are Mine; therefore I said, that He takes of Mine, and will disclose it to you." The Holy Spirit illumines our minds and brings God's Word to our remembrance to keep us close to Christ, to allow you and me to glorify Christ in what we say and do.

There's a great example of this in Matthew 10. Jesus was giving His disciples instructions before sending them out to preach the good news. In verse 19 He told them, "When they deliver you up, do not become anxious about how or what you will speak; for it shall be given you in that hour what you are to speak."

Notice what Jesus said. The apostles would have what they needed when the time came that they needed it. He didn't give them a book of speeches ahead of time. Many of us want God to enlighten us now about what will happen a year down the road. We worry about stuff that God has no intention of giving us in advance.

But Jesus says, "When you get there, the Holy Spirit will recall to your mind what you need. That's His job."

It's unfortunate that so many evangelicals limit this promise of the Spirit's guiding and reminding ministry to those first disciples. Well, if we are going to limit this promise to the men who heard it that night, then we need to limit the whole Upper Room Discourse to them, since this promise is embedded in the same context. That's something very few Bible expositors are willing to do.

But the promise of the Spirit's teaching and reminding ministry is for all believers, because Jesus' condition for benefiting from the Spirit's indwelling presence is obedience to His commandments (John 14:21–24). That's a condition you and I can meet.

In addition, this promise is in the very same verse (14:26) as Jesus' promise of the Spirit's overall enabling ministry. So to limit the promise and experience of the Spirit's teaching and reminding ministry to the first century is to limit the Spirit's role as the divine Helper to the first century.

## SPIRITUAL CONFIDENCE

Here's a third aspect of the Spirit's illuminating ministry. It gives you spiritual confidence. "For God has not given us a spirit of timidity, but of power and love and discipline" (2 Timothy 1:7).

### Know Where You're Going

We don't have to be timid as Christians, because through the illumination or enlightenment of the Holy Spirit, we can know where we're going and what's happening. When you know that, it gives you confidence.

I see an example of this in Acts 20:17–38, the story of Paul's farewell to the elders of Ephesus. In verses 22–23, Paul told these men that he was on his way to Jerusalem and that the Holy Spirit had revealed to him that he was in for a very rough time.

So why didn't Paul quit and turn back? Because, "I do not consider my life of any account as dear to myself, in order that I may finish my course, and the ministry which I received from the Lord Jesus, to testify solemnly of the gospel of the grace of God" (v. 24). Paul knew that God would see him through to the completion of his ministry. That's spiritual confidence.

### Not Necessarily Easy

Now confidence doesn't mean God is going to make everything easy. If it were all easy, you wouldn't need any confidence. You may be facing a rough time at home or at work right now. But when you are walking in the Holy Spirit and He tells you to go on anyhow, go on anyhow!

Stay in there and don't turn back. Even though it may be rough, He will go with you.

Some of us have not given the Holy Spirit the chance to go with us, because as soon as we step out and see that it's going to be rough out there, we turn and head in the other direction. But the Holy Spirit says He will never send us out there alone. He gives us His presence and power to step out by faith. He gives us spiritual confidence.

Holy Ghost confidence changes the way you see things and the way you feel about things. Let me give you an example of that, also from the book of Acts. In Acts 7, Stephen has just been rejected and condemned by the religious leaders of Israel. Verse 54 says these guys were really hot with anger.

Now notice verse 55: "But being full of the Holy Spirit, [Stephen] gazed intently into heaven and saw the glory of God, and Jesus standing at the right hand of God." In other words, he saw something the others did not see. The Holy Spirit illuminated Stephen's spiritual eyes so that he saw right into heaven.

Now mind you, he was about to lose his life. But it makes all the difference what the child of God sees versus what the world sees. Stephen saw Jesus standing up. Let me tell you, when Jesus stands up, something big is coming down!

Stephen saw Jesus, and he said so (v. 56). If all you see are your enemies, you are going to be scared. But if you see Jesus standing at the right hand of God, you are going to stop looking at your enemies and start looking at the glory of God.

### Seeing More

The reason many of us don't have confidence is that we are looking at the wrong people. We look at our boss as though he controls the bottom line. We look at the people who are against us as though they control events. But when you are full of the Spirit and He illumines you, you get to see things other people don't see. You get insights other folk don't have.

In Stephen's case, those other folk didn't see what he saw. So in their spiritual blindness they picked up stones and killed him, even as he prayed for them to be forgiven (Acts 7:59–60).

I'm afraid too many of us would have been cursing those people, praying, "Lord, they're stoning me. Kill them on the spot." Where did Stephen get the grace to pray, "Lord, they don't know what they are doing. Please forgive them"?

I will tell you where. The Holy Spirit illuminated him and filled him. Are you being abused and misused? Are you being "'buked and scorned and talked about sho' as you born"? What you need is the illumination and fullness of the Spirit, which gives you confidence in the midst of a crisis. Such confidence is what we mean by experiencing the Spirit.

I love the story of the Emmaus disciples in Luke 24:13–35. The two were dejected and downcast. Jesus had been crucified. But along came a Stranger who opened the Bible to them and then opened their eyes to His identity. Their emotions changed because Jesus showed them something other people didn't see.

That's illumination, and that's what the Spirit has come to do in our hearts. When He turns on the light of God's glory in you, then you'll have the joy of the Lord even if things are bad.

## SPIRITUAL DIRECTION

Here's a fourth and final aspect or benefit of the Holy Spirit's illuminating work: spiritual direction.

Life is full of tough decisions, the kind that make some people want to pull their hair out. Well, in the Holy Spirit you have a Guide who has been down this road before and knows where you are supposed to go and when you are supposed to get there.

We're going to talk about the Spirit's guidance later, so I don't want to steal too much of the thunder from that study. But we need to remember that even though we are dividing the Spirit's works into various categories for the purposes of study and analysis, in real life the Holy Spirit doesn't work in neat little compartments.

## A Few Examples

There is overlap and cross-fertilization between the aspects of His ministry, so it's OK for us to talk a little bit about the Spirit's guidance as a function of His illumination. But since we do have a fuller discussion of guidance coming up, let me just remind you of a few examples from the book of Acts.

In Acts 8, we meet Philip the evangelist, who went to Samaria and lit a revival. Just when things were going great, though, God pulled him out of Samaria and put him on a desert road, where the Spirit sent him to an Ethiopian official. Philip obeyed the Spirit, led the man to faith, and baptized him. Then the Spirit snatched Philip away for his next assignment (v. 39).

In Acts 10, a passage we keep turning to, Peter the racist who could not stand Gentiles was led by the Spirit to the house of Cornelius, where he wound up leading Gentiles into the kingdom. Now God had to go some to enlighten Peter, but the illumination of the Spirit overcame racism and culturalism.

When people are enlightened by the Holy Spirit, things like racial prejudice and classism go out the door. When the Spirit is pulling the strings, He can get people like Peter to relate to folk they would not normally relate to. The Spirit took Peter in a whole new direction because he was available to the Spirit of God in spite of his inbred prejudices.

In Acts 13:2, the Spirit called Paul and Barnabas to the mission field. In 16:6–10, Paul was heading one way when the Spirit said, "No, we need you over in Macedonia." I could go on, but you get the idea. The beauty of the illuminating work of the Spirit of God is that He redirects your life according to God's agenda. And when you're on God's agenda, you're on your way!

## An Observation

Let me make an observation here. Although the Holy Spirit's ministry of illumination is specifically tied to helping you understand the Scriptures, that does not mean the Bible has a specific answer for every detail of your life. The Bible does not deal with all the specifics. Instead, it gives you the basic principles that should govern all decisions.

How does the Spirit figure in this? The Bible gives you the objective standards. The Holy Spirit gives you the subjective leading. The Bible gives you the biblical parameters. The Holy Spirit guides you within the boundaries of those parameters to the specific goal God has for you.

Therefore, when your commitment to the objective Word of God is tied to a dynamic relationship with the Holy Spirit, He provides you with the subjective, internal illumination and direction you need to get you where God wants you to be.

So when Paul writes, "All who are being led by the Spirit of God, these are sons of God" (Romans 8:14), we need to ask, how does the Spirit lead? What does He use to illumine our human spirits? I want to suggest three general things.

### God's Word

This first one should be obvious. The Spirit uses the Word to lead us to holiness, to Christlikeness. Now here I am not talking about the specifics of whom to marry or where to work. I'm talking about the will of God for all believers that's clearly revealed in Scripture.

For example, the Spirit illumines the Word so we can see ourselves as we really are. He is going use the Word to show us that we're not as good and as attractive as we thought we were.

The Spirit does this for the same reason your doctor shows you your X rays. He wants you to see what's wrong so you will be willing to get on the operating table and let him cut out the mess. That's what the "Holy Ghost doctor" wants to do with the sin in our lives. The purer our lives, the clearer the signals and the leading of the Spirit will be to us.

The Spirit wants you to see that which is not what it should be so He can make it what it should be. He always starts with the Word. So if you do not have a commitment to the objective truth of Scripture, don't expect the subjective leading of the Spirit.

Don't expect Him to lead you to a godly mate if you don't have a biblical commitment to being holy while you are single. Don't expect the Spirit to reveal unknown facets of God's will if you aren't obeying the will of God revealed in His Word. Spiritual direction has to start with a commitment to the Word.

### Circumstances

The Holy Spirit also leads through circumstances. I don't think I need to quote Romans 8:28, except to remind you that it says "all things . . . work together for good" if we love God.

That's all things. So for the believer, there is no such thing as luck or coincidence or accident. All things work together for good. That means good things, bad things, up things, and down things work together for good.

God takes the good and the bad, stirs them together, and comes out with a pretty good meal on the other side. The negative thing you are experiencing right now is the thing He can use to achieve His positive results.

### Common Sense

Another thing the Holy Spirit uses is sanctified common sense. In Acts 15, the church had a controversy about what to do about Gentiles. James rendered a judgment, and verse 22 says it "seemed good" to the apostles and elders (see also v. 25). It just seemed like the right thing to do.

But that's not all. It also "seemed good to the Holy Spirit" (v. 28). That's sanctified common sense. Now notice that it didn't seem good until they held a meeting of godly people and talked it over. In other words, if God is leading you in a way that makes good sense, He's going to tell someone else. This plan didn't make sense just to one person. If the Spirit doesn't seem to be telling anybody but you, better go slow.

### Satan

No, that's not a misprint. You say, "Where's that one, Tony?" I see it in 2 Corinthians 12, the well-known case of Paul's "thorn in the flesh" (vv. 7–9). He called it a "messenger of Satan" and asked God three times to take it away. God's answer was, "My grace is sufficient for you" (v. 9). So Paul rejoiced in that answer to prayer.

God used Satan to keep Paul humble before Him. God allowed Satan to inject a negative thing into Paul's life to achieve His positive purposes. God may use negative things to achieve His will in us—even if the negative thing comes from the Devil.

### Other People

The Spirit's ministry of illumination may operate without human intervention. But He often uses other people in the process of illuminating us.

This happens, for instance, when the gospel is preached and the Spirit opens the eyes of unbelievers to their need for salvation (Acts 2:36–41). It also happens as Christians regularly place themselves under the ministry of a Spirit-filled teacher (1 Thessalonians 1:5–6; 2:9–13).

One of God's primary ways of answering our prayers for guidance (James 1:5) is through sermons the Holy Spirit uses to speak to our needs. On many occasions I have had the privilege and joy of being used by the Spirit to give Christians answers to issues they were seeking God's wisdom about. When such illumination occurs, an experience or encounter with the Spirit has taken place.

Allow me to tell a personal story here. According to my plan, I should not be in Dallas. I had already been accepted by a seminary in Indiana. We were preparing to move there the summer after I finished college. But during my last weeks of college, one of my professors asked me, "Have you applied to Dallas Theological Seminary?"

I said, "No, I don't need to now. I have already been accepted at another seminary."

He said, "You have been on my mind a lot lately, and I think you ought to apply to Dallas. I'll tell you what. If I gave you the application fee, would you be willing to apply?"

I replied, "Yes, but we are going to seminary in Indiana."

I sent in the application to Dallas and got a letter back stating that even though registration had been closed, the admissions committee had decided to let me come. Now I was confused about God's leading. I had already gone to the other seminary to look for housing and meet the faculty. Everything was ready.

The idea of attending Dallas Seminary came out of nowhere. But suddenly I was considering a larger city, where it would be easier to find employment, and so forth. One reason after another led us to choose Dallas, but that's all I had in mind. All I was looking at was Dallas Seminary.

But God could see things I couldn't see. He could see the full-tuition scholarship Dallas gave me, but which I didn't know about until I got there. He could see the formation of a little work in Oak Cliff with a handful of people that would grow to a church of thousands.

God could see the man, my longtime associate pastor Martin Hawkins, who came about a month after we started and spoke one line that transformed my ministry. I shared my vision and passion with Martin, and he said, "If you take that vision and focus on developing it here at Oak Cliff, you will reach the world from Oak Cliff Bible Fellowship."

That was more than sixteen years ago. Now, the messages and other resources go out from here to more than forty countries. Pastors and church leaders come from across America to learn about our philosophy of ministry. The Spirit used people in my life: a professor, a new friend. And He's used many others over the years.

He will do the same for you. The Holy Spirit is the Illuminator. His job is to help you understand God's Word and discern God's will. And He will shine the light of God on your path if you're committed to Him.

# EXPERIENCING THE SPIRIT'S ILLUMINATION

Since God's thoughts and ways are so much higher than ours, how thankful we should be for the illumination of the Spirit. Without it, we would be in the dark, maybe for eternity! I hope these ideas will help turn on the Spirit's light for you:

1. You've probably heard this before, but you'd be amazed how much of God's will, even His specific desires, is revealed for us in the Bible. Get out your Bible concordance— or get out and get one if you need it—and look up the word *will*. Then be prepared to obey what you find.

2. What situation or person do you feel the least confident in handling today? That may be exactly where you'll find the spiritual confidence we talked about. Try looking beyond just what you can see—the people, the events, the hurts, whatever. Ask the Holy Spirit to enlighten your spiritual eyes so you can see beyond the obvious to His purposes in your trial.

3. I used a satellite dish to illustrate our ability to receive and translate the things of God. You have the same capacity as every other believer to tune in, because you have the same Holy Spirit. Are you allowing outside interference, competing signals, to jam your spiritual receiver? Better do a "program check" to make sure God has your undivided attention.

4. When it comes to seeking direction, we usually just pray, "Lord, lead me today." That's not really what He wants to hear. Try praying this way and see what happens: "Lord, I am Yours today. Bring those influences and people into my life that You can use to keep me close to You and walking in Your truth."

# PART TWO

# THE HOLY SPIRIT'S PURPOSE

# CHAPTER SEVEN
# EXPERIENCING THE SPIRIT'S CONVICTION

A young boy was at Disneyland enjoying Mickey Mouse and Donald Duck and the rides and the popcorn and the fanfare and didn't notice that he had become separated from his parents. He was enjoying the hustle and bustle of Disney life until he looked up and discovered that his parents were not there.

Once this boy discovered he was not in fellowship with his parents anymore, Disneyland turned into a Disney disaster. All of sudden, the cotton candy wasn't sweet, the rides were not fun, and Mickey Mouse was no longer cute, because Mom and Dad were nowhere to be found.

That's the great tragedy of our world: people so busy enjoying the rides and the thrills and the bright lights that they haven't even noticed they are not in fellowship with God. They are so busy sucking on the cotton candy of life, riding the Ferris wheel of entertainment, and going up and down the roller coaster of pleasure that they haven't even noticed God is not in the vicinity anymore.

That young boy at Disneyland needed to come face to face with two realities before he could get help. First, he needed to discover he was lost. And second, he needed somebody to lead him back to his parents.

The Bible declares that, apart from God, all people are eternally lost. They are forever separated from the life of God. They need to know they are lost, and they need to know the way back home.

Enter the Holy Spirit. He is the champion of the lost and found. His unique task is to bring men and women front and center before Jesus Christ: to bring the unregenerate and the unconverted into a saving relationship with Christ and to keep the regenerate in constant fellowship with Christ.

As we begin the second part of our study, focusing on the purpose for which the Holy Spirit was given, let's open with His ministry of conviction.

## THE GREAT CONVICTER

One of the ministries of the Holy Spirit is that of conviction. That is stated quite clearly for us in John 16:8, particularly as it relates to the unregenerate world: "And [the Holy Spirit], when He comes, will convict the world concerning sin, and righteousness, and judgment."

The key word here is *convict*. When the Bible speaks of convicting someone of something, it is referring to a concept we could use synonymously with conviction— that of convincing. The job of the Holy Spirit is to make absolutely clear the spiritual issues of life and to call for a decision.

Unsaved people walk around in a spiritual fog or daze, not really understanding what God expects from them. You hear it every time you talk to an unbeliever. Just ask that person, "Are you going to heaven?"

"Well," he will usually say, "I sure hope so. I think so." When you ask him what he's pinning his hopes for heaven on, he may tell you, "I try to keep the Ten Commandments. I go to church. I'm doing the best I can." It's clear this person is lost in a deep fog.

Some unbelievers even try to argue that they'll go to heaven because they have a dear mother over there where Jesus is. But the real question is, "Does that mother have a son or daughter going over there where Jesus is?"

So great confusion abounds when it comes to the things of God. The Holy Spirit's job is to make the issue clear and to jar people loose of their misconceptions about the good news of the gospel. And we'll see later that His job is also to jar us Christians loose of our misconceptions about intimacy with God.

The Spirit is the great Convicter, the great Convincer, the great Explainer. But in order to do this, He must get people's attention. He has to break through the fog that blinds the unsaved because of their darkened hearts (2 Corinthians 4:3–4), and He has to dispel the sinful distractions that get the saved off the track of fellowship with God.

It's like the wasp that landed on a sandwich and began eating the juice of the jam. The wasp was so busy enjoying the sweet stuff it didn't even notice that the person on whose sandwich it had landed had picked up a knife to slice the sandwich in half. In other words, that wasp was suddenly in great peril. But you know something? It kept right on eating.

An unredeemed person is so busy eating the jam of this world order that it takes a disaster to get his attention. In fact, many people are believers today because God first got their attention in some unique way.

They were indulging themselves and enjoying the jam of this world until God sliced through their lives. Then it dawned on them that this world wasn't as tasty as they thought it was. This is the convicting work of the Holy Spirit. His job is to get our attention so that we take seriously the things of God.

## CONVICTION OF SIN

In John 16:9–11, Jesus went on to explain more about the three areas in which the Holy Spirit must do His convicting work. The first of these is sin, "because they do not believe in Me" (v. 9). Unsaved people don't understand two realities about sin.

## The Sinfulness of Sin

First, people do not realize how exceedingly sinful sin is. They will call it a mistake, a bad habit, a weakness—anything to soften the blow.

But God calls it sin. It is an affront to His holiness. The world does not understand that. Lost people do not understand that when you break one of God's commandments, you are held as guilty as though you had broken them all (James 2:10). People do not understand that salvation is not by works of righteousness they can do. They do not understand that they are powerless to cancel out their sin because they have offended a holy God.

And so the Holy Spirit must make clear to sinners the seriousness of sin. People must see that they have fallen short of the divine standard, that God is so infinitely holy there is no such thing as a "good" sinner versus a "bad" sinner. We are all sinners.

Only the Holy Spirit can bring that conviction, because most people are convinced they aren't all that bad. If you look hard enough, you can always find someone worse than you. So what most people do is look at their neighbor, the guy down the street, or a co-worker. If they find out they are better than these other people, they think they are OK.

The trouble is, people who do that are measuring themselves against the wrong standard. The measure of sin is not our neighbor. When God measures us, He measures us against Himself and His standard of perfect righteousness. That's why all of us fall short of the standard (Romans 3:23). It takes the Holy Spirit to convince a sinner that he's really as bad off as God says he is.

## Rejecting the Savior

But there is something more specific the Holy Spirit wants to convict the world of: the ultimate sin of rejecting the Savior. This is vitally important to understand, so allow me a brief excursion into biblical theology.

Before Adam plunged the human race into sin, God had already prepared a way to reconcile sinners to Himself and bring them into relationship with Himself. The way God did this was by providing us a Savior, Jesus Christ.

What the cross of Christ did on behalf of all sinners everywhere was to satisfy the demands and the wrath of a holy God against sin. That's why the Bible says "God was in Christ reconciling the world to Himself, not counting their trespasses against them" (2 Corinthians 5:19). In Romans 5:15, Paul says that in Adam the "many" died, but in Christ the same "many" have been made alive.

In other words, the death of Jesus Christ removed the barrier that kept sinners from being reconciled to a holy God, thus freeing God to save anyone and everyone who believes. Every person is still responsible to come to Christ in repentance and faith to be saved, but Christ's death makes that transaction available to all.

So the fact is that people do not go to hell simply because they sin. People go to hell because they reject the Savior. The lost are not separated from God forever because they did certain sins, because God provided a way of forgiveness for those sins by the death of Christ. The issue on the table is what a person does with Christ.

See, God was so satisfied with the death of Christ for sin that He, if I can put it this way, neutralized the effects of original sin. All of us are born in sin and shaped in iniquity (Psalm 51:5). We are born with the old Adamic nature, but the death of Christ addressed that.

This also explains how people who are incapable of believing, such as infants or those severely retarded from birth, can go to heaven if they die. Since they do not reject God's revelation, and since their original sin is covered by Christ's death, God can act in grace on their behalf. People are not separated from God simply because they were born with a sin nature.

The reason people are condemned is that they have rejected God's Savior and have chosen to be their own saviors. They have refused to accept the death of Christ as the only payment for their sins.

Instead, like the wicked queen in *Snow White*, they stand in front of the mirror and say, "Mirror, mirror, on the wall, who is the fairest of them all?" If they can get enough mirrors to lie to them, they will think they really are all right and never come to realize that Jesus Christ is the only One who can satisfy the demands of a holy God.

So the first thing the Holy Spirit does is convince men and women that they are sinners and convict them of the ultimate sin of rejecting Jesus Christ. That's why, when Peter stood up on the Day of Pentecost and preached, the Bible says that the hearers were "pierced to the heart" (Acts 2:37). The Spirit convinced them, and all they could do was ask, "What shall we do?" They had come to an understanding they did not previously have.

## CONVICTION OF RIGHTEOUSNESS

The second area of the Spirit's convicting work is "concerning righteousness, because I go to the Father, and you no longer behold Me" (John 16:10).

### Revealing the Standard

The Holy Spirit convinces the world of a new standard of righteousness, which is Christ. The reason the Spirit must convict men is that Jesus Christ is no longer on earth to demonstrate His righteousness. You can't see Him walk down the street. You can't watch Him cast out demons and make the lame walk. He has ascended to heaven.

So it's the Spirit's job to convince people that Jesus Christ is the only perfectly righteous One who has ever lived, the only One who has perfectly measured up to God's holy standard. This differentiates Christ from all other so-called Messiahs. You can go anywhere and find a self-appointed messiah, somebody who claims to have special acceptance with God. There are David Koreshes around every corner.

So the question is, what makes Jesus the real Messiah? What makes Him the righteous One? What sets Him apart? Jesus answered that Himself when He said, "I go to the

Father." The resurrection and ascension of Christ are what put Him in a class all by Himself.

See, no other person can claim that. Muhammad had a good rap and talked a good talk, but when he died nobody ever saw him again. Buddha looked very comfortable in his repose, but when he died nobody was able to locate him again. Confucius had many wise and creative sayings, but when he went to the grave nobody could affirm him again.

But Jesus died on Friday and got up on Sunday and showed Himself alive to more than five hundred brethren (1 Corinthians 15:6)! The thing that sets Jesus apart, and the reason I am a Christian today, is that the grave is empty. Jesus Christ is the only One who has beaten death and can lay claim to being the righteous standard of God.

### Accepting the Standard

Remember in school when you and almost everybody else messed up bad on a test? The teacher would throw a curve on those grades, which is what you were hoping for. But there was always one smart student who would ace the test. So you lost out because Mr. Know-It-All messed up the curve. You got mad at him because he passed, which made your failure unacceptable.

The problem with Jesus is He ruins the curve. You think you are OK spiritually until you run into Him. Then you find out that you and everybody else failed the test of meeting God's standard.

When they find that out, a lot of people simply get mad at Jesus and look around for some way to make their failure acceptable. But that is eternally fatal, so the Holy Spirit applies His work of conviction so that people know the real story and don't stumble on in their failure.

See, when I stand before God, I will have no excuse. I will not be able to cop a plea. There will be nothing I can offer God to pay for my sins. The fact that I was a pastor will be irrelevant. My twelve years of theological training will be meaningless. The fact that I didn't do some bad things other people did won't mean a thing.

Only one thing will matter. My only plea will be, "Father, I have accepted the righteousness of Jesus, your Son, as my righteousness. For You to reject me, You will have to reject Him, because I stand in Him. I have banked my eternal destiny on Your acceptance of Christ and His acceptance of me." As the old hymn says, "I need no other argument, I need no other plea. It is enough that Jesus died, and that He died for me."

Christ is the only standard of righteousness that satisfies God's demands. The Holy Spirit must convince us of this truth, because we would never arrive at this conclusion on our own.

## CONVICTION OF JUDGMENT

Jesus describes the third aspect of the Holy Spirit's convincing work in John 16:11. He convinces "concerning judgment, because the ruler of this world has been judged."

People run away from judgment. They do not want to talk about it. Some of us are Christians today because we became terrified of judgment. Well, if it took feeling the flames of hell to bring you to Christ, that's OK. It's OK to go into glory blistered, because judgment is real.

### The Reality of Judgment

How do we know judgment is real? Because Satan, "the ruler of this world," has been judged. If Satan did not get away with his sin, neither will any of his followers. If Satan did not get away with rebelling against the holy standard of God, then neither will any who adopt him as their father.

Hell was not prepared for human beings. Jesus said hell was prepared for Satan and his angels (Matthew 25:41). God never intended people to be separated from Him for eternity. However, if that is your vote, He will not turn down your request.

Someone says, "I never voted to spend eternity with Satan." Oh, yes, you did! Every time you sin, that's a vote for hell. Every time you think an evil thought, every time you act outside the will of God, that's a vote for hell.

You don't have to say, "Satan, you are my god." All you have to do is follow his lead. God will allow you to vote for Satan, but He wants you to know there is judgment to follow. To those who refuse to say to God, "Thy will be done," He says in judgment, "Your will be done."

### The Need for Judgment

You may wonder why Satan is still around bothering you if he has been judged. Well, Satan has been judged, but his full sentence hasn't been carried out yet (see Revelation 20:10). And he has a horde of demonic cronies who carry out his agenda in history. So his judgment becomes the judgment of anyone who rejects Christ. Even a decapitated snake can still poison you. Jesus Christ crushed the head of Satan on the cross, but his venom still spews out.

It's interesting to note how the Holy Spirit carries out His work of convicting. Jesus said in John 15:26–27 that the Holy Spirit would bear witness about Him, but that we would be His witnesses too (see Acts 1:8). In other words, the Spirit works in harmony with our witness.

But if you are not witnessing, you are not giving the Holy Spirit anything to work with, because He uses your lips to get His message of conviction across. Now don't misunderstand. You can't convict anybody of sin. Only the Spirit can do that. But it is your responsibility to declare the message, because the Spirit wants to use you to convince people of sin.

## CONVICTION OF THE SAINTS

But the convicting and convincing work of the Holy Spirit is not limited to sinners. It is also the Spirit's work in the lives of the saints. This work takes a slightly different form and has a different purpose in our case, but it is still very real.

### Making the Saints Uncomfortable

Because He is the *Holy* Spirit, His job is to make us uncomfortable with our sin. You have good reason to question your salvation if you never feel any guilt over sin. I don't care how many times you have walked down an aisle or how many forms you have filled out. If you can sin perpetually and never feel it, maybe your problem is not that you have backslid. Maybe your problem is that you have never "frontslid."

## The Sin of the Saints

The Bible is clear that believers sin. That is why the Scripture says, "Do not quench the Spirit" (1 Thessalonians 5:19). Don't throw water on the fire when the Holy Spirit is convicting you of sin, because this is the way the Spirit pricks you. Again, this reflects the unique, indispensable link between the Holy Spirit and your human spirit.

We are told in Ephesians 4:30 not to "grieve" the Spirit by our sin—in this context, the sins of the tongue. The Spirit is saddened by sinful speech, and He lets us know it because He lives within us. Your body is the Spirit's temple, and when your temple starts going places it ought not go and doing things it ought not do, the Holy Spirit, like a metal detector in an airport, goes off when He detects something illegitimate.

When that happens, the only way you can stop the beeping is either to unplug the system or get rid of the stuff alarming the heavenly sin Detector. If you don't want to do get rid of the junk, you have to stay away from the things of God. Because if you hang out where that Detector is, He will go off every time.

## The Fellowship of the Saints

The issue we're talking about for true Christians is not that of salvation, but that of fellowship. The Holy Spirit convicts the saints of sin that we might draw closer to the Lord and please Him. This is made clear in 1 John, a book written to answer questions like, How do you know you and God are close? How do you know you are on speaking terms with Jesus Christ?

John says in 1:5, "This is the message we have heard from Him and announce to you, that God is light, and in Him there is no darkness at all." Now verse 7: "If we walk in the light as He Himself is in the light, we have fellowship with one another, and the blood of Jesus His Son cleanses us from all sin."

Please note. It is when we are walking in the light that the blood of Christ does its work of cleansing us from all sin. It is only when you are in the light that you see sin as sin. When you are in darkness, you don't see anything wrong with sin. It's only when you turn the light on that you see the stain.

So don't feel bad if the Holy Spirit is convicting you. It means that you are sensitive enough to feel the conviction. It's true that you ought to feel bad about your sin. But you ought to feel good that you are still close enough to the Holy Spirit to hear His voice when He speaks.

The light of God's revelation, His Word, sensitizes us to sin. That's why the Holy Spirit wants to keep us in the Word.

## The Action of the Saints

When the Holy Spirit reveals that you have displeased God, then you ought to take action. That's the whole point of 1 John 1:9, the classic verse on confession of sin for the believer: "If we confess our sins, He is faithful and righteous to forgive us our sins and to cleanse us from all unrighteousness."

The Greek word for "confess," *homologeō*, means to say the same thing, to agree. If you are going to be in fellowship with God, you have to say the same thing about your sin that the Holy Spirit says about your sin. You must treat it like He treats it.

Far too many of us treat sin lightly. Like the unregenerate, we say, "Well, everybody does it." That's not what the convicting Holy Spirit says. He says, "You did it, and it's wrong." But confession is not simply saying glibly, "OK, so I sinned. I'm sorry." That's not the attitude of confession.

Confession means that I see this sin as God sees it, as something hideous and ugly, because I am measuring it against how God feels about it. When you have a conflict with someone and he or she blows it off as no big deal, that bothers you if it's a big deal to you. You want it to be important to the other person, especially if that person claims to love you.

Sin is a big deal to the Spirit, and He doesn't want us treating it like a little thing. When you do, you haven't practiced biblical confession. In fact, please note that the word in verse 9 is plural: "sins." John is talking about individual sins. That's how seriously God takes sin. He wants each one dealt with.

So a catchall, bedtime confession doesn't work. To say, "Lord, forgive me for any sin I have committed this day" is not the idea. The idea of confession is that when I think a thought or perform a deed that violates the character of God, I bring that specific thought or deed to the throne of grace and get it cleared up on the spot. I don't wait until bedtime.

The reason the Holy Spirit is so faithful to convict us of sin the moment we sin is that He knows God cannot fellowship with sin of any size or on any level. So when I think a wrong thought, I am to confess that thought as sin. When I do an evil deed, I am to confess that deed when the Spirit alerts me to it.

When I go around with unconfessed sin, I am out of fellowship with Jesus Christ. I am no longer in harmony with Him. Yes, I am still saved. It's not about relationship; it's about fellowship. Now you may ask, "Since God already knows I did it, why do I need to confess it?"

Well, suppose you walk into your home and discover your child taking money out of your wallet. You see the sin, but your child makes no attempt to deal with it. I don't think you will be satisfied to have your child say, "Well, since you already knew about it, I didn't see any need to admit it or ask your forgiveness."

That won't do the job. You two are going to have a serious problem until that sin is brought out in the open and somebody says "I'm sorry" and the other person says "I forgive you." Until there is confession and forgiveness, the fellowship in your family is broken.

You say, "What about all the sins that I did not know were sins, or the sins I forgot to confess?" That's covered too. If you take care of the sins you do know about, God will be faithful to take care of the sins you don't know about. If you take care of the ones you remember, He will cover the ones you forget. His grace is exceedingly graceful, and it cleanses us from all unrighteousness.

### Taking the Spirit Seriously

So the convicting work of the Holy Spirit lets you know when you are grieving Him or pouring water on the fire that He is placing on your conscience to bring you to confession.

The Holy Spirit is not to be trifled with. We must take seriously His call to holiness. None of us is perfect, don't misunderstand. We will always wrestle with sin. It's when we stop wrestling with sin, when sin doesn't seem all that sinful anymore, when we put off and ignore the Holy Spirit's convicting voice, that we invite the discipline of God—even to what John calls for believers "a sin leading to death" (1 John 5:16).

## AN ILLUSTRATION OF CONFESSION

I want to take a little time here to show you the Holy Spirit's convicting work in action and the proper response to it on the part of a believer. Psalm 51 is probably *the* great illustration of confession in all the Bible.

The background to this is David's sin of adultery and murder (2 Samuel 11). By the time Nathan the prophet confronted David (chapter 12), he had been covering his sin up for about a year. So it had plenty of time to eat away at him.

### Admitting the Sin

But when Nathan came to David, David came under conviction. That's why we must confront each other, by the way. If you see me in sin you ought to confront me, not tell my neighbor (Galatians 6:1). Don't pick up the telephone and tell the world.

So David was confronted by Nathan and was pricked in his heart by the Holy Spirit. We know it was the Holy Spirit because David prayed in verse 11 of Psalm 51, "Do not take Thy Holy Spirit from me." The Spirit had nailed David after a full year of rebellion.

David began his prayer of confession in Psalm 51 by saying, "Be gracious to me, O God, according to Thy lovingkindness; according to the greatness of Thy compassion blot out my transgressions." The Hebrew word for "lovingkindness," *ḥesed*, was derived from the actions of storks.

Storks build their nests on high peaks and are known for their tenacious protection of their young. God loves His children so much that He is tenacious for them. It's storklike love, loyal love.

David needed that love because he said, "I am dirty. I am stuck in the muck and mire of sin and only Your soap can clean this mess and make me zestfully clean. I understand the real deal. I know what I have done. I am not going to hide it or excuse it. I know my transgression. My sin is smack dab in front of my eyes" (vv. 2–3, Evans paraphrase).

### The Real Deal

David also realized that his sin was really against God (v. 4). Yes, he had messed over other people and that had to be dealt with. But David knew what the real deal was. He knew that his sin was an affront to God and a terrible evil in His sight. And he knew that God had the right to do anything with him that He chose.

See, confession recognizes God's right to spank us. It recognizes God's right to correct us. What it really does is acknowledge God as God in our lives and approve of His doing whatever is necessary to fix the problem.

Notice verse 6. David was saying, "Lord, I know what You are looking for in my confession. You are looking for truth in my innermost being. You don't want me just to mouth some words. You are looking for heart-wrenching confession, for something that is coming from a bleeding heart."

### The Need for Cleansing

Then David prayed, "Purify me with hyssop" (v. 7). Hyssop branches were dipped in blood and used to sprinkle it on the altar. David was asking God to sprinkle the blood of His grace on him. For us today, this is the blood of Christ which keeps on cleansing us from all sin.

In verses 8–11, David's plea is that God will restore him to the intimate fellowship they had once enjoyed together. As I said above, David pleaded with God not to remove the Spirit from him. The essence of this prayer we must pray today as well. Since the Spirit maintains our fellowship with God, we too must ensure that His work of intimacy not be lost, but we can never lose His indwelling presence.

### Sharing the Good News

What would be the result of God's answer to David's prayer of confession? David said, "I am going to tell sinners how good You are so they will come to You and be saved too. Show me Your grace and I will be a dispenser of Your grace."

One reason God loves to forgive is so that through us He can let others know that He is in the forgiving business. And He knows how to do it right, because He promises never to turn anyone away who comes to Him with a heart broken over sin.

True confession is brokenness over sin. If that is not how you are treating your sin, no matter what you say you are not confessing it. The Holy Spirit is not achieving His goal of convincing you to confess and put away your sin. The Spirit never wastes His energy. When He does His convicting work, He doesn't want a half-hearted confession.

When it comes to the conviction of the Spirit, we are like the general who was defeated in war and said to the victorious general, "I have come to negotiate the terms of my surrender."

The victorious general replied, "No, I will give you the terms of your surrender." On this matter of sin, God is not negotiating. He has set the terms of forgiveness and restoration of fellowship. Those terms are "a broken and a contrite heart" (Psalm 51:17).

Let me make one more observation about this psalm. In verse 8, David prayed, "Let the bones which Thou hast broken rejoice." The New English Version translates it this way: "Let these bones that you have broken dance again."

David was saying, "God, You have broken my bones. But if You will just set them and make me right, I will be able to dance again. I can't dance now. My heart is too broken. I can't express any excitement about You because You have broken my bones. But You also do orthopedic surgery, so please set these bones so I can dance again."

That means a lot to me because I have a steel plate in my right leg. In 1970, from my linebacker position, I intercepted a pass and took off with it. But I was hit with a cross-body block. My leg did not come up out of the dirt. You could hear the snap of my tibia and fibula all over that football field.

With my leg broken literally in half, I lay helplessly on the ground. The ambulance took me off the field and I was rushed into surgery. I still have the scar and the steel plate. If you were to see my leg, you would know something happened to me. You would know this man was once broken.

But I have good news for you. The surgery was successful. They put in a steel plate that is held together by screws. I know it's there, but no one else knows it's there. The good news is I can move. I can walk. I can jump up and down—not because I was never broken, but because the doctor knew how to set my bones.

David said, "O God, my life has been broken. But I believe that if You will take me to Your hospital, perform surgery on me, and put the steel plate of Your grace in my leg, these bones that were broken will be healed, and I will be able to dance again."

That, my friend, is good news. The convicting work of the Holy Spirit is designed to put you on your feet again. The good news is that if you will let the Spirit do His work, no matter how broken you may be, you will dance again. You may have a scar to remind you of how broken you were, but when the Spirit gets through operating on you, you'll be able to kick up your heels, even with a scar!

# EXPERIENCING THE SPIRIT'S CONVICTION

The Holy Spirit's conviction over sin isn't a pleasant experience. But it is pain with a purpose. God wants you to feel bad about sin so you will do something about it. The ideas below will help you deal with yourself and others on this issue:

1. The first thing to remember is that the Holy Spirit is the Convicter, not you. You just need to be faithful in presenting the gospel. So free yourself from the responsibility of trying to make people believe by the force of your persuasion.

2. Having said that, there are a lot of things you can do to help your unsaved friends think clearly about the issues involved in salvation. Since most people try to justify themselves, jar them from their complacency by asking questions like, "Just how good do you have to be to make heaven? How will you know when you've been good enough? What standard are you using to measure goodness? Do you live up to your own standard all the time? What happens when you don't?"

3. Since the Holy Spirit's job is to convince unbelievers of sin, we had better keep the discussion centered on sin. People don't need Christ because they need fulfillment, joy, or peace. Those are by-products of salvation. People need Christ because they are lost sinners under God's judgment.

4. What about your own sin? If you don't have a broken heart toward your sin, ask God to give you one. If you don't feel bad about your rebellion, ask God to make you feel bad about it so you can do something about it. God can handle your honesty, but He cannot tolerate sin.

# CHAPTER EIGHT

# EXPERIENCING THE SPIRIT'S POWER

All it takes is about a two-hour power failure to make us realize how much we benefit from an invisible resource called electricity. Electricity has power within itself. Stick a piece of metal in one of your home's electrical outlets and you will *become* one of the lights in your home!

Electricity is also exceedingly powerful in its visible effects. It cools and cooks our food. It can freeze water and make bread pop out of a toaster. When it's dark the lights come on, all because we have available to us an invisible power.

Wind is another good analogy for the Spirit (we've seen that the Hebrew word for spirit means wind). Wind has a life of its own (John 3:8). Sometimes it is so gentle and still that we hardly know it exists. At other times it blows so viciously that nothing can withstand its power. Trees, buildings, boats, and people are tossed around when the wind blows hard. Yet the same wind helps to sustain life, supports an airplane in flight, and moves a sailboat toward its destination. So in likening the Holy Spirit to wind, Jesus was speaking of a Person with enormous power.

The powers of electricity and wind are very real and readily available, whether or not we choose to draw on them. And if we mess with them in the wrong way, these powers can discipline us as well as help us.

But the invisible, available power we have in our homes is nothing compared to the power that all of us who know Jesus Christ have in our lives in the Person of the Holy Spirit. He is the invisible presence and power of God. He is God, in fact. The Spirit is deposited in the life of every believer at the moment of salvation (a subject we discussed in the previous chapter on the baptism of the Spirit) and will never abandon us (we've discussed the matter of security too).

So we have a royal Resident in our lives, the indwelling Holy Spirit. As we saw in the opening chapter, one of the Spirit's chief roles is to empower believers to live supernatural lives. He is also the invisible power source for the church as the collective body of believers. Let's talk about the Holy Spirit's power, beginning in Acts 1 with a classic passage that addresses this topic. The centerpiece of this text is a very familiar verse:

> But you shall receive power when the Holy Spirit has come upon you; and you shall be My witnesses both in Jerusalem, and in all Judea and Samaria, and even to the remotest part of the earth. (v. 8)

The clear implication of Jesus' words here is that the disciples would not have power until the Spirit came: Power is not simply a concept to be understood but a reality to be experienced. So you can't talk about spiritual power without simultaneously talking about the Holy Spirit. I want to show you four truths from Scripture that will give us a good perspective on this powerful One who has been made available to us.

## A POWERFUL PRESENCE

Notice first of all that the Spirit provides Christians with a powerful presence. In verse 4 of Acts 1, Luke says that after His resurrection Jesus gathered the apostles and "commanded them not to leave Jerusalem, but to wait for what the Father had promised, 'Which,' He said, 'you heard of from Me.'" Jesus then repeated the promise of the Spirit's coming: "You shall be baptized with the Holy Spirit not many days from now" (v. 5).

So Jesus told the apostles not to go forward until they had experienced the fulfillment of the promise. In other words, don't leave home without the Holy Spirit, because the power promised in verse 8 can only be realized when a person has the presence promised in verse 5.

### The Spirit of Christ

We already know from John 14–16 that Jesus told His men He would be leaving them soon, but would send them a Helper just like Him. In John 14:18 He promised, "I will not leave you as orphans; I will come to you." The way Jesus was going to come to them was through the Holy Spirit. That's the way Jesus comes to us too.

See, if you have the Holy Spirit living within you, you have as much of Jesus as those first disciples had, even though Jesus lived among them for more than three years. You do not have to go back in time to be with Jesus. He is with you right now in the Person of the Holy Spirit. There is no such thing as wishing Jesus were here. He is.

That is why the Holy Spirit is often called "the Spirit of Christ." You can see the relationship between the Spirit and Christ in the letters to the seven churches of Revelation 2–3. In the letter to Ephesus, for example, the apostle John writes that "the One who holds the seven stars in His right hand" is the One speaking to the church (Revelation 2:1).

We know from Revelation 1:16 that this Person is the risen and glorified Christ. He delivers His message to the church, then He warns, "He who has an ear, let him hear what the Spirit says to the churches" (2:7). This same pattern is repeated in each of the seven letters. So here is Jesus Christ speaking to the churches by means of the Spirit. They speak with one voice.

I've said this before, but I think it's important. Don't spend too much time trying to figure out how the Holy Spirit and Christ relate to each other or you'll jump out a window. The mystery of the Trinity is beyond our human ability to comprehend.

But as we learned in the first chapter, the Holy Spirit can do what Jesus could not do in His flesh since Jesus was limited by His human body. When Jesus went home with little Zaccheus that day, He couldn't go home with anyone else. It was either Zack's house or someone else's house.

But the Holy Spirit is not subject to any limitations of location or time. Now the presence of God in Christ is with each of us equally through the Spirit. We are at no disadvantage for not having seen Christ. In fact, Jesus Himself said the Spirit's coming was to our advantage (John 16:7).

You can see this in 1 John 1. John wrote to a second generation of believers who had not seen Jesus. Yet, even though John had seen and touched Jesus (v. 1), he wrote that these later believers "may have fellowship with us" (v. 3). In other words, John was saying, "You can have what we had."

The point is, you and I are not second-class Christians when it comes to experiencing the reality of Jesus Christ. We have been endowed with the Holy Spirit, who brings to us a very powerful presence: the presence of Christ Himself.

In 2 Corinthians 3:17–18, Paul writes:

> Now the Lord is the Spirit; and where the Spirit of the Lord is, there is liberty. But we all, with unveiled face beholding as in a mirror the glory of the Lord, are being transformed into the same image from glory to glory, just as from the Lord, the Spirit.

Jesus Christ and the Holy Spirit are distinct Persons in the Godhead, but Paul spoke of their work as synonymous because they belong to the same Godhead. So, when you have the Spirit, you have Christ.

You have as much spiritual potential as any other believer, because you have the Spirit in all His fullness. He can take you into a realm that you in your natural state could never enter: the realm of spiritual power.

This is why the apostle John spent so much time reminding Christians to abide in Christ as well as in the Spirit (1 John 2:6, 24, 27; 3:24); that is, to live in the realm of the Spirit. It is the Spirit who brings you into the reality of the experience of the living, resurrected, and ascended Jesus Christ. If you want to be close to Christ, you must be close to the Spirit.

### A Higher Realm

I am amazed at how far electronic science has come, particularly in the video market. The games our kids can buy are simply staggering. So are the claims for what has come to be known as "virtual reality." The makers of these products invite us to enter another realm of reality. But it's electronic hocus-pocus. You're there in the race car or in the battle or whatever, but you're not really there.

The Holy Spirit is far more than virtual reality. If man with his feeble mind can take you into the video realm, how much more can God the Spirit, by His unlimited power, take you into the spiritual realm. This is "real reality." The Holy Spirit has taken you into the very presence of God, "the heavenly places in Christ" (Ephesians 1:3), where you are in another realm.

If I were in the right realm, I could easily lift a ton. My problem, however, is that I cannot do it in this realm because there is a law that works against me called the law of gravity. But if only I could get on a space shuttle and travel in outer space, I could lift the weight.

Why? Because I would be living in a higher realm where the law of gravity does not operate. The reason some of us can't lift our heavy problems is that we are living in the wrong realm. The Holy Spirit wants to take you to the nongravitational realm of spiritual places.

But in order to pull that off, we must be living in the realm of the Spirit. What the Holy Spirit does is place us where we can do the supernatural rather than simply living in the realm of the natural.

So the Spirit provides you a powerful presence because it is God who lives in you through Christ by means of the Holy Spirit. When you pray, when you work, when you do whatever you do, you have the presence of the Trinity working through the Person of the Holy Spirit.

If you are one of those people who says, "I've got to see it before I'll believe it," you are going to be in spiritual trouble. It's like waiting to see electricity before you use it. You are going to freeze to death and your food will spoil, because electricity is not designed to be seen. It is only designed to be used. We live by faith, not by sight. In fact, get worried if you do start seeing things!

The spiritual realm is a different realm, a higher realm. It's the powerful presence of God, made real to us by the Holy Spirit.

## A POWERFUL PROGRAM

The Holy Spirit not only provides a powerful presence. He is accomplishing a powerful program:

> To [the apostles] He also presented Himself alive, after His suffering, by many convincing proofs, appearing to them over a period of forty days, and speaking of the things concerning the kingdom of God. (Acts 1:3)

We know that the kingdom was on their minds because they were asking Jesus, "Lord, is it at this time You are restoring the kingdom to Israel?" (v. 6). This is very important because this is the context in which Jesus promised the coming of the Holy Spirit.

### Building the Kingdom

The question was not whether Jesus was going to establish His kingdom. It was just a matter of when. So the ultimate goal of the Spirit's coming at Pentecost to indwell believers is the building of God's kingdom.

One of the great problems we are facing today, particularly in the abuses coming from various groups regarding the Spirit, is that the Holy Spirit is made an end in Himself. But the Spirit is not an end in Himself. He did not come just so you could know Him and experience His power.

The Holy Spirit came to provide you with power to accomplish a great program called the kingdom of God. So if you are one of those Christians who goes around Spirit-hunting, you need to know that God does not simply give His power to show off, to flex His muscles. God has a specific program in mind that He uses the Spirit's power to accomplish.

See, God is not David Copperfield. He doesn't do magic shows. He is not simply trying to strut His stuff and say, "Look what I can do!" Jesus' earthly miracles were pointed and purposeful because they were all related to the kingdom. (In his gospel, John calls them "signs.") When the Bible talks about the kingdom of God, it is talking about His rule or reign; that is, the sphere in which God will demonstrate His control.

The Bible declares that God's kingdom is the universe. Then it narrows it down and says God's kingdom is the earth. "The earth is the Lord's, and all it contains, the world, and those who dwell in it," the psalmist declared (Psalm 24:1). But we live in a universe that does not recognize its rightful King.

That's going to change someday, however. God will set up His kingdom. Throughout the Old Testament, God's prophets kept prophesying that one day His Servant, who is Jesus Christ, would come to set up a kingdom where God Himself would rule and reign on planet earth.

Even though the kingdom is not yet physically established on earth, the primary biblical concept of the kingdom is not a place. The Greek word for kingdom, *basileia*, means rule or authority. God's kingdom is first of all His sphere of authority, His rulership. So when you become part of God's kingdom, the concept is that you come under God's rule.

I have a kingdom. It's my house, located two blocks from our church. I don't have much, but I have that. Make no mistake about it, I am the king in my kingdom. It's not a big kingdom, but it's mine. (I can say that because my wife, Lois, isn't reading this!)

Now in my kingdom, I have rules. For example, if a person comes to my kingdom and he is smoking a cigarette, he will have to put it out before he enters my realm. First of all, I do not have any ashtrays for him. Second, I have asthma. Third, I don't like it. The same goes for any alcohol he might have with him.

He may say, "Well, in my kingdom I smoke and drink anywhere and any time I want." Fine. But once he comes into my kingdom he will have to adjust, to rearrange things, because in my kingdom these things are unacceptable.

My oldest son is now driving. Recently, a friend of his came over to the house, and they said they wanted to go out. So I said to my son, "Tell me where you are going and when are you coming back."

He hit me with this heavy line. "Dad, I'm almost a man." In other words, "Why do you have to know, Dad?"

I can remember saying that to my own father. So I just had to explain some kingdom theology to my son. "Because I am the father and you are my son, and I want to know." This is my kingdom.

Well, this whole thing is God's kingdom, and it's a powerful program because it's energized by a powerful Holy Spirit. His job is to bring people to recognize God's right to rule as King and to submit to His authority. God does not want you bringing your rules into His house. The worst thing in the world, and you know this if you're a parent, is having kids who want to build their own little kingdoms in your house.

So Jesus told the apostles that God will indeed establish His kingdom someday, but in His own time. In the meantime, God has decided to set up His own kingdom within a kingdom. That is called the church, brought into being by the Holy Spirit.

## The Church's Goal

The ultimate goal of the church is not itself, but the kingdom. The church has become ingrown when we equate the church with the kingdom. The church is the vehicle to deliver the kingdom that is to come.

That is, we are to model, reflect, and illustrate the kingdom, so that anybody who wants to know what the kingdom that is to come will look like can look at the kingdom in miniature that has already come in the form of the church. That is why the witness of the church is so critical, and that is why the church has been given Holy Ghost power.

So the church is being established as the kingdom of God on earth to reflect the kingdom that is to come. Church is a bigger issue than just going to a building. It is part of the powerful program of God, His kingdom rule. We listen to the Word of God that we might understand the rule of God. It is His house.

God's kingdom is God's plan and program, and we as the church are the vehicle to deliver it. So if you want to see Holy Ghost power, make sure you are involved in the kingdom. If you are not doing kingdom business, don't expect Holy Ghost power.

See, if you are only asking the Spirit to bless your kingdom instead of building God's kingdom, the Holy Spirit is not interested in blessing you or empowering you. He is here to do kingdom work only.

So if all you want is another miracle so you can feel better or have more money, that is not kingdom work. That's the problem with so-called prosperity theology. It is not about the kingdom. It is about *me*. God is after the kingdom.

## A POWERFUL PEOPLE

The power of the Holy Spirit is also evident in that He creates a powerful people who have His powerful presence carrying out His powerful program.

The disciples were a weak group of men. Peter denied Jesus. The other disciples left Him because they feared the Jews. They ran until the Spirit came.

### The Holy Spirit Difference

But when the Spirit came upon them, those weak-kneed wimps who ran when the going got tough received some spiritual courage. They got Holy Ghost power, the Holy Spirit difference.

It didn't happen because of changes in their environment. They did not get it by taking a Dale Carnegie course or by enrolling in a class on the power of positive thinking. The only difference was Holy Ghost power, but what a change took place. Peter was drastically changed. Something happened to the boy.

According to Acts 4:13, the Jewish authorities marveled at the courage shown by Peter and John, who were "uneducated." I like that because it means they hadn't been to formal school. They hadn't been to Bible college or seminary. But they *had* been with Jesus.

The power of the Holy Spirit has nothing to do with the degrees you have on your wall. It has nothing to do with your theological training or background. You can have it all and still be a defeated Christian. But if you have been with Jesus, somebody else is going to know it. If you have been with Jesus, it's going to become evident that something powerful is at work in you.

We spend all this time trying to change our personalities, trying to fix ourselves. We go to our therapists to help us work through who we were, who we are, and who we will be. But the Bible says when the Spirit took over the apostles, there was a personality change. All of a sudden these spaghetti Christians stood up with shoulders squared and spoke for Christ.

Threats couldn't scare or stop them (Acts 5:27–29). The same guys who had run away stood eyeball-to-eyeball and toe-to-toe with the authorities. Even after the apostles were beaten and ordered to stop preaching, they went out rejoicing for the opportunity to suffer for Christ (vv. 40–41).

### The Spirit's Control

Where did they get that kind of power? The Holy Spirit. The Holy Spirit will change your personality if He can get hold of you. So if you and I don't have a relationship with the Spirit, we are going to be defeated spiritual wimps, always running to the next conference or program to see if it can do for us what only the Holy Spirit can do.

Sometimes, people come for counseling and say, "I don't know what's wrong with me." I know what's wrong. The Holy Spirit is not in control yet. Because if He would ever take over, people would do things they would not normally do and say things they would not normally say.

The Spirit is infinitely bigger than all your attempts to fix yourself. He brings about a real change. He can change your personality. You may say, "I am a worrier. I was born that way. My mother was a worrier. I have worry in my genes."

That means you need a personality change. That's the Holy Spirit's specialty. He can make the insecure person secure, the fearful person confident. That's what He did with the apostles. But He only does it if you are doing kingdom work. He is not going to do it so you can win a personality or popularity contest. But when the Spirit goes to work, things change.

I shared this illustration in an earlier book, but it fits well here. I saw a clip of the first *Crocodile Dundee* movie, in which Dundee is walking down the street in New York with his girlfriend. Some guys jump out to rob them, and one guy pulls a knife and says, "Give me your money!"

Dundee's girl screams, "Oh, he has a knife!"

But Dundee is cool. He says, "That's not a knife." Homeboy reaches behind his back and pulls a huge knife out of his belt and says, "*This* is a knife." The thief looks at Dundee's knife and takes off. What would normally bring fear did not bring fear to Crocodile Dundee, because he had something bigger and better working on the inside.

You have something, or rather Someone, bigger and better working on the inside. Therefore, God does not want you to be intimidated out of being the person He has saved you to be. If you are doing the powerful kingdom program God has called you to do and you have the powerful presence of the Holy Spirit, you are a spiritually powerful person.

## A POWERFUL PROCLAMATION

Finally, the Spirit of God leads us to make a powerful proclamation. This is Acts 1:8, the Spirit-given power to be Christ's witnesses.

The first word of verse 8, "but," is instructive, because in the original language this is a very strong adversative. When Jesus said, "but you shall receive power," He was telling the apostles in a strong way, "Get your minds off what you were just talking about. Stop being preoccupied with it. I'm changing the subject."

We already know what the apostles were preoccupied with: the arrival of the kingdom (v. 6). They were hoping the kingdom would come right then. But Jesus said, "That's not your concern" (v. 7).

### Kingdom Power

The apostles wanted the kingdom to come because they knew that with the kingdom would come the power. After all, had not Jesus Himself taught them to pray, "Thine is the kingdom, and the power, and the glory, forever" (Matthew 6:13)?

But Jesus said He was not going to give them the political kingdom they were looking for. Instead, He was going to give them the power of the kingdom in the Person of the Holy Spirit. Now this was some power because the Greek word used here is the word from which we get our English word "dynamite." Notice that this power would enable the apostles to become something, Jesus' witnesses. They were not just going out to do witnessing.

See, one of the ways you know the Holy Spirit is taking over is that you are being Christian when nobody is telling you to be Christian. You are representing Jesus when nobody is telling you to represent Jesus. You are taking a stand for Christ when nobody has to tell you because that is what you have become. When this happens, you don't really need an evangelistic program.

But if you can go day in and day out and never bring up the name Jesus Christ in a serious way; if you can go day in and day out and Jesus Christ does not emanate from you on your job; if you can go day in and day out without Christ being the dominating influence of your life, the problem is not that the church needs to come up with a new evangelistic program. The problem is the Holy Spirit doesn't have control of your life yet. When the Holy Spirit gets hold of you, a transformation occurs.

## Christ's Witnesses

Now I like what happened to old Peter when the Holy Spirit came upon him. On the Day of Pentecost in Acts 2, the people were making fun of the disciples, accusing them of being full of "sweet wine" (v. 13), the good stuff.

But Peter took his stand, raised his voice, and boldly declared the Word of God to the crowd (v. 14). It was Peter's finest sermon, and God used His formerly wishy-washy witness to bring revival in Jerusalem. When the Holy Spirit controls us, we will be Christ's witnesses.

Let me make an observation about the Spirit's power. He gave the gift of tongues on Pentecost so the apostles could proclaim "the mighty deeds of God" (v. 11). It's amazing to me how many people want the gift of tongues today so they can speak for God in heavenly languages when they aren't even speaking for Him in the earthly language He's already given them.

It does not make any sense in the world to come to church and speak in another language if you are not willing to witness for Jesus Christ in English. The idea is that God has called us to represent Him and He wants us to be witnesses.

People ought to know you have become intoxicated with Jesus. They ought to mistake your love for Jesus for a drunken man's obsession with alcohol because you are not ashamed of the gospel. I can assure you, in Dallas people are not ashamed to speak about the Dallas Cowboys football team. We'll talk about "Da 'Boys." Just ask us.

But when it comes to Jesus Christ, too many of us have nothing to say. We become intimidated. We back off. That's not the Spirit of God at work, because when He takes over, you have to get up and say, "We are not drunk as you suppose. This is that which the Bible speaks of."

## Turning On the Power

My friend, you don't need more power. You have the Holy Spirit. You just need to let the Spirit loose in your life. We are going to talk about the specifics of how to do that when we cover the filling of the Spirit in a later chapter.

My point is, don't go looking for power. Your car has a power source already in it, called your battery. That battery empowers all the other parts of your car to work. You do not need to sit in your car and say, "If I only had power to get this thing going. Just give me some power so I can move."

No, you already have all the power you need in your battery. Power and battery go together. If the battery works, you have the power. If you have a working battery but you are going nowhere, it's not because your power source failed. It's because you never engaged the ignition.

Many of us are going nowhere in our spiritual lives, not because there is something wrong with the Holy Spirit, but because we have not engaged His power. We're trying to get somewhere by using the Spirit's power only when we feel like it or when we're in trouble.

But it doesn't work that way. If you are going to experience the benefits of the Holy Spirit's power, He must have more of you. You don't need more of Him. The key to enjoying the Spirt's power is obedience. This is why Jesus told His disciples that their love for Him would be measured by their obedience. When you and I obey, the Holy Spirit empowers, because through obedience we join with the Spirit's agenda of glorifying Christ.

The "Holy Spirit" battery is waiting on you. He's waiting for you to take out your relationship key, put it in the ignition of obedience, turn the key, press the accelerator, and take off. Don't blame the battery if the driver doesn't know what to do. And don't blame the Spirit if you are not doing what He wants you to do. His power is guaranteed. He never runs down, and He is available to make you all He wants you to be, but only as you obey.

# EXPERIENCING THE SPIRIT'S POWER

I hope you got the point: when we're dealing with the Holy Spirit, we're dealing with power! His power is manifested in His presence, His program, His people, and His proclamation. I believe the ideas below will help you tap into that power:

1. Wouldn't it be great to live in that spiritual realm where the gravitational pull of sin doesn't work against you? Well, the Spirit can take you there. He already lives within you. All He's waiting for is your cooperation. If you have any sin in your life pulling you down, confess it right now and claim Christ's cleansing (1 John 1:9). The Spirit will reveal any such sin to you if you'll ask Him to search your heart.

2. Jesus said we are to be His witnesses, beginning right in our own Jerusalem. The trouble is, most of us never get started where we are, so we can't move out to wider spheres of witness. Is there someone in your Jerusalem—your neighborhood, your street, maybe even your house—who you know needs the Lord? Put that person on your prayer list, asking God to give you a witnessing opportunity. Remember, you have the Spirit's power to help you be effective.

3. Maybe you can identify with the disciples in their fear of the Jewish authorities. But the Holy Spirit who replaced their fear with courage is the same Spirit you have within you. What or whom do you fear most today? Write down your biggest fear, then ask the Holy Spirit to give you a new dose of spiritual courage. Carry this piece of paper with you until the Spirit helps you conquer your fear, then tear the paper up and give God thanks.

4. The Holy Spirit's power is totally available to you. Why not appropriate it in a new way by praying something like this: "Holy Spirit, I am Yours. I give my life to You. Have Your way in me. I will do what You want done as You want it done. I will seek to glorify Christ and build His kingdom. Be real in me because I want all of Your power expressed through me. I give You all of me."

## CHAPTER NINE

# EXPERIENCING THE SPIRIT'S AUTHORITY

L et me begin this chapter by making two statements that I hope are patently obvious to you by now.

First, there is no victory in the Christian life apart from the power of the Holy Spirit. Second, this means that any attempt to live the Christian life by any authority other than that which the Spirit supplies is doomed to end in abysmal failure.

I make these statements lest we forget—because we do tend to forget. Someone has said that the Christian life is not a matter of our ability, but of our *avail*ability. The ability is all from above, made real to us in our day-by-day lives by the indwelling Holy Spirit.

I want to show you how you can experience the Spirit's authority by surveying the heart of the book of Romans, God's comprehensive statement on the Christian life. We will be surveying Romans 6–8, three of the most important chapters in the New Testament. In these chapters Paul sets forth the sanctification of the believer; that is, how we as Christians are set apart by the Spirit to a spiritually victorious experience.

If we can grasp what Paul is saying in Romans 6–8, we will have a good understanding of the spiritual life. Now we can't go verse by verse through all three chapters. That would be a book in itself. What I want to do is underscore and summarize Paul's argument as we pursue the goal of discovering and experiencing the Holy Spirit's authority to live the Christian life. Just to give you a taste of the good stuff up front, let me say that the way you tap into the authority of the Spirit is by living under the law of the Spirit. Now let's unfold what that means.

## YOUR NEW IDENTITY

Paul opens the sixth chapter of Romans with a handful of questions and a couple of powerful declarations:

> What shall we say then? Are we to continue in sin that grace might increase? May it never be! How shall we who died to sin still live in it? Or do you not know that all of us who have been baptized into Christ Jesus have been baptized into His death? Therefore we have been buried with Him through baptism into death, in order that as Christ was raised from the dead through the glory of the Father, so we too might walk in newness of life. (vv. 1–4)

At least a dozen times in Romans 6–8, Paul refers to what we do know, what we don't know because it's beyond us (see 8:26), and what we should know but don't. Three of those references are right in front of us here in chapter 6: verse 3, which I quoted above, and also verses 6 and 9.

The point is that successful Christian living is predicated on what you know about how you ought to live because God has revealed it to you. Therefore, if you don't know what you need to know, you will be handicapped in living successfully. Why? Because it is our knowledge of our identity in Christ that allows us to interpret life from a divine frame of reference.

## What You Need to Know

Many Christians either do not have this knowledge, or else they do not understand it, so they operate from a false identity. Whenever you identify yourself falsely, you will act falsely.

Many of us are like the eagle's egg that got knocked out of its nest and fell among turkeys on a turkey farm (don't ask how it happened; just take it by faith).

So the turkeys hatched this eagle egg. The eaglet came out, looked around, saw all these turkeys, and came to a logical but false assumption: He must be a turkey too, even though he didn't look like the other turkeys. So the eaglet began to walk and talk like what he thought he was, a turkey.

But one day an eagle soared over the turkey farm. The eaglet looked up and saw the eagle, and something stirred within him. He felt like they were related somehow, but he figured, "Well, he's up there and I'm down here." So he would have forgotten about it except that the eagle saw the eaglet, swooped down, and asked, "What are you doing down here?"

"I'm hanging out with my family, the turkeys," the eaglet replied.

"What makes you think you're a turkey?"

"Well, I was born with turkeys. I was raised with them. I eat with them. I sleep with them. I must be one of them."

The eagle said, "Somebody has lied to you! Stretch out those wings." The eaglet stretched out its wings. "Now flap those wings." So the eaglet flapped his wings and began to rise. "Flap them harder," the eagle said. The eaglet flapped them harder and went higher.

Then the eagle said, "Now, follow me." He took off with the eaglet right behind. One of the turkeys looked up and saw the eaglet flying away and said, "Where do you think you're going?"

The eaglet looked back and said, "I'm going to be what I was created to be, you turkey."

See, a lot of us are hanging out with the turkeys when we ought to be soaring with the eagles. A lot of us have been satisfied with waddling through the Christian life rather than soaring through the Christian life. We have gotten so used to being with turkeys that we think we are one of them.

You say, "How do I get the real picture of my identity in Christ so I can live like who I am?" Good question. Answer: The Holy Spirit gives you the authority to know it and live it. Your identity as a believer begins here in Romans 6. You must know and understand that you have been co-crucified, co-buried, and co-resurrected with Jesus Christ.

You are no longer a slave to sin. You no longer belong to this world order. Your old self was crucified (v. 6). That means dead. So you need to get this down: If you know Christ, you are not who you used to be. You are totally different.

## What You Need to Consider

Not only must you know who you are in order to understand your identity in Christ, you must also *consider* who you are. "Even so consider yourselves to be dead to sin, but alive to God in Christ Jesus" (v. 11). This means you must add up the facts and come to the right conclusion about your new identity. You must count it as a reality.

The Greek word translated "consider" is an economic term that means to add up the figures and arrive at the proper answer. It's one thing to know something factually or academically. It's quite another thing to consider or count or reckon it to be true.

Paul is saying it's not enough to know who you are in Christ because the Bible tells you it's true. You can put it in the bank and count on it. In fact, it's crucial that you do so, for only then will you really start drawing on your new identity and experiencing it.

Let me illustrate the difference between knowing and considering as Paul is using the latter term. You know I have a steel plate in my right leg because I told you so at the end of chapter 7. You have factual knowledge of my repaired leg.

But I *consider* that fixed leg! That is, I remember it being broken. I can recall the pain. Every day when I put on my socks, I see the long scar. I can feel the lump of the plate. And you can be sure that I take that leg into account before I try something that may rebreak those bones.

So I not only know I have a repaired leg, I consider it to be so. I add up my memories of the event and the scar and the lump and come to the proper conclusion. And when I am tempted to try something that might jeopardize that repair job, I act on what I know and walk away. To consider a biblical fact to be true is to begin the process of experiencing that truth in your life.

Now remember, we're talking about experiencing the Holy Spirit's authority to enable you to live a victorious Christian life. But before we can jump to that truth in Romans 8, we need to lay the foundation in chapters 6–7. So stay with me, because this stuff is bedrock you can build your life on. Besides, it doesn't do much good to talk about the Spirit's authority until we have answered the question, His authority to do what?

So you need to know that you are identified totally with Christ in His death, burial, and resurrection. And you need to go the second step and consider or count it to be so.

## What You Need to Do

When you have done that, then you're ready to take the third step, which is found in 6:13:

> Do not go on presenting the members of your body to sin as instruments of unrighteousness; but present yourselves to God as those alive from the dead, and your members as instruments of righteousness to God.

If you are going to live victoriously, you need to make an offering (see Romans 12:1). You need to offer your body to the doing of that which you know and count to be true. You've already taken the truth of your new identity to the bank. This is where you draw on that bank account and spend it in righteous living, not as a slave to sin (v. 14).

When I am performing a wedding and we come to the part where the bride is to be given away, I ask, "Who gives this woman to be married to this man?" It's generally the father who says, "Her mother and I."

At that point, the groom steps up and takes the father's place. The father presents the bride to another man, who now becomes the primary male influence in her life. Once they say "I do" and I pronounce them husband and wife, the father has lost his dominant influence in his daughter's life.

Her primary obligation is no longer to her father, even though that was true all her life until that day. She has been presented to another. Her obligation changes.

Since you know you have been married to Christ, and since you are banking on it, don't present yourself to the person you used to belong to, the Devil. Present yourself to your new love, Jesus Christ.

Paul is saying that the only way you will be able to stop living the way you used to live is when you get hold of the fact that you are not who you used to be. Where does that authority to know, consider, and do come from? From the ministry of the Holy Spirit in your life.

## YOUR NEW PROBLEM

But you have a new problem too. You say, "Come again?" No, you have it right. The latter half of Romans 7 deals with a problem I call new because you've only had it since you've been a Christian. Let Paul spell it out for you:

> For we know that the Law is spiritual; but I am of flesh, sold into bondage to sin. . . . For I know that nothing good dwells in me, that is, in my flesh; for the wishing is present in me, but the doing of the good is not. . . . For I joyfully concur with the law of God in the inner man, but I see a different law in the members of my body, waging war against the law of my mind, and making me a prisoner of the law of sin which is in my members. (vv. 14, 18, 22–23)

### Same Old Address

So what's the problem? The problem is, only the inner you was made brand-new in Christ. Your spirit was dead in sin, and now it is alive in Christ. But this new you is still living in the same old house at the same old address: the flesh.

In other words, the new invisible you—your redeemed inner person, your spirit—is still hanging out in the old visible you—your body. Why is that a problem? Because the old you, which Paul calls the flesh, has been utterly contaminated by sin. It was born in sin. It is so messed up that God is not even going to try to fix it. We need to keep reminding ourselves that the flesh is only good for worm food.

What's more, the longer you were a sinner before you came to Christ, the more time your flesh had to get contaminated by sin. That's why we try to win people to Christ when they are young, so that by God's grace they can be spared the ravages of sin.

If you got saved when you were five, praise God. You were probably spared a lot of exposure to the contamination of sin. But if you did not get saved until you were twenty-five or thirty-five, your flesh had plenty of time to be controlled by your sin nature.

Our flesh is like the structure of a house that has been eaten up by termites. You can paint the inside, put down new carpet, and buy new furniture, but you have not fixed the structural problem. The flesh is like a bad in-law; you can't get rid of it. It just keeps hanging around.

Now don't misunderstand. Our physical bodies and our physical desires are not evil in themselves. God gave them to us. When Paul refers to the flesh, he's talking about our bodies and appetites under the destructive control of our old nature inherited from Adam and thoroughly ruined by sin. Since the body is our vehicle to get around on the planet, it is through the body that we express the sins of our old or fleshly nature.

### Nothing Worth Saving

This is a hard one to get hold of, because we have a hard time really believing what the Bible says about the flesh. See, we spend so much time making the outer shell look good that it's hard to believe it's all bad. Paul, you mean there's nothing of the flesh worth saving? "There isn't one good thing in my flesh" is Paul's answer in Romans 7:18.

So you may as well mark it down. There is nothing of value to God in your flesh. Your old address has been condemned. That's why it must die. God doesn't want it in heaven, and you can't fix it here on earth.

Now if you don't understand this, you are going to waste your time trying to improve your flesh, whether through New Year's resolutions or by sheer effort, gritting your teeth and giving it your best shot.

It's true you may be able to make a few minor improvements that way. The authority to do what we're talking about, however, doesn't come from you. It comes from the authority of the Holy Spirit in you.

But a lot of us are like lion tamers, trying to whip the flesh into shape. It cannot be done. The flesh is totally diseased. It attracts sin like a magnet. Sin appeals to the flesh because sin pleases the flesh. The thing that makes the flesh so bad is that it seeks to serve and please self rather than serve and please God. But your new inner person seeks to please God.

## Growing the New You

You say, "Then why is my flesh so dominating?" Because it has been in control of you so long. That's why the only way to overcome the flesh is by growing the new you, not by trying to fix the old you.

How do you grow the new you while shutting down the old you? You do it by feeding your spirit while you starve your flesh—those old, corrupt impulses and desires and habits. You cannot feed the flesh, neglect the inner you, and expect to have victory over the flesh.

But too many Christians are like people in a cafeteria line. They get a steak smothered with brown gravy, mashed potatoes, bread with plenty of butter, and a big dessert covered with whipped cream. Then they come to the end of the line and get a diet drink, hoping somehow that it will cancel out the effects of the other stuff.

This is what happens to a lot of us. All week long we feed the flesh, then we come to church for "diet worship," hoping that two hours on Sunday will cancel out all the feeding the flesh we did Monday through Saturday. It won't work. The only answer for the flesh is "putting to death the deeds of the body" (Romans 8:13). And guess who gives you the authority to do that? The answer is right there in verse 13: the Holy Spirit.

"Putting to death the deeds of the body" is what I call starving your sinful flesh. You starve it by not feeding it the sinful stuff it craves and thrives on. The flesh is so bad that Paul cries out, "Wretched man that I am!" (7:24a). Notice this is present tense. This is the apostle Paul talking about his present struggles. So he asks, "Who will set me free from the body of this death?" (v. 24b).

The imagery Paul uses here is very interesting. In his day, if you killed someone, one of the ways you might be punished was by having the dead body of your victim tied to your body. You would be face-to-face with the person you killed.

When they tied that dead body to you, that cadaver signed your death warrant because as decay set in on the cadaver, it would begin to penetrate the pores of your skin, poisoning your blood and ultimately killing you. So you were looking death in the face as you dragged a dead body around with you. What you wanted more than anything was release from that body.

That's a gruesome image, but it pictures well what Paul is saying here. He was dragging around the dead carcass of his sinful flesh. It was dead because it had been put to death by Paul's co-crucifixion with Christ, but it was still weighing him down.

You are trapped in your flesh until Christ releases you. That's what Paul gives thanks for in verse 25. Jesus alone can release you from "the body of this death." And He does it through the power and authority of the Holy Spirit. Once you realize the flesh can't be salvaged and is destined for dust, it will radically change your approach to the Christian life. You will give up trying to tame or fix the flesh and concentrate on building up your inner person by the power of the Spirit.

## YOUR NEW LAW

Now we are ready to move to Romans 8 and the law of the Spirit, by which He gives us authority to live victoriously:

> There is therefore now no condemnation for those who are in Christ Jesus. For the law of the Spirit of life in Christ Jesus has set you free from the law of sin and of death. For what the Law could not do, weak as it was through the flesh, God did: sending His own Son in the likeness of sinful flesh and as an offering for sin, He condemned sin in the flesh, in order that the requirements of the Law might be fulfilled in us, who do not walk according to the flesh, but according to the Spirit. (vv. 1–4)

What God did when He saved you was to transfer His power from the outside of you to the inside of you.

### A Power Transfer

You have probably had the experience of using jumper cables to jump-start a car with a dead battery. It's a pretty simple procedure. You just connect one battery's positive and negative poles to their counterparts on the other battery and rev the good battery's engine.

At that moment there is a power transfer. The power of the living battery is transferred to the dead battery, so that the dead battery becomes as alive as the living battery. Now this did not happen because that dead battery had any life in it. It got connected to another battery that had life.

I think you get the picture. Jesus died and rose from the dead, so He has all the power we will ever need. When we are connected to Him by the "jumper cables" of the Holy Spirit, we receive Christ's life as our dead spirits come alive.

The Holy Spirit is there to empower you with the life of Christ, not to help you fool around trying to get the dead battery of your flesh going again on your own. The Spirit hooks you up to the living battery called Christ.

You say, "Wait a minute. If I am connected to the living and powerful Christ by the living and powerful Holy Spirit, how come I still seem so dead? Why am I so weak? How come I am losing, not winning, the battle?"

Well, even with a living battery working for you, even when life is flowing from the living to the dead battery, a jump start doesn't do any good until you turn on the ignition. In other words, there is something you must do in order to authorize the benefits of the power and the authority that are being transferred to you by the Holy Spirit.

### Walk by the Spirit

You'll find your responsibility in the latter half of Romans 8:4, where Paul says the Spirit's authority is made available to those "who do not walk according to the flesh, but according to the Spirit." There's that familiar word *walk*, a favorite euphemism of Paul's for our daily conduct, the way we live our lives. The imagery of walking has at least three concepts embedded in it.

First of all, walking assumes you are going somewhere. It means there is a destination. There's only one destination to pursue if you want to experience the Holy Spirit's power and authority, and that is the will and glory of God. If you are not committed to living for God's glory and doing His will, there will be no transfer of power. This is turning on the ignition.

That's why the Bible tells us not to pray with a double mind (James 1:6–8), a mind that can't decide whether or not it really wants to do God's will. God is not going to waste His time revealing His will to somebody who is not sure he wants to obey it.

What we want to do is say, "Lord, show me Your will and if I like it, I will do it."

God says, "No deal! I am not here to negotiate. You must be willing to do My will before you know My will. Only then will I reveal My will to you." So walking "according to" or by the Spirit means pointing toward the destination of God's will.

Second, walking implies dependence. When you walk, you place one foot in front of the other, putting all your weight on each foot for each step. To walk by the Spirit, you must rest your weight on Him, depending on His power and not your own.

One thing God hates to hear Christians say is, "Well, I'll try." You know why? Because that means you are going to use your own efforts to pull off what God has asked you to do.

God wants to hear you and me say, "In dependence on Your power, I *can*."

He responds, "You're right. You can. Here's My power."

Then you can turn around and say like Paul, "I can do all things through Him who strengthens me" (Philippians 4:13). Now that means you can't do it through your flesh, so don't even try it through your flesh. Instead, present the members of your body to God as "slaves to righteousness" (Romans 6:19).

This gets really practical when you start saying, "Holy Spirit, I can't love that person in my flesh, but You can give me the ability to love him. So I am going to depend on You to give me the love I don't have in my own strength."

How about this one? "Holy Spirit, I don't have patience. But You do. So rather than trying to work up the patience I don't have, I am going to rest in Your ability to express Your patience through me." See the difference this makes? You can take that same prayer and fill in your particular need, whether you need to control your temper, your passions, or whatever.

Then when God does through you what you could never do on your own, guess what? He gets all the glory and all the praise. But you don't get this kind of Holy Spirit authority by tossing a few mumbled sentences God's way every couple of days. If you want His power, you start your day with prayer and you call on Him throughout the day. That's true dependence.

The third aspect of walking is that it is continuous. You don't take one step and sit down, not if you want to get anywhere. Walking is repetitive. Walking in the Spirit is something you are to do all the time.

That's why, for instance, 1 Thessalonians 5:17 says, "Pray without ceasing." This thing of depending on the Holy Spirit's enablement is a way of life. This is the way the Christian life is supposed to be lived.

In fact, God has set it up to run this way. That's why Paul calls it the "law of the Spirit of life" in Romans 8:2. A law implies authority, something that has real teeth in it. Well, the law of the Spirit is so powerful that even though your flesh has been enslaved to the "law of sin and of death" for ten, twenty, thirty, or more years, this law, this principle, this enabling from the Spirit is so strong it will release you from your slavery.

### The Power to Soar

My favorite illustration of this principle is the law of gravity. Gravity pulls you down. It dictates that what goes up must come down. It's the reason we can't soar with the eagles. The gravitational pull of the earth always seeks to bring us down. The law of gravity demands it.

The law of sin and death seeks to pull you down too. It wants to send you crashing down mentally, morally, spiritually—every way possible. The law of sin wants to addict you to sin so it can drag you down, all the way to hell if possible.

Although you can't get rid of the law of gravity, you can transcend it. If you have ever been on an airplane, you have whipped gravity. When you move at a certain speed with a certain degree of power and upward thrust, you are propelled upward so that gravity no longer controls the agenda. It no longer has the last word. You transcend one law with a higher law.

This works in the spiritual realm too. When the combustion of the Holy Spirit is combined with the power of an obedient life, you transcend the gravitational pull of sin and soar in your spiritual life. That's what God is after, but it only comes when you are walking in the Spirit as a habit of life, drawing on His power and authority.

When you see the Spirit's authority at work giving you victory over sin, you will have experienced the Spirit.

You cannot feed the flesh all week and expect a two-hour Sunday service to get you soaring. You may leave church soaring. But you will crash-land on Monday unless you feed your spirit. When you get a cold, someone will always ask, "Is it 'Starve a cold and feed a fever,' or 'Feed a cold and starve a fever'?"

Well, there may be a debate about the best remedy for a cold. But there is no debate about the remedy for fleshly living: Feed the spirit, and starve the flesh!

### Mind Control

"The mind set on the flesh is death, but the mind set on the Spirit is life and peace" (Romans 8:6). Paul says this because whatever controls the mind controls the feet. You walk where your mind tells you to walk. So if the flesh controls your mind, your feet are going to follow. If the Spirit controls your mind, your feet will follow the Spirit.

If you pump fleshly impulses into your mind all day long, don't be surprised if your feet turn aside to fleshly activities. But if your mind is being pumped with spiritual reinforcement all day long, don't be surprised if your feet start following in spiritual activity.

Whoever controls the mind runs the show. Do you feel weak and rundown spiritually? Have you been feeding your spirit or your flesh? If you are expecting a Sunday morning meal to keep you going all week, you are going to be in trouble. It's like expecting a diet cola to cancel out a huge buffet.

No wonder Paul says in Romans 8:12–13, "So then, brethren, we are under obligation, not to the flesh, to live according to the flesh—for if you live according to the flesh, you must die; but if by the Spirit you are putting to death the deeds of the body, you will live."

### Fleshly Desires

Now let me try to correct a very common misunderstanding. The Bible is not saying that when you walk in the Spirit, you will no longer have any of the desires of the flesh. What the Bible says is, "Walk by the Spirit, and you will not carry out the desire of the flesh" (Galatians 5:16).

There's a big difference between not having a desire and not acquiescing to that desire. All of us will go to our graves carrying fleshly desires. When we are tempted to fulfill them in illegitimate ways, the Spirit gives us the authority to say no to the flesh. But He does not necessarily kill those desires.

So if your flesh craves drugs because it has been trained to crave drugs by ten years of addiction, becoming a Christian doesn't necessarily mean that your body will no longer crave drugs. It does mean that you have the power not to give in to that craving.

By the same token, a strong desire for tobacco or alcohol or immorality will not always disappear overnight just because you became a Christian. It's true that God does immediate miracles in some people's lives. I would never discount that.

What I'm talking about is the guy who is disillusioned because he thought when he became a Christian he wouldn't have any more sexual temptation. So he feels guilty because his flesh still wants to sin.

Guess what? That's what flesh does. So don't feel bad that your flesh wants to sin. Feel bad when you don't draw on the power and authority of the Spirit to say no to your flesh.

### DOUBLE JEOPARDY?

There's a principle in law called double jeopardy. You can't be tried twice for the same crime. Jesus has already been tried for your crime. He was condemned, sentenced, and put to death to pay for your sin. And He rose from the dead to prove that His sacrifice was all-sufficient.

So don't let Satan try you again. You have already been convicted, but Christ has satisfied the demands of a holy God. So now, you and I are to walk in newness of life. When we mess up, we need to get up. Don't stay down there. When you mess up, get back on your feet. Start soaring again. Remember, you used to live with turkeys, but now you are an eagle. Count it to be so. Stop letting Satan tell you you are something other than who you are.

The story is told that Frederick the Great, the king of Prussia, was once on an inspection tour of the prison in Berlin. All the prisoners except one man fell on their knees before the king, vigorously protesting their innocence. But that one prisoner stood, silent and aloof.

The king called to him, "Why are you here?"

"I'm in prison for robbery, Your Majesty."

"And are you guilty?"

"Yes, Your Majesty. I entirely deserve my punishment."

Frederick immediately called the guard and said, "Release this guilty wretch at once. I will not have him kept in this prison where he will corrupt all the fine innocent people who occupy it." I imagine that brother hit the road!

Those who are busy trying to protest their innocence to God aren't going anywhere. But if you have admitted your guilt and come to Christ for salvation, you are no longer under the authority of the law of sin and death. You need to get up out of that prison of the flesh and hit the road. The Holy Spirit has unlocked your cell!

# EXPERIENCING THE SPIRIT'S AUTHORITY

I really hope God through this chapter will take some of the weight off your shoulders, because if you are trying to move forward as a Christian under your own power, you are carrying a very heavy load. The Holy Spirit comes equipped with the power and the authority. Just make yourself available to Him. These suggestions should help:

1. Maybe you realize you've got a dead body tied to you, some sin you've never really confessed or asked the Spirit's help to overcome. Cut that cadaver loose! Confess that sin as sin, turn from it, and claim your cleansing (1 John 1:9). Show the Devil Romans 8:2, and tell him to get out.

2. Want to starve your flesh and feed your spirit? Try putting down that remote control and picking up your Bible. Get off the phone and get on your knees. Turn your eyes away from that book or magazine and turn them on Jesus. Stop indulging your whims and start listening for the whispers of the Spirit.

3. Quit trying to subsist spiritually on "diet worship." Make time each day for a worship service. Sing a hymn to the Lord on your way to work. Use the last five minutes of your lunch hour to read a chapter of a gospel, a psalm, or a chapter of Proverbs. Take a few minutes somewhere to be totally still in God's presence and allow the Holy Spirit to speak to your spirit.

4. Maybe it's time you looked around at the folk you're hanging out with. If you're an eagle, you can't afford to spend a lot of time with those other birds! Now I'm not talking about spending time with unbelievers so you can get to know them, care about them, and share with them the gospel of Jesus Christ. I'm talking about letting yourself be unduly influenced by unsaved people who are pulling you away from your commitment to Christ.

# CHAPTER TEN

# EXPERIENCING THE SPIRIT'S FREEDOM

On New Year's Day, 1863, a proclamation was issued declaring that all slaves in the states of the Confederacy were now free. This document, known as the Emancipation Proclamation, resulted in the passage of the Thirteenth Amendment on December 18, 1865, when all slaves were formally set free.

However, for various reasons many slaves did not experience freedom. Some chose to stay enslaved to their masters because they preferred the security of slavery to the risk of freedom. Other slaves remained enslaved in their minds, even though they left the plantation, because they kept thinking and acting like slaves.

Still other slaves, like those here in Texas, didn't get word until many months later that the Emancipation Proclamation had been signed.

My point is that it's a terrible thing to be free and not be able to enjoy it. Whether it's due to "Jim Crow" structures that seek to keep people in bondage or simply a failure to understand that freedom has indeed been granted, it's a terrible thing to be free and yet not be able to throw off the chains.

That's true spiritually too, because when Jesus Christ saved you, He made you free (John 8:36). Therefore, one purpose of the Spirit's ministry is to help us experience the freedom Jesus purchased for us. We need this even as believers, because many of us are trapped and held hostage by all manner of things.

Some of us are trapped in our past. Things that happened a long time ago still control how we function today. Maybe it was abuse by an insensitive parent or a mistake we made that we can't seem to shake off. Others of us are bound by our fears and insecurities and worries. We spend so much time worrying about what might happen that we never get around to enjoying what is happening.

We could expand the list indefinitely, but let's get to the good news. No matter what form of slavery a believer may be under, he or she can be liberated, because the Spirit of God is the Great Emancipator. His job is to set you free, to release you from those things that hold you hostage.

Let's define freedom biblically before we go any further. Freedom never means you are free to do whatever you want. That's license. Freedom means that God has liberated us to fulfill the purposes for which He saved us. He has freed us up to become what He redeemed us to become.

## FREE TO BECOME

In Galatians 5:1, Paul writes, "It was for freedom that Christ set us free; therefore keep standing firm and do not be subject again to a yoke of slavery."

God did not set you free so you could go back to slavery. He did not release you so that you could get bound up again. Paul states emphatically that when Christ set you free, He intended for you to stay that way. You are free to be free. So if you are a Christian and yet you are bound, you have a fundamental misunderstanding of what happened at the Cross.

Christ died to set us free. So why are we still wearing those handcuffs on our minds, those chains around our attitudes, those shackles on our actions? Don't let anyone clap you in spiritual irons again, Paul is saying.

The reason Paul was so worked up about this matter of freedom is that he knew something a lot of Christians today still aren't clued in on. That is, there will always be someone around who wants to clap chains on you and drag you back into slavery.

You say, "Oh, yeah, I get it. You mean those nasty sinners out in the world and the forces of Satan." Well, they can put you in bondage, but they're not the ones I'm talking about. Many times the enslavers are sitting in church with you.

See, Paul was being hounded by a group called the Judaizers. These men followed Paul around, trying to get his Gentile converts to put themselves under the Mosaic Law by undergoing circumcision as the sign of the old covenant. But it was a form of spiritual slavery, an attempt to take these believers out of the right environment and put them in the wrong environment.

### Freedom Within Rules

Imagine a fish saying, "I want to be free. Get me out of this water. I want to roam with the lions and hang out with the bears and run with the deer." So we take the fish out of the water and put it in the jungle.

Now we have done that fish a great disservice by fulfilling his foolish quest for false freedom. Freedom for a fish is not roaming in the jungle. That's death for a fish. Freedom for a fish is fulfilling its purpose in the water because God created fish to live in water.

Let me say it again. Freedom is becoming what God created you to be. It does not mean there are no rules. Without sidelines and foul lines, a football game or tennis match or baseball game would be nothing but chaos. The only thing that makes the game work is that there are restrictions.

Within those boundaries, there is still an awful lot of room for creativity and energy and action. That's what makes sports enjoyable for many people to watch. Within God's boundaries, we still have a lot of flexibility in how we go about becoming what He saved us to be. So don't let anyone tell you that Holy Spirit freedom is just another form of slavery.

There is a form of so-called freedom which is just that: a form of slavery. It's the kind of freedom the world peddles all the time. When a drug addict says he wants to be free to take drugs, what he is literally saying is, "I want the freedom to become a slave of drugs."

When a man without morals says, "I want to be free to pursue any and every woman I can find," he is saying he wants to be free to be a person who has no control over his passions and is therefore a slave of his passions.

If I said to you, "I want to be free to play the piano," you should run for cover, because I don't know the rules of piano playing. So all I could do is make bombastic sounds with no rhythm or harmony. If I want to be free to play Bach, then I need to know the rules of the piano. Freedom never means throwing out all the rules. But it does mean you have a lot of room to move within the rules.

Remember when Sammy Davis, Jr., sang "I've Got to Be Me"? It was a call for freedom. Now that's OK as long as you know what you are supposed to be. But if you don't know who you are supposed to be and yet you are singing "I've Got to Be Me," then how will you know when you have found yourself?

There is a lot of confusion today about freedom. But God is not confused at all. When He talks about freedom, He means the ability to become what He created you and saved you to be. And God is not confused about where the dynamic of freedom is located. It comes to us "through the Spirit, by faith" (Galatians 5:5). Your freedom comes when the Holy Spirit is at work in your life.

### The Supply Line

In 2 Corinthians 3:17, Paul writes, "Where the Spirit of the Lord is, there is liberty." What a declaration of freedom! So if you are all bound up, the Spirit is not having His free flow in your life for some reason. The supply of freedom is there, but something is cutting off the supply line.

Some believers are, to use the psychological term, co-dependent. That is, they are slaves to somebody else. Somebody else is playing God in their lives. If this is true for you, then one thing is sure. God can't be God in your life. And if God isn't God in your life, there is no Spirit control.

That explains why Paul tells the Galatians, "If you receive circumcision, Christ will be of no benefit to you" (5:2). If these believers let the Judaizers dictate to them—play God in their lives—they would forfeit their spiritual benefits.

In fact, Paul didn't leave the issue there. He went on to say in verse 4, "You have been severed from Christ . . . you have fallen from grace."

What does he mean? He means the supply line of the Spirit who gave them the ability to be all that God wanted them to be had been cut off. They had allowed something to bring them into bondage. It's like stepping on the air hose of a diver in one of those old diving suits. You cut off his oxygen supply, and he's in big trouble.

You say, "I can't help the way I feel. I don't feel free!" There is only one reason for that. You haven't learned to think free, because your emotions are always controlled by your mind. If your mind is not a mind of freedom, then your emotions will not experience freedom.

Marriage is a good analogy of what I'm talking about. Sometimes you have to remind people they are married. They may tell you they don't *feel* married. They may not even want to *be* married anymore. But the reality is, they are married. Their challenge is to enjoy the marriage they are in rather than spending so much time not wanting to be married.

It's easy to lose our focus. If you are in bondage as a believer, you are losing your spiritual focus. The Holy Spirit has not been allowed to set you free, even though Christ has purchased your freedom.

## ENJOYING YOUR FREEDOM

Think about it. Jesus Christ looked down through history, saw you trapped in sin and death, and gave His life to save you and set you free. That's something to shout about.

But like a "lifer" in prison, we have gotten used to being locked up in our flesh all these years. We have been bound in old relationships and old dependencies and old habits so long that when the Holy Spirit swings open the cell door and says, "Come out," we shrink back because we are not used to freedom. For many freed slaves, it was a lot easier to stay on the plantation in the South than to take the trail north.

We purchased our family dog, Cassie, from the pound a couple of years ago. We took the boys down there and looked over all the dogs. They came to this mutt and immediately fell in love with her. "We want this one."

After a family huddle we decided she was the one, so I went to the desk to find out how much it would cost to purchase her. I took the bill, reached into my wallet, pulled out the money, and paid the price for Cassie's freedom.

Now it was time to set Cassie free from her cage. She was already a free dog. Her freedom was paid for. But when the attendant opened her cage and we reached in for Cassie to confer on her the freedom that had been purchased for her, she began to shrink back into the corner of the cage.

Why? Because she was so used to being locked up in a cage that when freedom showed up, she didn't know what to do with it. When we came in love to release her, she pulled back, preferring to remain a slave in familiar surroundings rather than take the risk of becoming free in unfamiliar surroundings.

But Paul says if you don't operate by the freedom Jesus purchased for you and the Holy Spirit delivers to you, if you shrink back or choose any other route, you are severed from Christ. Many of our attempts to get free from whatever is holding us in bondage are futile because we are trying to operate apart from Christ and the Holy Spirit.

## The Spirit's Freedom

Listen, my friend. Any attempt at freedom that does not draw on the power and reality of the Holy Spirit's freedom is built on a faulty foundation.

By the time you read this, our church in Dallas will be in its new facility. One use we have planned for our new building is a community counseling center. It will be a biblical counseling center, a ministry not only for the body of Christ at Oak Cliff, but for people in the community who are hurting in any way.

What we mean by that is that all of our counseling will be founded on biblical presuppositions concerning how God defines who we are as human beings. One important part of this biblical counseling agenda is the work of the Holy Spirit in setting people free.

See, without the Holy Spirit I can give you advice. It may even be beneficial to you. But without the Holy Spirit, you do not have the power to sustain whatever changes you may make. Any counseling program that is going to be Christian must be rooted in the conviction that only the Holy Spirit can set people free.

Now let's get to the fun stuff—a survey of some of the things the Spirit has either set us free from, or wants to set us free from.

## The Flesh

Since we just spent an entire chapter covering this one, I only want to mention it here. Remember I said earlier that the Spirit's ministries aren't as neatly divided in actual experience as we have divided them for this book. So we keep running into certain concepts under a number of different headings. This is one of those occasions.

I do want to make one point here. If you remember the trouble in Haiti a few years ago, you recall that an army general kicked the elected president out of the country and took his office. Then, after agreeing to leave and give the presidency back, the general balked when the time came to leave. He liked being in control, and he didn't want to give it up.

That's a perfect description of your flesh. It doesn't want to leave town. But your life is now Jesus Christ's territory to rule. If you let the "general" called your flesh stick around, you will always be in spiritual exile and will never enjoy the privilege of being free in your rightful home.

Paul makes this insightful observation: "We have this treasure in earthen vessels, that the surpassing greatness of the power may be of God and not from ourselves" (2 Corinthians 4:7). You will only be free when you recognize that there is another, surpassingly great, power at work in you—the Holy Spirit—and yield yourself to His control.

Most of the time we try to get free using all the power we can muster, which isn't much. So we stay in bondage. Only the power of Christ through the ministry of the Holy Spirit can free us from the sins of the flesh.

That brings us back to a Christian foundation for counseling. I may be able to give you some information about your problem, help you trace the history of it, help you understand it, and provide some suggestions for dealing with it. But if I don't help you understand how the Spirit works, how you are to walk in the Spirit, what it means to depend on the Spirit, and how you can engage the Spirit, then I am asking you to do the impossible: to use your human resources to solve a problem you haven't been able to solve yet. If you had, we wouldn't even be talking about it.

## People's Expectations

Another thing God sets us free from is the expectations of others. "The kingdom of God is not eating and drinking, but righteousness and peace and joy in the Holy Spirit" (Romans 14:17). In God's kingdom, freedom comes from what He tells you on the inside, not what people tell you on the outside.

But we spend so much time worrying about what people think that we never get around to finding out what

God thinks. People who need people to validate them in this way are the unhappiest people in the world.

Don't get me wrong. God expects us to be people lovers—but not people pleasers. Look at how Paul addresses this elsewhere in Romans 14:

> Now accept the one who is weak in faith, but not for the purpose of passing judgment on his opinions. (v. 1)

> Who are you to judge the servant of another? To his own master he stands or falls; and stand he will, for the Lord is able to make him stand. (v. 4)

> He who observes the day, observes it for the Lord, and he who eats, does so for the Lord, for he gives thanks to God; and he who eats not, for the Lord he does not eat, and gives thanks to God. (v. 6)

> For if we live, we live for the Lord, or if we die, we die for the Lord; therefore whether we live or die, we are the Lord's. (v. 8)

Pretty impressive lineup, isn't it? Paul says your first responsibility is not to please the crowd, but the Lord (2 Corinthians 5:9; 1 Thessalonians 2:4). We can work so hard seeking acceptance with people that we lose acceptance with God. If you lose that, there is no power, because the Spirit of God is only here to glorify Christ.

In the early days of our ministry, people-pleasing occupied a major part of my time. I pulled it off then because there were only about twenty-five people in the congregation. But as we grew, people-pleasing became tough. Now, with more than 3,500 people, pleasing everyone is impossible. I've also learned it's not my job. One day the Lord hit me with this: "I already died for them, Evans. You don't need to die for them too." Bam!

You can listen to people, learn from people, and benefit from people, but when it comes to living your life, God is not going to ask you whether you did what John or Jane told you to do. Paul goes on to say in Romans 14:10–12 that we will all stand before the judgment seat of Christ where "each one of us shall give account of himself to God."

When some of us stand before Christ, He is going to say, "This was my plan for your life. But I see a large percentage of it went unfulfilled."

"Well, Lord, You see, I had a problem. All these people kept telling me what to do. There was John, who kept telling me I should do this and do that."

God might look at us and say, "John isn't even up here. You should not have been listening to him."

Let's be careful here. The Bible does not say don't judge. It says don't judge one another over things that God has not addressed. Here's what I mean. If you are blatantly sinning, I should come to you and say, "God says that is wrong." As God's representative, I can judge issues of right and wrong.

But I do not sit in judgment on matters of opinion. That's what Romans 14:1 is all about. God loves variety. You are unique. His plans for you are unique. I cannot take what God is doing in and through me and make it the standard for you. The Spirit is perfectly capable of telling you what He has for you.

That's why when we seek God's will and allow the Spirit to do His work of setting us free from human expectations, the result is righteousness, peace, and joy. Here is the cure for envy, frustration, irritation, exasperation, and all those other problems that arise when we try to please everyone. Now, this freedom comes with the warning that we not use it to stifle the spiritual growth of someone else.

When I was growing up, we could not go to movies. When my father got saved, one of the things he cut out was movies. That was many years ago, and Dad still does not feel free to go to movies.

My family goes occasionally, but I would not try to impose my freedom on my father by trying to take him to a movie so he can get free like me. In his opinion, movies are out. I cannot sit in judgment on that opinion.

Some ladies look at the way other ladies are dressed and say, "She thinks she is something." Well, you are not

God, so you don't know who thinks what. Besides, you don't have to wear what she wears if you don't like it.

Now, if the clothing is immodest, you can say something. If we're talking about an X-rated movie, you can say something. God has specific guidelines on that kind of thing. Immodest clothing creates an illegitimate allure. X-rated movies only exist to stir lust and put people in sexual bondage. So we have a biblical rationale there. We can judge that. But we cannot judge other people's opinions. Let them be free.

Lois had to wrestle with people's expectations for the pastor's wife. Lots of folk had a job description all prepared for her. We had some frustration points because of these expectations until we came to the realization that there is no biblical job description for a pastor's wife. All Lois Evans has to be is a good Christian and Tony Evans's wife.

## THE PAST

Another thing the Holy Spirit has freed us from is the past. (I think I hear a few amens here.) One reason so many of us are not free is that we are living in the past. We are reliving past failures and mistakes—either ours or someone else's. It happened ten years ago, but we have never forgotten it.

Computers are programmed with commands by which you can either erase or retrieve and display what is stored in the computer's memory. Since your brain is like a computer, you can send it either an erase or a retrieve command when it comes to something painful in the past.

Now by "erase" I don't necessarily mean that you can completely wipe a bad memory out of your brain as if it had never happened. I realize that human memory is more complex than a computer's memory. We can erase the past, however, when it comes to its power to control our lives today.

But what many of us do instead is keep sending the retrieve-and-display command so we can recall and relive past events at will. We tell our brains to save that information. We store it in our memories and keep recalling it so we can look it over and remind ourselves how much it hurt.

That way, every time we see the person involved, we can remind ourselves of what he or she did to us. We can take some satisfaction in hanging on to the past instead of erasing it, especially if we are looking for an opportunity to pay back the hurt. So the cycle just goes on and on.

But when you do that, you have just severed yourself from Christ. He taught us in the Lord's Prayer that we would be forgiven of our trespasses as we forgive those who trespass against us.

This means that if you don't hit the erase command for that other person, God will not hit the erase command for you. Thus you will find yourself in bondage to something that happened years ago. The Holy Spirit wants to cut you free from the shackles of the past.

## Worry

I wonder how many Christians are in bondage to worry and need the Spirit to free them from this cage. I suspect the numbers are legion. We humans are great at worrying. We look for new worries to take upon ourselves. We get worried when we are not worried. We worry about what there is to worry about next.

That can only mean the Spirit of God is not being allowed to have full sway in our lives. Jesus told us to quit worrying (Matthew 6:25, 34). Paul wrote, "Be anxious for nothing" (Philippians 4:6). Jesus' reason for commanding us not to worry is that we are under the watchful care and eye of our heavenly Father. Paul could tell us not to worry because God will supply all of our needs (4:19).

Not worrying does not mean being unconcerned about the issues of life. Worry happens when you are so dominated by a concern that it impedes your ability to function and be what God wants you to be. That's when worry becomes sin.

Whenever you talk about worry, the answer people come back with is, "It's normal." No, for the Christian worry is abnormal. God gave you the Holy Spirit to calm you and give you peace in the midst of the storm, not to stir you up and get you worried.

Lois does not like to fly. So when we were on a flight together that hit some turbulence and started bouncing all over the place, I looked over and saw that Lois was in great turmoil, although she was trying to stay cool. She was gripping the seat with her fingernails.

So I simply reached over and put my hand on her hand. That's all I did. I did not say anything. The turbulence didn't stop, but I noticed she was calming down. She was relaxing.

The Holy Spirit does not always remove the turbulences of life, but He does put His hand on your hand. Or better yet, He puts His hand on your heart so that He calms you down even though life is bumping you up and down. That's His job.

## Materialism

Finally, the Holy Spirit can free us from materialism. Hebrews 13:5 tells us not to fall in love with money, but to be content with what we have.

When you set your affections and your hope and your desires on material things, those things can sever you from a vital and growing relationship with Christ. Then you lose out on two counts. First, you sacrifice intimacy with Christ. And second, that need you have which He would have met, He is no longer free to meet because you are out of His will.

Some people don't want to be set free from their materialism. But it's critical that we allow the Spirit to break the chains that tie our wallets to our hearts. God has something infinitely better for us. Hebrews 13:5 closes with God's promise, "I will never desert you, nor will I ever forsake you."

The only time God stops meeting your legitimate needs is when it is time for you to die. David testified, "I have not seen the righteous forsaken, or his descendants begging bread" (Psalm 37:25). If you believe that, God can give you peaceful sleep tonight because you won't be up all night wondering how you are going to pay the bills (Psalm 127:2).

Jesus said to consider the birds in the sky. They don't work, but God feeds them. People who have experienced the Spirit's freedom in relation to their earthly goods can give because they know their heavenly Father has them covered. Free people don't have to hoard or to rob God because they know He has them under His protective care.

## HOW TO EXPERIENCE YOUR FREEDOM

What can you do to make the Spirit's freedom real in your day-to-day experience? Let me briefly suggest three steps you can take toward a new experience of the Holy Spirit's freedom.

First, you have to believe God's promise of freedom. In John 8:36, Jesus said, "If therefore the Son shall make you free, you shall be free indeed." You need to claim the reality of Romans 8:2, that the law of the Holy Spirit has set you free from the law of sin and death.

In other words, there must be a renewing of your mind (Romans 12:2). You have got to begin to think free so that you can live free. You must tell yourself what the Holy Spirit tells you. He says you are free.

Second, you must commit yourself to discipleship. You can only be free when you are committed to Christ's call on your life, which is to follow Him with your whole heart. If you compromise on that, you will never be free. God will not free you so you can half-step on Him. All of you must be committed to all of Him before you will know the Spirit's freedom.

Third, forgive whomever you may need to forgive so God can set you free by forgiving you. This may be the hardest step for you to take, but the more radical the step of obedience God asks you to take, the greater the reward when you take it.

The story is told of a young lady who married a charming and handsome young man named John. They had a wonderful life together until John suddenly died. His wife could not bear to face life without him. She could not stand the thought of not being with John anymore, so she had him embalmed and brought him home.

She put him in bed with her every night and sat him at the breakfast table every morning. She would say, "Good morning, John. What would you like for breakfast?" She sat him in front of the TV the way they used to do and asked, "John, what show would you like to watch?" The poor woman was enslaved to John, even though John had nothing to offer her.

About a year later, she left John at home and took a vacation to Europe. There she met Bill. Bill was alive! Bill could talk and walk and move. She fell in love with Bill, and after a whirlwind romance they married. Bill brought her back to the States. As he carried her across the threshold into her home, he almost dropped his new bride as he looked into the face of John. "Who is this?" he asked.

She answered, "That's my old husband, John."

Bill said, "Let me tell you something right off. John and I cannot occupy the same premises. Someone has to go. Either we take John out and bury him and I become your new husband, or I'll go back to Europe and you can keep living with a dead man."

That's the way a lot of us live our Christian lives. We've got a "John" somewhere, something dead holding us hostage. But Jesus is our Bill. Now, do you want John, or do you want Jesus? The Holy Spirit will bury that old life for you and set you free. And that, my friend, is the experience of a lifetime.

# EXPERIENCING THE SPIRIT'S FREEDOM

There's not a whole lot more to say. Freedom is your privilege and your birthright as a Christian. You have been set free by the Holy Spirit. Why go back to any form of slavery again? Instead, apply these steps to help restore or preserve your freedom:

1. Second Corinthians 3:17 is such a crucial declaration of our freedom in the Holy Spirit that I encourage you to copy it on a card and put it where you'll see it often, write it on your heart, store it away in your memory—whatever it takes to get the truth of this great verse active in your life.

2. If God lays someone on your heart who needs your forgiveness, write the person a letter or make a call to re-establish contact. If the person previously asked for forgiveness and you refused it, tell him or her now that you have forgiven the offenses, and ask forgiveness for any wrongs you may have committed in the relationship. (Don't tell a person "I forgive you" if from his or her perspective no wrong has been committed.) By the time you put the letter in the mailbox or dial the number, your burden will lift, and you'll be free.

3. Got any worries, especially financial ones, that are keeping you awake at night? I don't mean to dismiss lightly a real concern, but if we really trust God there comes a point at which we say, "Lord, this worry is Yours. I'm going to bed." If it has been awhile since you prayed that way, try it tonight.

4. That closing illustration may seem to be extreme, but there's a lot of reality behind it. Are you carrying around a dead weight from the past? Ask the Holy Spirit to take it out and bury it for you—and on the headstone write Galatians 5:1.

# CHAPTER ELEVEN

# EXPERIENCING THE SPIRIT'S FELLOWSHIP

If you and I are powerless Christians, it is directly attributable to the lack of fellowship between us and the Holy Spirit. If you and I are anemic, if there is little joy and peace, if there is little of anything in our lives that seems to demonstrate the Spirit's reality, it is because our fellowship with the Spirit is not as it ought to be.

I have included fellowship in this section on the Holy Spirit's purposes because I believe that if we want to enjoy intimate fellowship with Him, we must be serious about carrying out His purposes for our lives. So let's talk about these purposes as they relate to experiencing intimate fellowship with the Holy Spirit.

## PRIORITIZE THE SPIRIT'S PASSION

First of all, if you want to enjoy the Spirit's fellowship, you need to make His passion your priority. What is the Spirit's passion? We have seen it repeatedly. Jesus said it best in John 16:13–14: "He will not speak on His own initiative. . . . He shall glorify Me; for He shall take of Mine, and shall disclose it to you."

The Spirit's passion is to glorify the Son. In the mysterious and wonderful inner workings of the Trinity that we talked about in an earlier chapter, it was determined that the Spirit would come to magnify Jesus Christ.

That's what the Spirit is doing in this age, which means if you want to hang out with Him, He is going to take all your energy and all your aspirations and focus them on magnifying Christ. Wherever you see Christ being glorified and lifted up, look for the presence of the Holy Spirit.

### Putting Christ First

So if Jesus Christ is a low priority in your life, then you will be a low priority in the Spirit's work. If Jesus Christ is an extra in your life, then you will be an extra in the Spirit's work. I'm not saying the Spirit will quit convicting and drawing you, and He certainly won't stop loving or indwelling you. But don't expect to enjoy dynamic fellowship with Him if your commitment to Christ is anemic.

In fact, if you want to know how much attention you are getting from the Holy Spirit, ask yourself how much attention you are giving to Christ. If there is little attention to Christ, there will be little attention from the Spirit.

Why? Because the Holy Spirit finds His greatest joy in showering attention upon those who get up in the morning and go to bed at night having lived for Jesus Christ.

So is Christ your passion? I don't mean is He your Sunday experience. I mean is loving and serving Christ your driving passion? Is glorifying Him what gets you up in the morning and keeps you going all day? If it is, you won't have to hunt for the Spirit. He has already tracked you down.

When Christ is your passion, He rewards you with the presence and power of His Spirit.

### Living Water

Let me point you to another passage we studied earlier, John 7:37–39. I won't quote it again here, but to refresh your memory, Jesus promises that those who believe on Him will experience a river of living water flowing out of their "innermost being" (v. 38). John then tells us in verse 39 that Jesus was talking about the Holy Spirit, who would come on the Day of Pentecost to indwell and energize believers.

What I want to note is Jesus' description of the Spirit's presence as "living water." The Holy Spirit is a life-giving Spirit. When He dominates your life, He will make you more alive than you ever thought you could be. You will not only be fulfilled yourself, but the river of living water flowing out of you will overflow so others can drink from your life as well.

The ones who enjoy the flowing river of the Holy Spirit are those who make it the passion of their lives to glorify Christ. Do you want the presence, power, and intimate fellowship of the Holy Spirit? Then run after Jesus Christ. Make knowing, loving, and serving Christ your passion. In other words, get thirsty.

## Developing a Thirst

One reason we have so little spiritual power in the church of Jesus Christ today is that we are not thirsty Christians. God only satisfies folk who are thirsty. If you are not thirsty, you don't get to drink.

What we need is to develop our spiritual thirst. We need a generation of Christians who are passionate for Christ. Unless that is your goal, studying the Bible is a waste of time; coming to church will make little or no difference in your life. The life-giving, thirst-quenching fellowship of the Holy Spirit is enjoyed where the passion of Christ is sought.

So make it your prayer every day, "Lord, give me a thirst for You." Isn't that what Jesus said in the Beatitudes? "Blessed are those who hunger and thirst for righteousness, for they shall be satisfied" (Matthew 5:6). See, if you are self-sufficient, you don't need God. If your life is filled with other things, you won't seek Christ the way a thirsty man seeks a drink of water or the way a deer "pants for the water brooks" (Psalm 42:1).

### Being Transformed

But when you prioritize the Spirit's passion, the provision is awesome:

> Now the Lord is the Spirit; and where the Spirit of the Lord is, there is liberty. But we all, with unveiled face beholding as in a mirror the glory of the Lord, are being transformed into the same image from glory to glory, just as from the Lord, the Spirit. (2 Corinthians 3:17–18)

Notice how the Lord and the Spirit are used interchangeably. This means that when the glory of Christ becomes your passion, the Spirit of God transforms your life. If you really want to see your life changed, let Christ become your passion. When the Spirit sees that you feel about Christ the way He feels about Christ, He will allow the glory of Christ to transform your life.

When you start making your decisions and your choices based on whether they bring Christ glory, you will automatically see the Spirit changing you. You will automatically see the fruit of the Spirit being developed in you. But don't get me wrong. Automatic does not mean magic. We're talking about a process.

We usually want the change to be instantaneous, like the farmer and his family who went to a mall for the first time and were astounded by its size and number of stores. As the farmer's wife began to shop, he and his son took off in the other direction.

At the other end of the mall was a bank. The farmer and his son went inside, and the farmer stared in amazement at two huge steel doors that stood open at the back of the bank. He had never seen a bank vault before and wasn't quite sure what it was.

As the farmer watched, he saw a little old lady barely able to walk with a cane go through the steel doors. A few seconds later, a very attractive young woman came out of the vault. The farmer looked at his son and said, "Boy, go get your mother!"

The Spirit's transformation does not occur like that. It's neither magic nor instantaneous. But as you learn to make Christ the measure of your life, ever so surely you will find yourself being transformed into His image.

This transformation has some wonderfully practical benefits. You will start experiencing victories in areas where before you tasted one defeat after another. You will have joy where there was misery, harmony where there was conflict, and power where there was impotence. A passion to glorify Jesus Christ is transforming.

During the football season, we in Dallas see a weekly illustration of what happens when people get a passion. Every Sunday, personalities are transformed over the Dallas Cowboys. People who are normally of quiet demeanor become energized. Folk set their alarms and get up for the early service so they can be home by noon and not miss the opening kickoff.

Others who usually sit peacefully in church become agitated, wishing the pastor would hurry and finish. Meals are eaten in the den in front of the TV to avoid distraction. Everything is geared around the Cowboys kickoff at noon, because people are so captivated by an event that everything else has to adjust.

If Christ could just get a little bit of that passion! If we could become that captivated by His glory, we would find the Holy Spirit giving us some excitement where before we were lethargic. We would find the Spirit bringing us our spiritual meals in the den. Does that sound good to you? Make a bee-line to Christ, and you'll find the Spirit waiting with good things.

## PRESERVE THE SPIRIT'S UNITY

A second thing we must do to enjoy the Spirit's fellowship is preserve His unity. This is critical because the Spirit of God only operates in a context of spiritual harmony. This is why Paul writes:

> [Be] diligent to preserve the unity of the Spirit in the bond of peace. There is one body and one Spirit, just as also you were called in one hope of your calling; one Lord, one faith, one baptism, one God and Father of all who is over all and through all and in all. (Ephesians 4:3–6)

Please note that we only "preserve" the Spirit's unity; we do not create it. This is because unity was already created for us when we were baptized by the Spirit into one body. Our job then is not to allow anything or anyone to divide the new family into which we have been placed. While there may be disagreements within the family over issues like the definition of the gift of tongues, modes of baptism, and the role of women in the church, and so on, which may affect the degree to which one part of the body relates to another (in every family there are members who are closer to some than to others), these differences must never be allowed to affect our central oneness. Since it is the Spirit's unity, then our relationship with the Holy Spirit is the essential ingredient that assures that our oneness goes undisturbed.

### At All Costs

Paul says we should preserve at all costs the unity of the Spirit. In the Bible, unity does not mean uniformity. It does not mean trying to make everyone else like me. It does mean commonality of purpose, everybody going in the same direction.

What's the point? If you are a divisive Christian, you negate the Spirit's working in your life. If you are disrupting the fellowship in God's family, His Spirit will not fellowship with you. Why? Because in God's family, you are not an only child. That's why the Lord's Prayer begins with "our" Father, not "my" Father.

See, God's relationship to you is inextricably linked to your relationship to other saints. Let me say again we're not talking about salvation here. We aren't saved in groups. We're talking about the day-by-day reality and experience of the Spirit's fellowship.

If you cause conflicts or divisiveness, not over issues of sin and righteousness but over preferences and opinions, you are breaking down the body rather than building it up. You are not preserving the unity of the Spirit.

Many husbands and wives are not in fellowship with the Holy Spirit because they have disrupted their unity with their spouses. The same can be said of many parents and their children. It goes both ways. Whenever we allow illegitimate distinctions to occur in God's bigger family, we lose out on the benefit of being in that family. For example, Scripture warns a husband that if he does not tenderly love his wife, instead of aiding his prayers the Holy Spirit resists them (1 Peter 3:7).

So if you are a cantankerous Christian, if you are a Christian who is bringing division and tearing down rather than building up the body of Christ, the Spirit's fellowship is not yours until you use His resources to fix that mess.

## The Spirit's Sensitivity

Let's go further on in Ephesians 4, where Paul gets down to talking family talk:

> Therefore, laying aside falsehood, speak truth, each one of you, with his neighbor, for we are members of one another. Be angry, and yet do not sin; do not let the sun go down on your anger, and do not give the devil an opportunity. Let him who steals steal no longer; but rather let him labor. . . . Let no unwholesome word proceed from your mouth, but only such a word as is good for edification. . . . And do not grieve the Holy Spirit of God, by whom you were sealed for the day of redemption. Let all bitterness and wrath and anger and clamor and slander be put away from you, along with all malice. And be kind to one another, tender-hearted, forgiving each other, just as God in Christ also has forgiven you. (vv. 25–32)

I want to let you in on a secret. The Holy Spirit is extremely sensitive. He is grieved when we engage in the things Paul lists in these verses, which have to do primarily with our relationships with other members of God's family.

This is not talking about salvation, because verse 30 says we are sealed until the day of redemption. So to grieve the Holy Spirit is not to lose your salvation, but it is to lose the enjoyment of your salvation, which is the fellowship of the Spirit.

Unresolved anger toward other members of God's family grieves the Spirit. This also has long-term consequences.

If you are still angry about what your father did to you when you were five, then you may be negating the Spirit's freedom to work in you today. That's why dealing with hidden hostility is such a major issue in counseling. If you prolong your anger, you block the free flow of the Spirit.

It's OK to own your anger. It's not OK for your anger to own you. That's why you have to come to grips with these attitudes before God. They are not only personally destructive, but they are divisive to the body of Christ. They not only tear you down spiritually, but they also tear down the body. And they sadden the Holy Spirit.

When you got saved, the Holy Spirit came to live within you and give life to your human spirit. As we have discussed, there is a linking of your human spirit with the Holy Spirit. What that means is when you grieve the Holy Spirit, who is now indwelling your human spirit, your human spirit is grieved too.

To put it another way, when the Holy Spirit within you is made joyful, He is going to give you joy. But when the Spirit within you has been saddened or wounded by sin, then of necessity you are going to be unhappy in your spirit. When fellowship with the Holy Spirit is blocked, when He is sensitive to sin in your life, His sensitivity will become your sensitivity.

### Resisting the Spirit

In his bold message before the Sanhedrin, Stephen told the religious elite of Israel, "You . . . are always resisting the Holy Spirit" (Acts 7:51).

Can mere human beings resist God? Stephen said so under the inspiration of the Holy Spirit. The unsaved can resist God and refuse to hear His Word, just as the Sanhedrin did in Stephen's case. They even stoned him in an attempt to silence the Spirit's witness through him of their condemnation.

As believers, we have already yielded to the call of the Spirit for salvation. But we can get ourselves into a state of mind and heart where we say no to the Spirit's promptings to deal with unconfessed sin and get back into intimate fellowship with Him. We can keep Him from giving us joy.

Do you know Christians who have been miserable for years because they have created their own misery? It's not that God doesn't want to change them. It's that they don't want to change on His terms.

For example, if you adopt an attitude that says, "I was angry, I am angry, and I am going to remain angry," you are one dangerous loose cannon on the deck of God's ship. You need to know that you will have a very unhappy Holy Ghost inside of you. And He is going to make you an unhappy person because you share in the emotions of the Spirit. When you resist Him, when you stiff-arm His promptings, you are headed for a struggle.

You say, "Tony, would a Christian actually make a statement like that?" Believe it. It happens all the time. For some people, bitterness is the sin they cling to. Others hold on tight to malice or some other sin from Paul's list in Ephesians 4. But the result is usually the same: a deep wound in Christ's body, the church.

Once you decide, "This is the way I am, I intend to stay this way, and nobody is going to make me be any other way," you leave the Spirit little option but to take hard steps to overcome your resistance.

Why? For two reasons. First, for the sake of your own spiritual life. Second, because there are a lot of other kids in the family. The Spirit can't have you disrupting the family and making everyone else miserable. So He does whatever is necessary to break your rebellion and resistance. The job becomes misery, the marriage is drudgery, the kids start acting up.

I can't predict how the Spirit may deal with a particular Christian. But I do know the problem can get so bad He has to take out the sinning believer to preserve unity in the body.

How do I know that? Because of Ananias and Sapphira in Acts 5:1–11. They lied to the Spirit, and they died. It wasn't an accident. They schemed together to cheat the Lord out of a portion of the proceeds from the sale of a piece of land they owned.

Was lying to the third Person of the Trinity the total reason for what happened to Ananias and Sapphira? No. If you back up and read carefully Acts 4:32, their sin looks even more hideous in its context.

Why were some believers selling property? To help fellow believers who were destitute and hungry. So Ananias and Sapphira were lying to God about how much they wanted to help His family. That was a serious breach of the unity the Holy Spirit is so intent on preserving. So the pair paid with their lives.

What an object lesson of how serious the Holy Spirit was about this business of unity in the body of Christ (Acts 5:11)! When you hurt the body, the Spirit hurts you (1 Corinthians 3:17).

No wonder the writer of Hebrews says, "If we go on sinning willfully after receiving the knowledge of the truth, there no longer remains a sacrifice for sins" (10:26) because we have "insulted the Spirit of grace" (Hebrews 10:29). When you resist the Spirit, the Spirit resists you.

Isaiah 63:10 says, "They rebelled and grieved [God's] Holy Spirit; therefore, He turned Himself to become their enemy, He fought against them." Ever feel like God is fighting against you? Everything you do, God seems to undo. Every prayer you pray, He seems to do the opposite. Every time you think you see daylight, darkness engulfs you. Every time you look for joy, there is sadness.

Could it be that the Spirit is fighting against you because you are resisting Him? I certainly can't judge what is happening in your life. But I would be less than fair to you if I didn't point out the danger of resisting the Spirit, particularly in relationship to what He wants to do in the rest of the family of God. If you want to experience maximum fellowship with the Holy Spirit, make sure there are no walls of your making between you and your brothers and sisters in Christ.

## PRACTICE THE SPIRIT'S DISCIPLINES

The third and final path to experiencing full fellowship with the Holy Spirit is to practice His disciplines.

Let's return once more to Romans 8, this time to verses 5–7:

> Those who are according to the flesh set their minds on the things of the flesh, but those who are according to the Spirit, the things of the Spirit. For the mind set on the flesh is death, but the mind set on the Spirit is life and peace, because the mind set on the flesh is hostile toward God; for it does not subject itself to the law of God, for it is not even able to do so.

Here is the key to the successful practice of spiritual disciplines: Discipline your mind to focus on the realm of the Spirit. Discipline is a matter of setting your mind on "the things of the Spirit." The writer of Proverbs put it this way: "As [a man] thinks within himself, so he is" (23:7).

If you are walking wrong, it is because you are thinking wrong. If you are talking wrong, it is because you are thinking wrong. To the extent that the Spirit of God controls your mind, He is able to lead you in new spiritual directions.

If I were to take out my pen and begin writing, I could record anything I wanted to record. But if I remove my hand, the pen would simply fall on the paper and lie there. My pen has no life of its own.

My pen contains all the raw materials I need to write with, but it has no writing ability of its own. In order for this pen to function, it must be joined to the life in my hand. When that happens, my pen can form letters it could never form by itself. It can compose clauses and phrases and put them together to make sentences because it is in my hand, and my hand is alive.

When you connect your life to the life of the Holy Spirit, He can write things that you could never write on your own. He can achieve things you could never achieve on your own. But if you live in the flesh, if you set your mind "on the things of the flesh," you will drop like a discarded pen because there is no spiritual life in your flesh, your unredeemed humanity.

Our challenge, then, is to cultivate minds that are set on the things of the Spirit. How do we cultivate minds fixed on the Spirit? By practicing the Spirit's disciplines. As we do these things, they become avenues over which the Holy Spirit guides us to the practical, daily experience of the fellowship, the "life and peace" that God's Word promises to those who set their minds on Him (Romans 8:6).

So let's consider three of what I consider the most crucial spiritual disciplines. I don't have any surprises for you here. The Holy Spirit isn't playing hide-and-seek with us. If you want to pursue intimate, enriching fellowship with Him, the path is clearly marked in His Word.

## Prayer

The first discipline I want to consider is prayer. The simplest definition of prayer is communion and communication with God. Let me show you why the practice of prayer is so crucial as it relates to enjoying the fellowship of the Spirit.

Prayer takes you out of your realm, the realm of the flesh, and transports you into another realm, that of the Spirit. Remember, we are seeking the mind of the Spirit so that we might fellowship with Him. To do that, you must enter the Spirit's realm. Prayer takes you there.

See, as long as you are self-centered, you can't be God-centered. Prayer replaces your self-focus with a God-focus. Whether you pray silently or audibly, prayer lifts you out of yourself to a sphere inhabited by the Holy Spirit. When you enter His realm, He meets you for fellowship.

Our discipline of prayer should include thanksgiving, because that relates to what God is already doing for us. As the song says, "Count your blessings." Thanksgiving reminds us that we are talking to a God who keeps us when we want to throw in the towel, a God who stands by us when we do not think we are going to make it. If He hung with us yesterday, He'll be there today. Thanksgiving reminds us of that.

And when you pray, include confession. Confession brings you back into fellowship with the Spirit. Confession pleases Him because it means you feel the same way about your sin He feels about it—that it's wrong and has to be dealt with. Sin is a huge barrier to experiencing the Spirit's fellowship. Confession tears down that barrier, and along with thanksgiving it prepares the way for you to bring your petitions and needs to God.

There is nothing mysterious about prayer. The only reason we don't feel more comfortable in prayer is that we don't pray enough. But if you are serious about cultivating the mind of the Spirit and entering the realm where He lives, you need to put some muscle in your prayer life. You need to practice the discipline of prayer.

But you say, "Tony, I don't like to think of prayer as discipline. It sounds too much like a duty, like a job I have to do. Aren't you supposed to pray because you want to instead of because you have to?"

That's a good question. It is important that we make prayer something other than just a duty we perform because we have to, like mowing the lawn on a hot day. How do you keep prayer from becoming just another duty on your daily spiritual "to do" list?

Well, let me say first that prayer *is* a duty in the sense that it is a vital part of the Christian life. God's Word tells us to pray—to pray without ceasing, in fact. There's nothing wrong with practicing prayer as an act of daily discipline until you get to the place where it becomes your daily delight.

But the question is still valid. The best way I know to keep prayer from becoming routine and automatic is to turn your focus from prayer to God. Here's an example of what I mean.

Eating is a duty in the sense that we have to eat to sustain life. But most of us don't approach eating as a chore. We take great delight in it. We eat when we need to eat, and we eat when we don't need to eat. Some of us even eat when we aren't supposed to eat.

Why is this? Because we enjoy the act of eating itself. We prepare food to look appetizing, and we season it to taste good. We make meals a time of intimate fellowship with family and friends. We look forward to our next meal.

When you start approaching prayer the way you approach eating, something will happen. Prayer is your time to gather around the table for warm, close fellowship with the Holy Spirit who can comfort and help you in any situation, with Jesus Christ your elder Brother, and with a Father who delights to hear from His children.

There is delight in the act of praying itself as you pour out your heart to God and sense His presence and His loving attention. See, prayer is not an end in itself. It is our invitation to fellowship with the Holy Spirit, to seek His mind on the things we face. Communication and communion with God is the goal of prayer.

So the question is not whether you feel like praying today. The question is, do you want to know the mind of the Spirit? Do you want to worship and adore God? Do you feel like talking to Somebody who can do something about your situation? Do you want to talk to Somebody who can change a desperate circumstance for a fellow believer or meet the deepest need in your family?

If you do, prayer will be no problem. You'll pray, and you'll find joy in it because you are fellowshiping with Someone who can put sugar in your tea and sweetener in your coffee.

### The Word

The second discipline of the Spirit is reading and studying the Bible. If you want to cultivate a mind set on the things of God, you need to get in the Spirit-inspired Word. The Spirit says, "If you want to fellowship with me, spend time in My Word to you."

See, we often do with the Bible what we do with prayer. That is, we make it something other than what it was intended to be. The Bible was not written as a religious textbook. It is a love letter from the Holy Spirit to you. A lot of us won't read a textbook, but not many of us will pass up a love letter.

Try opening your Bible and saying, "God, what is it that You want to say to my heart today? What do You want to change about me today? What do You want me to understand about You today?" Now you have a love letter and not a textbook.

When you receive a love letter, you carry it around with you and read it again and again. You linger over the words. You hear in them the voice of your loved one. You meditate on their meaning.

You probably know by now that I'm big on Scripture meditation. I like to compare it to marinating a fine cut of meat. Meditation is marinating the truth of God; letting it sit, allowing it to penetrate every fiber of your being. When you do that, suddenly you're not just reading verses like John 3:16. You're saying, "Wait a minute. That means me. I can put my name in there. God has given *me* eternal life. Fantastic!"

You get the idea. See, if you're an old hand around the divine corral, you don't need another harangue about how you should be praying and reading your Bible. You just need to hunger and thirst for fellowship with the Holy Spirit.

## Trials

A third discipline of the Spirit is trials. Trials are what happens when God removes the "training wheels" from your spiritual life.

Training wheels give a child's bike a nice, steady feel. But they're meant to be temporary. When you remove them, there is a risk that your child may fall and get a skinned elbow or knee. But unless you take off those training wheels, your child will never really go anywhere.

Unless the Holy Spirit takes the training wheels off our spiritual lives, we will never learn how to get our balance. We will never learn to pedal for the glory of God. We will never learn to steer like we ought to steer our lives.

So the Spirit has to remove the training wheels. Far too many Christians are living off the spiritual success of others rather than developing spiritual vitality for themselves.

When I broke my leg, the doctor told me, "I'm going to have to snap your bones back into place. This is going to hurt. You may want to look the other way." Every now and then, God allows us to be broken so we can experience the release of the Spirit.

When we're broken, we need to have that broken part reset. So the Holy Spirit says, "This may hurt a little bit, but it's necessary. Look the other way. Set your eyes on Jesus."

## BY THE SPIRIT

Romans 8:13 says, "If you are living according to the flesh, you must die; but if *by the Spirit* you are putting to death the deeds of the body, you will live" (italics added).

There it is, the secret to a life of intimate fellowship with the Holy Spirit. It's you doing it, but not by your own power. You do it by the Spirit's power. So whatever you need to do on the positive side or put away on the negative side, you can do it because your human spirit is harnessed to the Holy Spirit.

Now this is not the power of positive thinking. This is not making New Year's resolutions. This is a Holy Spirit resolution. A New Year's resolution says, "This is what I am going to try my best to do this year." But a Holy Spirit resolution says, "This is what I am going to do by the power of the Spirit."

One day I was on my way to catch an airplane, and I was late. By the time I got off the escalator to catch the shuttle train that would take me to my terminal, the door had closed and it was gone. I had missed my ride. But I still had a plane to catch, and I was still late. There was no time to wait for the next shuttle, so I decided to go for it. Grabbing my briefcase and suitcase, I began running to my terminal. As I ran, I noticed something. I was flying by some people who were walking fast, and even by other people who were running.

In fact, I got to the terminal ahead of the shuttle train I had missed! And I wasn't even sweating that much. Do you want to know the secret of my speed? Do you want to know where I got the ability to move so fast even with luggage in my hand?

Well, underneath me was one of those airport moving sidewalks. I was running, but the sidewalk was carrying me along a lot faster than I could have gone on my own.

My friend, the Holy Spirit is your moving sidewalk. When you start running, He comes alongside and underneath and gives your feet wings to take you where God wants you to be. You have to get on the sidewalk through prayer and obedience and Bible study, but it's the Spirit who is carrying you.

And when you see that you are making up lost ground in your life—having strength where you would normally be weak and having victory where you would normally know only defeat—you will then know what it's like to experience the fellowship of the Holy Spirit.

# EXPERIENCING THE SPIRIT'S FELLOWSHIP

**F**ellowship with the Spirit is what gives warmth and life to your spiritual life. It's like the blood in your body through which you receive the nourishment you need. And there's more at stake than your personal spiritual life, because as we have seen, your fellowship also affects the other members of Christ's body. Do you need a "fellowship boost"? Try these ideas:

1. Since the Spirit's passion is to glorify Christ, guess what your passion should be? If you can't honestly say the goal of your life is to exalt Jesus daily, better put that at the top of your prayer list.

2. Are you doing your part to preserve the Spirit's unity? We can hinder the unity of the body by our absence as well as by the wrong kind of presence. If you're not a full participant in a local church, you're leaving a void that causes the body to suffer. You don't just fellowship with other believers because you need it. You do it because the body needs it.

3. Prayer is a challenge for most of us, because it doesn't come naturally. Many people who have trouble focusing in prayer say that praying with a friend or praying out loud even in private help a lot. You may want to try it if you find it hard to keep yourself focused.

4. Remember how good it felt as a kid when your dad removed the training wheels from your bicycle and you really took off? That's what the Holy Spirit longs to do for you spiritually, but He can't do it if you aren't willing to accept the scrapes and scratches too. Ask Him to help you see your trials through His eyes.

# CHAPTER TWELVE
# EXPERIENCING THE SPIRIT'S RESTRAINT

One reason we do not get everything we deserve is the restraining ministry of the Holy Spirit.

This chapter may be breaking some new ground for you, because my experience has been that the Spirit's ministry of restraint is not as well known and appreciated as the other aspects of His work we've been talking about. It's something we tend to take for granted, like the air we breathe.

I use that analogy because the Holy Spirit's restraint of sin is like the atmosphere around us. It's helping to sustain this world as we know and experience it. The only reason worldwide sin isn't as bad as it could be is because of the Spirit's restraint.

In fact, the only reason you and I are not as bad as we could be is because of the Spirit's restraining ministry. So we need to understand and appreciate what the Holy Spirit is doing to hold back sin in this age so we can cooperate with rather than resist His work.

## RESTRAINING SIN

The first thing I want you to see is that the Holy Spirit limits the operation of sin in the world. In 2 Thessalonians 2, Paul is comforting the believers in Thessalonica who had been scared to death by false teachers telling them the Lord had already come and they had missed it (vv. 1–2).

In the process of correcting this error, Paul unveils for the Thessalonians and for us the picture of a future time when, quite literally, all hell will break loose. There will be a great departure from the faith, culminating in the revelation of the "man of lawlessness" (v. 3)—Satan's false Christ, the Antichrist—whose coming will usher in the time of the Great Tribulation that will devastate the earth.

### The Principle of Restraint

That's the context of the verses I want us to examine, because as Paul explains this future time, he makes reference to the restraining ministry of the Holy Spirit:

> And you know what restrains him now, so that in his time he may be revealed. For the mystery of lawlessness is already at work; only he who now restrains will do so until he is taken out of the way. (vv. 6–7)

This is a very interesting and enlightening passage because it tells us a lot about the Spirit's restraining ministry even though He is not mentioned by name. We'll see, in fact, that the restrainer couldn't be anyone else but the Spirit.

Look how Paul puts this together. The word *what* in verse 6 is actually a neuter word, meaning that the restraint referred to here is not a person, but a principle. However, in verse 7 Paul uses the masculine equivalent of the term, "he who now restrains," so what we have here is a complete picture of the Spirit's restraint.

That is, the Person of the Spirit uses a principle of restraint. There are different ideas as to what Paul means by this. Some say the reference is to the Spirit's restraint through the church or through human government or through some other agency. I think these are all included in the idea, and in fact I want to suggest below that the Spirit uses a number of means to hold back the full expression of sin in our world and in our personal lives.

As I mentioned, the Spirit is not named as the restrainer here. But notice that this person and his means of operation were known to the Thessalonians (v. 6). Notice too that this restrainer is holding back the "mystery of lawlessness" which is already at work in the world and which will ultimately be given full expression when the man of lawlessness is revealed.

We know from elsewhere in Scripture that this lawless one is the emissary of the Devil, his imitation Christ (see Revelation 13:1–10). Satan would love to turn this guy loose on the world now. Satan would love to see sin have its maximum expression. But the restrainer is holding this back, so the restrainer has to be more powerful than the Devil himself.

When you put it all together, you realize that the restrainer has to be God Himself. In particular, He is the third member of the Godhead, the Holy Spirit.

## The Benefits of Restraint

Think about it for a minute, and you'll start praising God for this work of the Spirit. His restraint keeps sin from overflowing its banks and flooding the world. It's bad enough now, but think what things would be like if the Holy Spirit did not intervene and curb the full expression of human sinfulness.

We often look at life backwards. If we get sick, we say, "Lord, why am I sick?" It's a natural response. But a more biblically accurate response would be, "Lord, as sinful as I am, why did You allow me to stay healthy for so long?"

Or if we are robbed, we say, "That's not fair, Lord. I don't deserve to get robbed." What should confound us is the fact that God allows us to live so long in this sinful world without getting robbed. The same holds true for tragedy and other painful circumstances that come upon us because we live in a very sinful world.

See, we are taught to be thankful for God's grace. The restraining ministry of the Holy Spirit is the flip side of that coin. His job is to prevent Satan from doing all that Satan wants to do whenever he wants to do it. The Spirit holds sin back, like a dam restraining a mighty river so that it is not fully unleashed.

But the time is coming when God will remove the restraints on sin by removing the Restrainer (2 Thessalonians 2:7). That's at the Rapture, and—praise God—we will be removed with Him! But until then, the Spirit is restraining sin in a number of ways. Let's look at seven of them.

### Seven Means of Restraint

The first way the Spirit restrains sin is by direct intervention. He will intervene in a circumstance and say to Satan, "No, you can't do that." In the case of Job, Satan wanted to bring total ruin to his life, but God intervened and told Satan exactly what he could and could not do. God controlled the agenda in Job's life. He limited what Satan could do to Job (Job 1:12).

A second means of restraint the Spirit uses is godly leaders. Time and again Moses intervened with God on behalf of Israel after the people sinned and God wanted to destroy them (Exodus 32; Numbers 14). In Exodus 32:11–35, Moses acted very directly to restrain the people's sin by breaking up their golden calf "worship service" and dealing out judgment to the offenders. His actions preserved the nation. The Spirit will often use God's appointed leaders to restrain sin.

The family is a third vehicle or means the Holy Spirit uses to hold back sin. One thing God expects the family to do is lay down guidelines for children to give them a track to run on and to keep them from doing everything they want to do.

Most of us probably can't imagine what kinds of things our children would do if they thought they could. No, wait a minute. We can imagine it, because at one time or another in life, they try. But family is meant to exert a restraint.

Eli the priest lost his two sons to death at God's hand of judgment because he would not restrain them (1 Samuel 2:34; 3:13). He left them free to pursue their evil desires, and it not only cost them their lives, but it cost Eli his life as well (4:18). He failed to be God's representative because he did not obey when God told him to restrain his sons. The family is one of God's intermediate means of restraint.

Here's a fourth means through which the Holy Spirit restrains sin: our internal restraining mechanism called the conscience. In order for you to sin, you have to climb over your conscience. Now if you are a redeemed person whose conscience has been informed by God, the more sensitive your conscience is to sin the higher you have to climb to get over it.

That's good, because when you can sin and not think about it, feel it, or worry about it, you're in trouble. The Holy Spirit will sensitize your conscience to alert you to sin. The conscience can thus become a valuable restrainer.

A fifth means of the Spirit's restraint is through the church. In fact, many Bible commentators believe the church is what Paul had in mind in 2 Thessalonians 2:6. That fits the picture of the Rapture in verse 7, because when the church is taken out of the world, the Holy Spirit will go too.

The Spirit won't cease being the all-present God, but the unique relationship He began with the church at Pentecost will end when the church's ministry on earth is complete and she is caught away.

If Jesus Christ were to come right now and take us to be with Him, think of the free hand Satan would have to propagate sin. The presence of the people of God means the multiplied presence of the Spirit of God, for every member of the true church is a temple of the Holy Spirit (1 Corinthians 6:19). When all that righteous influence is gone, Satan will unveil his man of lawlessness, the one through whom he will work.

Since every Christian is a temple of the Spirit, that means His restraining work will be wherever God's people are—and God's people are everywhere. By the way, this is why when we stop being salt and light in society, society deteriorates. We stifle the Spirit and His restraining work. So things begin to collapse because there is no more restraint.

A sixth mechanism of the Spirit's restraint is the Bible. When individuals, families, or entire cultures follow the Word of God, they will have guidelines to govern them that will help establish a righteous mentality in society, even if the people involved are not all Christians. Cultures that adopt biblical principles benefit from the application of those principles, one of the primary benefits being the restraint of sin that God's Word provides.

Take, for example, an unbelieving man and woman who get married. They can still have a relatively happy marriage, even though they are not Christians, by practicing biblical principles such as loving one another, being considerate and kind to one another, forgiving one another, and placing the needs of the other person ahead of their own.

This man and woman may not even realize they are practicing marriage principles taught in the Bible, but they can benefit from them. And society benefits from the reduction of evil because here is one less troubled marriage.

Now don't get me wrong. I'm not talking about salvation here. I'm talking about the general benefit of the restraint of sin that comes to a person or a society when the Bible is honored. "Righteousness exalts a nation, but sin is a disgrace to any people," says Proverbs 14:34. When the Bible is allowed to infiltrate society, its restraining influence is felt as an expression of God's grace that He makes available to all.

When you kick God out of the schools and the government, when you try to erase the Bible from the minds and hearts of a nation, you no longer have a moral frame of reference operating in your institutions. Moral chaos breaks loose because there is no restraint. Everybody does what is right in his or her own eyes. Sound like any nation you know?

So let's talk about government as the seventh means the Holy Spirit uses in His restraining ministry. Government is the God-ordained mechanism for the management of society and the maintenance of peace and order. Romans 13:1–7 makes it abundantly clear that the primary responsibility of government is to restrain evil.

I believe in limited government, but not because of my political preferences. I believe in limited government because I believe the Bible is very specific about government's role. Above all else, the Bible says that government is a "minister of God" to punish evil (v. 4). In other words, wrongdoers must fear the repercussions of their evil, or they will feel no restraint. Evil must be punished if society is going to be orderly.

A nation is in a dangerous situation when those who do wrong stop fearing punishment. When your kids stop being afraid of being spanked or punished, you are in trouble. Paul says that evil men should view government as a terror to them (vv. 3–4). So when government does not take that as its primary role in society, violence rules.

God established the death penalty back in Genesis 9:5–6. It has nothing to do with our opinions about it— whether we find it distasteful or arrogant to assume that society has the right to take a person's life. All of that is an irrelevant discussion. God has clearly addressed the matter. The Bible says that anyone who deliberately and with premeditation takes a life, his life shall be taken. It's a bottom-line issue. In fact, not only is capital punishment biblical, but public capital punishment is biblical so that those watching will say, "I don't want that to happen to me" (Numbers 16:30–34; Joshua 7:24–26).

So the job of government is to bring terror to evildoers in order to restrain and prevent evil if possible and to deal with it when it is committed. The Holy Spirit uses government to create restraint in society.

When people, whether leaders or family or government or even the church, refuse to allow the Holy Spirit to carry out His ministry of restraint through them, the repercussions are staggering, because they are removing the only true source of restraint.

So we need to make sure we are not hindering, or quenching, the restraining work of the Spirit. It's as much a part of His ministry as salvation or sanctification or any other work He is carrying out today.

## RESISTING THE SPIRIT'S RESTRAINT

Having said all that, however, we need to see that it is possible to resist the Holy Spirit's efforts to restrain sin. We noted in the previous chapter the occasion where Stephen, one of the original leaders in the church at Jerusalem, was hauled before Israel's governing council, called the Sanhedrin, to explain his ministry (Acts 6:12).

Beginning in verse 2 of Acts 7, Stephen launched into one of the most powerful sermons in the Bible. Then he concluded by laying the charge of resisting the Spirit at the feet of these men who were the religious authorities of Israel: "You men who are stiffnecked and uncircumcised in heart and ears are always resisting the Holy Spirit" (7:51).

### The Danger of Resisting

So it is possible to resist the Holy Spirit, to tune out His voice. Have you ever been talking to someone who suddenly tuned you out? You are trying to communicate, but it's clear that the other person isn't paying any attention.

It is possible for someone to say no to the work of the Holy Spirit so often and so completely that He takes the person at his word, and his next no becomes his final no. It is very dangerous to say to the Holy Spirit of God, "No. I hear You and I know it's You. But I am not going to listen."

That's why the Bible repeatedly says, "He who has ears to hear, let him hear." It's even possible for a church to resist the work of the Spirit. In Revelation 2:5, the risen Christ had to warn the church at Ephesus that He would remove its lampstand if the people didn't return to Him.

It's also possible for a society to resist the restraining work of the Holy Spirit—but as we said above, that society will pay a dear price. We in America should know, because this is exactly what is happening in our culture today.

One of the greatest biblical illustrations of this is ancient Egypt in the days of Moses. All through the long process by which Moses sought to free God's people from Egyptian bondage, Pharaoh heard Moses' warnings that he was defying the God of Israel by his stubbornness. But Pharaoh resisted ten times, and ten times God wreaked havoc on Egypt. In the end it cost Pharaoh the life of his son, and then it cost him his own life.

Now think about it. Pharaoh's soldiers followed him in his foolishness and lost their lives too. Their leader led them to their deaths. I often try to imagine what it would have been like to be one of Pharaoh's men.

I have just seen the Red Sea open up. The walls of water are towering above me. I would have thought twice about going through that sea. No matter how loyal I was to Pharaoh, when he said, "Follow me, boys," I think I would have gone AWOL on that one. Pharaoh resisted God time and time again, and he and his people paid dearly.

We see this happen every day in the child who resists his parents' attempts to restrain his bad behavior, or in the criminal who resists the police officer's attempt to arrest him for his crime and put him in restraints so he cannot commit future crimes.

People can resist the Holy Spirit's attempts to restrain their sin. This leads to the Spirit making a momentous decision. When sinful people resist Him to the point of no return, the Holy Spirit gives them over to practice their sin and suffer the awful consequences of their resistance.

### Given Over to Sin

That's the picture we have in Romans 1:18–32. This passage is the epitome of what happens when sinful people resist the Spirit of God and He gives them over to their sin. This is a very important passage because of its repercussions, so I want us to note several things about these fifteen crucial verses.

Verse 18 is the key: "For the wrath of God is revealed from heaven against all ungodliness and unrighteousness of men, who suppress the truth in unrighteousness." Notice that these people have the truth, but they hold it down. God is trying to speak, but they are saying, "I don't want to listen."

So they try to put a lid on God's truth. They don't do it by accident; it's a purposeful act of unrighteousness. Suppressing the truth means that the people referred to here must stop their ears to the voice of the Holy Spirit, because He is the Spirit of truth (John 14:17).

When you suppress the Spirit of truth, you are suppressing the only One who can hold back the full explosion of evil. When you suppress the Spirit of truth, the dam of sin breaks. It breaks in your personal life, in your family life, in your church life, and in the life of the culture. No person or society can handle the pressure of suppressed truth.

What follows in Romans 1 only makes sense when you realize that there is such a thing as truth. There is a standard by which all reality is measured. We must start there.

You say, "I know that, Tony. I believe the Bible is God's standard of truth."

That's great, but I hope you realize we are living in a society that has given up the concept of truth. We could almost take the word itself out of the dictionary, because most people today do not believe that there is an absolute standard of truth that is the same for all people at all times. And even some people who claim to believe in truth live as though it doesn't exist.

The thing that increasingly marks Christians as unique is the fact that we believe in truth. We believe there is an unchanging standard by which all things can be measured. The interesting thing is that when it comes to their pocketbooks and their lives, people want truth to prevail.

For example, no one wants his boss to say, "Well, I know I said I would pay you five hundred dollars a week, but I didn't mean literally five hundred. You can't hold me to that rigid a standard of truth. What I really meant was around five hundred dollars. So I'm going to pay you four hundred this week." Nobody wants that kind of truth.

But when it comes to issues of spiritual truth and morality, people suppress the truth and the Spirit whose job it is to reveal the truth to human hearts. And when you suppress the Holy Spirit's ability to restrain sin, God takes the lid off and sin breaks loose. Let's pick this up in Romans 1:

> Therefore God gave them over in the lusts of their hearts. . . . God gave them over to degrading passions. . . . God gave them over to a depraved mind. (vv. 24, 26, 28)

Paul says that God gave these people over to sin in three basic ways. First, He gave them over to follow their lusts, to do their own thing. "You want to be your own God? Go right ahead." So the first layer of Holy Spirit restraint was removed.

Doing one's own thing may not sound like judgment to some people. It sounds more like fun. Yes, it is fun until it's time to pay up. Some people use credit cards like this. They go shopping and pull out all the cards. They're like Solomon in Ecclesiastes: they don't deny themselves any pleasure. They just say, "Charge it."

And when the credit card companies see that these people like to spend, they raise their credit lines. More fun! But then a few weeks pass, and it's payment time.

If you've been caught in that trap, you know you will be paying for the stuff for years to come. That's true in the spiritual realm too. You may think you are free to indulge yourself, but the payment will always come due, with interest. So God says to those who refuse the Spirit's restraint, "You want freedom from Me? You've got it!"

Then they take a step down to the next level, "degrading passions." In this particular context, Paul talks about homosexuality. Notice that he doesn't argue lifestyle, hormones, what a person may be born with, or any of that. All of that is smoke to cover the real issue. The real issue, according to the Bible, is that homosexuality is a degrading sin that invites God's judgment.

Verses 26–27 talk about homosexual behavior among both men and women. All of those who engage in this sin will receive "in their own persons the due penalty of their error." God is saying, "If you are determined to follow your degrading passions without any restraint, you will reap the consequences."

Now to many of us, this may sound like the bottom of the barrel. But according to verse 28, there's another step below degrading passions: "a depraved mind." You're in bad shape when you lose your mind concerning issues of sin and morality.

How do we know when people arrive at this point? Verse 32 tells us:

> And although they know the ordinance of God, that those who practice such things are worthy of death, they not only do the same, but also give hearty approval to those who practice them.

That is, they want to legalize depravity. You know people have gone crazy when they try to wrap their depravity in a cloak of respectability by making it legal. So what do we have today? People wanting to make same-sex marriages legal, to make adoption by a homosexual couple legal, to give all same-sex practices the full protection of the law.

Paul says that when a society reaches this point, it has gone stark raving mad. If you want to see people who engage in degradation of every kind, just tune in to the talk shows. The people on the platform are bad enough. But the audience applauds their depravity, giving it "hearty approval." What is the question that occurs to most of us when we hear about this stuff? The first thing we ask is, "Have these people lost their minds?" Then we say, "The TV people must be out of their minds to put this kind of trash on television."

Well, Paul would say yes to that question and amen to that statement. People go mad spiritually and morally when they reject the Restrainer and His attempts to hold back sin. God says when people give their hearty approval to sin, you are looking at a culture gone mad.

The sad thing is that our society has not yet paid the full bill for this madness. We haven't seen anything yet when it comes to problems like crime and disease and all manner of societal dissension.

What then is the cause of this "devolution" of society? It's because people said no to the restraining influence of the Holy Spirit, and He said, "You want unrestrained sin? You've got it." It's like the prodigal son. His father said, "You want to leave? Go ahead. Call me when you are tired of the pigpen."

You say, "People don't think they're depraved." Well, fish don't think they're wet either. People get so immersed in this stuff they don't even feel it. But no combination of bad eggs can make a good omelet. And no combination of sin can make a worthwhile life.

## REAPING THE RESULTS

People can resist and refuse the restraining Holy Spirit for only so long. As we have seen, those who resist the Spirit are turned over by Him to the consequences of their refusal, until those consequences become their final judgment.

There is a great illustration of this in Genesis 6:1–13, the description of the society that fell under God's judgment in the Flood. In verse 3, God says, "My Spirit shall not strive with man forever." The Hebrew word *strive* means to shield or protect. God is saying, "I am not going to keep on protecting mankind forever."

Why? Just read verses 5–7 and 11–13. It sounds like Romans 1. It sounds like today. The people of the ancient world had thrown off all restraint of sin and were indulging themselves in degrading passions and violence.

But notice the last half of verse 3: "Nevertheless his days shall be one hundred and twenty years." God was saying, "You have one hundred and twenty years to get this mess straight, because I am not going to keep going through this year in and year out with you. You are either going to take Me seriously or pay the price."

They paid the price. The whole world was judged except Noah and his family. It's interesting what Jesus said about this. In Matthew 24:36–39, He said the people of Noah's day were so intent on their sin that they were clueless as to what was going on until they felt cold water coming up over their ankles. They had lost their minds spiritually. They had gone mad.

What's the point? When God says, "My Spirit will not always be around to restrain sin," we had better take the clue! God isn't going to keep holding this messy world together forever.

My mother used to say to me, "You are trying me, boy!" Did your mother ever say that to you? "You are trying my patience." Sometimes my mother would just say, "Uh-huh, uh-huh." Or she would say, "Keep on. Just keep on."

I never knew when it was going to hit, but my mother had the fastest right hand in the world. BAM! What she was saying was, "Don't keep playing with me. Don't keep messing with me." Then judgment would fall.

For another classic example of the judgment of God falling, I would refer you back to Acts 5:1–11, the story of Ananias and Sapphira. Since we discussed this in the previous chapter, I won't go through it again here. Let me just make a couple of observations about that sad event and its aftermath.

The first thing I want you to see is that the church in Jerusalem was a happening place. The people were unified (see Acts 4:32). They were compassionate and unselfish, sharing what they had. And it was a powerful church (v. 33).

What a great church to belong to: Jerusalem Bible Fellowship! But even in this great church, they had a problem. Why? Because it is only in a church like this that they will call sin what it is. It's only in a context like this that the restraining ministry of the Spirit is taken seriously.

See, if Peter and the others had just treated the sin of Ananias and Sapphira lightly, brushing it aside as a small lapse of good judgment, the Holy Spirit would have taken a giant step away from the church at Jerusalem. Remember, it was the Spirit who was lied to; He's the one who was wronged.

See, there are believers who come to church on Sunday knowing in their hearts that they have sin planned for

Monday. The Spirit is seeking to restrain them, but they have already worked out how they are going to climb right over Him to get to their sin.

But the Holy Spirit is to be taken seriously. The Spirit certainly took Ananias and Sapphira dead seriously. Notice that in Acts 5:11, "great fear came upon the whole church." I guess so. Other believers started reworking their plans. This was healthy fear. The problem we face today is a generation that doesn't fear anything. We even have Christians who don't fear God.

But there was another response to this judgment: "None of the rest dared to associate with them" (v. 13). To put it another way, the people said, "We aren't going to that church. You die in that church!"

We hear something like this all the time in our ministry. People say, "We are not going to that church. They tell you you have to live right! They hold you responsible and accountable." Well, we aren't trying to scare anyone off, but we aren't playing games either. We take the restraining ministry of the Holy Spirit very seriously because we believe *He* wants it taken seriously.

The end of verse 13 says the people held the believers in Jerusalem in high esteem even though they did not join with them. They respected the church. If we want people to take the things of God seriously, we in the church had better be doing it. We need to be grateful for the Spirit's restraining ministry. And we need to pray that people will not resist and refuse His restraint, lest He withdraw it and leave us to ourselves.

# EXPERIENCING THE SPIRIT'S RESTRAINT

The world doesn't appreciate or understand the Holy Spirit's restraining ministry, but it is still desperately needed. Allow the Spirit the freedom He needs to exercise His restraint in you and through you to others, whether at home, in the church, or in the society at large:

1. This is another of those occasions when it would be good to check around and make sure there are no influences coming into your home that you don't want to be there. For most of us, learning the restraint of the Spirit started at home.

2. You can also help your church be salt and light and a restraining influence in your community by your faithful prayer support and active involvement. Drop your pastor a note to encourage him in his preaching and teaching of the Word.

3. If you're like most Christians, you have some unsaved friends and family members on your prayer list. As long as they are still here, you know they haven't said their final no to the Holy Spirit, so keep up your prayers for their salvation.

4. A lot of Christians simply get angry or frustrated when they think of government. But let's not make the mistake of thinking that if we can't do something really big and noticeable, we won't do anything at all. If you need to get informed about the issues and know who your local leaders are, start there. If you need to make your voice heard on an issue, don't hesitate to speak up, but also be alert for an opportunity to turn the situation into a witness for Christ.

# PART THREE

# THE HOLY SPIRIT'S PROVISION

# CHAPTER THIRTEEN

# EXPERIENCING THE SPIRIT'S FRUIT

We've come to the third section of the book, the provisions of the Holy Spirit. For these final six chapters, we are going to talk about the unbelievable experiential benefits the Spirit makes available to all believers without exception.

The key word is *available*, because I hope you know by now there's nothing automatic about the Spirit's ministry. Every believer is baptized by the Holy Spirit into the body of Christ, and every believer is indwelt by the Spirit. But neither of these guarantees that we will experience all the Spirit's benefits.

In this chapter I want to walk you through the Spirit's "orchard" of ripe fruit, those qualities of the spiritual life that the Holy Spirit will produce in us if we submit to His filling and control.

Paul delineates the fruit of the Spirit in Galatians 5:22–23, two tightly packed verses that are worthy of extended study. It would be great just to turn there and let the sweet juice of the Spirit's fruit run down our arm, so to speak, as we dig in and enjoy the good things He has for us.

But to do that, we would have to climb over the verses that precede verses 22–23, which means ignoring the context in which Paul's discussion of spiritual fruit occurs. But more important, if we skip over verses 16–21 of Galatians 5, we will miss a truth about the Christian life that is critically important to understanding and experiencing the Holy Spirit's fruit.

## WHETTING OUR APPETITE

What verses 16–21 do is whet our appetite for the juicy, sweet, and satisfying fruit of the Spirit by giving us a taste of the dry, rotten, and unsatisfying deeds of the flesh. Sometimes you don't develop a real hunger for the good stuff until you've gotten your fill of the bad stuff. If you've ever tried to live the Christian life in the energy of the flesh, you know what I'm talking about.

The believers in Galatia were trying to live the life of the Holy Spirit in the energy of the flesh, and Paul was astounded:

> You foolish Galatians, who has bewitched you, before whose eyes Jesus Christ was publicly portrayed as crucified? . . . Are you so foolish? Having begun by the Spirit, are you now being perfected by the flesh? (Galatians 3:1, 3)

This last question in verse 3 is one we all have to ask ourselves as Christians. Giving the correct answer is easy: no, we can't be perfected by the flesh. Living out that answer, however, is not always easy because we are engaged in a battle between the flesh and the Spirit.

We have already looked at the fact that the flesh, meaning our unredeemed humanity, is unfixable. It will never change. It cannot be reformed. Our humanity has been infested with spiritual roaches that, given the right amount of darkness, will come out of hiding. Our flesh is like a magnet for sin. It attracts sin because it was trained to do that in its unredeemed state.

No wonder God puts a condemned sign, called death, on the flesh. Its destiny is the grave. There is nothing in your flesh inherited from Adam that is going to help you live the life of the Spirit. Thus Paul could say that there was "nothing good" in his flesh (Romans 7:18).

This explains why Paul was so astonished at the foolishness of the Galatians. They were in danger of losing their moorings because of a serious misunderstanding of the spiritual life. The false teachers among them had convinced these believers that the way to pull off the Christian life was by taming the flesh and making it behave.

In other words, the Galatians were being tempted to substitute rules for a dynamic relationship with the Holy Spirit. This idea is still with us today. We have all met Christians who have a list of rules for us to follow if we want to be victorious: "ten steps to the abundant Christian life"; "twenty-five things you've always wanted to know about spiritual victory but were afraid to ask."

The Christian life does include rules. There are definite do's and don'ts. But the power for victorious Christian living is not in the rules. It's in the Spirit. Paul clarifies how it works in this classic passage in Galatians 5.

What he does is give us a good taste of the rotten fruit of the flesh so we will sincerely desire the fruit of the Spirit. We need to begin with Galatians 5:16–18:

> But I say, walk by the Spirit, and you will not carry out the desire of the flesh. For the flesh sets its desire against the Spirit, and the Spirit against the flesh; for these are in opposition to one another, so that you may not do the things that you please. But if you are led by the Spirit, you are not under the Law.

Paul is saying that you live in a war zone, and the war zone is *you*. This zone consists of two opposing realities: your unredeemed humanity, which we have already described, and the indwelling Holy Spirit.

## OLD HOUSE, NEW OCCUPANT

When you came to Christ, the Spirit of God came to take up residence in your life and give you a new nature.

He placed your new nature in the old house of your flesh—and your old house doesn't want a new occupant! It is comfortable in its current dilapidated status.

But the Spirit of God comes in to set up a whole new program, take control of your body, and run the show. Your flesh says, "Not here, You won't. I have been running this show for all these years, and I am not about to give it over to You." The presence of the Holy Spirit in your life does not mean your flesh no longer desires to sin.

The flesh will desire to sin until it is laid in the grave. But the Holy Spirit gives you the ability not to give in to the cravings, appetites, and demands of the flesh. That's why we are told to walk by the Spirit (Galatians 5:16), a command Paul repeats in verse 25 and which we will talk about briefly later.

Notice how verse 17 describes the outcome of this war: "You may not do the things that you please." I think of it as being like a football game, where the other team opposes you across the line. As you try to go forward, this other team—captained by the flesh—says, "If we have our way, you will make no forward progress. In fact, try to run the ball this way and you are going to lose yardage."

Many of us have experienced that in our Christian lives, haven't we? We keep getting pushed back. We can't even seem to maintain our line of scrimmage because the flesh is opposing us. But that's not the way it has to be anymore because we have a powerful force on our team who opposes the flesh. We have the Holy Spirit, who knows how to resist the flesh.

The Holy Spirit runs interference for us, like a pulling guard in football who pulls out of his position to block for the running back as he comes sweeping around the end. The reason they call it running interference is that the guard is there in front of the running back, ready to interfere with any attempts by the opposing team to tackle him.

My friend, God has given you a powerful "pulling guard" in the Holy Spirit. It is the Spirit's job to run interference for you so that when your opponent the flesh seeks to tackle you for a loss, the Spirit is there to knock the flesh on its backside and clear your path to the goal.

## NO NEED FOR LAW

In Galatians 5:18, Paul says the Holy Spirit is so good at His job that if you are led by the Spirit, if He runs interference for you, "you are not under the Law." We didn't pick this up in verse 16, but Paul's contrast between the Law and grace goes all the way back to chapter 3. His point has been to show the Galatians that no amount of Law-keeping, which is really the effort of the flesh to live the life of faith, will do the job.

Law is good and necessary because we are rebellious. The Mosaic Law, which is the revelation of God's perfect standard, was given to show us how sinful we are and how far short we fall of God's demands (Romans 3:23).

No police officer is ever going to pull you over, come up to the driver's window, and say, "I couldn't help but notice on my radar that you were going the speed limit. So I just wanted to pull you over and let you know how blessed the police department of this city is to have a law-abiding citizen like you. Here, let me write you a thank-you ticket."

That's not going to happen. That police radar is not there to congratulate you for obeying the law. It's there to catch you when you exceed the speed limit. It's there to condemn you, because that is what law does. The problem with the law is that it doesn't give you the power to obey it. All it can do is give you the guidelines and punish you when you have broken them.

That's why, if you try to live the Christian life by keeping a list of rules in the power of your flesh, you are doomed to failure and misery. All the law can do is condemn. It can give you the guidelines, but it can't give you the power to follow the guidelines.

So law is necessary to restrain evil, but it's not the way to experience the Spirit-filled, Spirit-directed life. Paul says if you let the Holy Spirit take over in your life, then you are going to be pleasing God because you want to, not because you have to.

It's sad but true that a lot of believers are living the Christian life because they have to. They feel like it's what they are supposed to do, what they are expected to do. They worry about what people will think if they don't do the right thing. So the Christian life becomes a burden instead of a joy. We may *have* burdens in our lives, but the Christian life is not meant to *be* a burden.

The same thing happens in many marriages. When a couple is newly married, they do things for each other because it is a joy, not because there's a law that says they have to do these things. The wife cooks a meal for her husband because she enjoys pleasing him, not because there is a "cook for me" rule.

The husband goes to work out of a sense of delight that he can meet his wife's needs and provide for her, not because there's a law that says, "Someone has to pay the bills around here." Marital intimacy is a delight, not a duty that is forced upon either partner.

But when the partners allow the love to fade in their marriage, a sense of duty sets in. The wife feels like she "has to" find her husband something to eat. She'd better get the laundry done or she'll hear about it if he doesn't have a clean shirt. And the husband drags himself to work because he "has to" earn a living and pay the bills or be out in the street.

What happened? Being a marriage partner ceased to be a delight and became a law. The marriage is now governed by law; "you have to" or "this is what you're supposed to do" replaces serving one another out of love.

This scenario describes the way many Christians live. But when the Holy Spirit takes over, we don't function by law. We function by relationship. That's why we need the Spirit. Many of us are faltering because we are trying to do in our own might what only God the Holy Spirit can do in and through us.

## THE WORKS OF THE FLESH

In Galatians 5:19, Paul says, "Now the deeds of the flesh are evident." You read the list that follows in verses 19–21 and you realize that no truer words were ever spoken. You can know whether you are a spiritual Christian or a fleshly Christian at any given moment. You don't have to wonder, because if you are producing the rotten "fruit" of the flesh, you will know it.

Paul's list of the works of the flesh can be broken down into three categories of sins. I want to survey these, both because they are part of the text and because I hope that just a taste of this mess will make us hunger for the fruit of the Holy Spirit.

### Moral Sins

The first category of fleshly deeds has to do with morality: "immorality, impurity, sensuality" (v. 19). Immorality is the Greek word *pornēia*, a word that should look familiar because it's the root of the English *pornography*. You are definitely living in the flesh if you are seeking to satisfy your sexual desires either by direct, illegitimate sexual contact with another person outside the boundary of heterosexual marriage or by feeding yourself with illegitimate sexual material.

See, if you are fulfilling your sexual desires by going to X-rated movies, you don't have to guess whether you are going in the flesh or in the Spirit. Paul says the answer is evident.

You say, "I don't go to those movies!" OK, but what reels do you play in your own mind? Impurity has to do with your thinking. It means creating your own movie, a thought life that is putrid and contaminated. The word translated "impurity" was used for that which oozed from a sore. It means to be controlled by nasty thinking. The desire to do that comes from the flesh. It means you have rejected the Spirit at that moment.

In this context sensuality has to do with flagrant sexual activity. Immorality can be hidden, privatized. Nobody knows it but you. Sensuality means that you have gone public. You have come out of the closet. When you "progress" to sensuality, you have little concern about who knows.

Now let me remind you that Paul is talking about Christians here. Christians are the only ones in whom the

Holy Spirit struggles against the flesh, because only Christians have the Spirit. The Spirit can't wrestle with the flesh if you are not a Christian.

The difference between a Christian and a non-Christian committing these sins is that the Christian is going to experience a terrific inner war, because the Spirit is going to wage war on the flesh. The non-Christian has no such war, because he's already Satan's prisoner of war.

### Religious Sins

Paul's next category is religious sin: "idolatry, sorcery" (Galatians 5:20a). Idolatry is worshiping other gods. Israel regularly did this. The nation went after other gods even though it knew the true God. Many of us go after other gods. We may even ride in them or live in them. Whatever takes the place of God in your life is your idol. When you fall into idolatry, worshiping the true and living God is not that big a deal anymore.

I remember that as I grew up there was no such thing as my father ever saying, "The car is not running, so we won't be going to church today." No such configuration of nouns, verbs, adverbial clauses, or prepositional phrases existed in my father's vocabulary that would make him say something like that.

If the car broke down, we walked. Our church was about four miles away, but we walked if that was the only way we could get there. The only time we got out of walking was when the weather was so bad it would impede our ability to do so. My father's philosophy was that we would not have a car to be broken down if it were not for God.

But now we come up with the puniest excuses for missing worship. That's because we have other gods competing for our devotion. That comes from the flesh, along with "sorcery," *pharmakēia*, another Greek word that should look familiar as the root of the English word *pharmacy*. In this context, it has to do with the use of drugs in religious ritual. Some versions even translate the word as "witchcraft."

You may be old enough to remember the sixties, when hippies were using drugs and calling it a religious experience. They even used religious terms. But the "religious" use of drugs goes back to biblical days.

People use drugs to get illegitimately what God wants to give us through His Holy Spirit: inner peace, fulfillment, the ability to cope with life's trials. The problem with drugs is that they make you dependent on somebody other than God to meet your needs.

Drug use uniquely opens a person to demonic influence. This is why Satan is always cooking up a new drug more addictive than the previous one.

### Social Sins

Paul's final, and longest, category is what I call social sins: how you relate to others (Galatians 5:20b–21). I count at least ten items on this list. One reason may be that these are the kinds of fleshly sins that Christians are most likely to fall prey to. Not too many true Christians are going to take a hit of crack cocaine to get high, but how many of us are guilty of "outbursts of anger"? OK, that's too convicting! Let's move on.

Actually, it doesn't get any better. If a married couple is having "disputes" (v. 20), fussing and fighting all the time, one or perhaps both partners are operating in the flesh.

You say, "Well, we can't get along." That's evident. What may not be so evident is the fact that your fussing means the flesh is in control, and that means your conflict is spiritual. It's not just that you have different personalities or that you were raised differently.

All of that is ancillary. At the heart of it, the flesh is in control. All of us come into marriage and other human relationships with a lot of baggage and junk from the past. That's why we have to walk in the Spirit.

Paul says he is not giving us an exhaustive list (v. 21), but just a taste of the flesh. What living in the flesh does is disqualify us from inheritance in the kingdom, which I take to be a loss of full reward and full participation in the kingdom, not a loss of salvation.

## THE FRUIT OF THE SPIRIT

Now we come to the Holy Spirit's fruit orchard (Galatians 5:22–23). The deeds of the flesh are evident, but so is the fruit of the Spirit. Let me tell you three things you need to know about the Spirit's fruit.

### Fruit Is Visible

The first thing you need to know about fruit is that fruit is always visible. Watch out for that tree in your backyard that is giving you invisible fruit! When fruit is ripe and luxurious, you know it.

So don't tell me that you are walking in the Spirit in your heart, or that you are full of the Spirit in your heart, if nothing is evident in your life but the works of the flesh. Jesus said that we can tell false prophets by the fruit they produce (Matthew 7:16, 20). The same is true for believers. If you are walking in the Spirit, others will know it.

### Fruit Is Recognizable

The second thing you need to know about fruit is that fruit always reflects the character of the tree or vine that is bearing it. "Grapes are not gathered from thorn bushes, nor figs from thistles," Jesus said (Matthew 7:16). Apple trees produce apples, orange trees grow oranges, and so forth. The fruit that comes from a life controlled by the Holy Spirit will reflect the character of Jesus Christ.

### Fruit Is for Others

A third fact about fruit is that fruit is always borne for the benefit of others. The seed in a fruit is designed for reproduction. So as you bear the fruit of the Spirit, others not only enjoy the "taste" of your life, but also the seeds of spiritual growth are planted in their lives.

Fruit is always meant for someone else's enjoyment. You never see fruit chewing on itself. In fact, fruit that only exists for itself gets rotten. Suppose an apple begins to jump bad and say, "I don't want to be picked. I don't even want to be touched, let alone eaten. Just let me hang here on the tree." That apple is going to rot, because one reason for fruit is so that somebody can take a bite.

The Holy Spirit wants to control us so that our families and friends can take a bite out of our lives and say, "Um, that's good!"

Notice that all the deeds of the flesh are selfish. The flesh says things like, "You made me mad. I'm upset. I'm not happy. You have what I want. You are irritating me." When you walk in the flesh, you are at the center of the program. But the Spirit's fruit is always God-centered and other-directed.

Although the word *fruit* in Galatians 5:22 is singular, Paul lists nine varieties or flavors, those wonderful qualities that grow out of a Spirit-controlled life. Why are the singular and plural together here? Because all of the Holy Spirit's fruit grows out of the same tree. This is no ordinary fruit tree.

What this means, for example, is that you don't have to go to the Holy Spirit for your religion and then look elsewhere for love. You don't have to go to the Spirit for your religion and then depend on some other relationship to give you joy. The fruit of the Spirit is singular because His "fruit tree" can produce everything you need for every area of your life.

### Spiritual Fruit

Paul says the fruit of the Spirit is love (Galatians 5:22). Godly love is the ability to seek the highest good for another, regardless of that person's response. See, the flesh says, "You aren't being loving to me, so I'm not going to show you any love." The Spirit says, "Even if you are not loving me, let me show you what real love looks like." That's the Holy Spirit.

How about joy? The world can only offer you happiness, which is driven by circumstances. In other words, if you can show me a good time, I will be happy.

But the joy of the Spirit has nothing to do with happiness. It has to do with a well of living water on the inside, not the circumstances on the outside. Joy is the overflow of the life of God within you. If you have an empty well within, you will have to go all over the place to find happiness.

But if you have joy, you can turn a bad situation into a playground. Joy is inner stability regardless of external circumstances.

The fruit of the Spirit is also "peace" (v. 22). The Holy Spirit can bring harmony where there is conflict. He can take two different personalities and cause them to live together in peace. He can take two factions that are at war and bring them together in harmony.

The fruit of the Spirit also consists of "patience," that quality that allows us to be "long-fused" instead of short-tempered. It removes a vengeful spirit toward those who have wronged us.

"Kindness" is thinking of ways you can help others, not ways you can hurt them. "Goodness" means deeds that benefit others, not deeds that destroy. "Faithfulness" is the ability to be consistent, not there one day and gone the next. It means we are dependable.

"Gentleness" or meekness (v. 23) is the ability to bring yourself under the control of another, the ability to submit to the will of God. Finally, "self-control" is the ability to say no to wrong and yes to right, no matter how tempting the wrong is.

## WALKING BY THE SPIRIT

Go through that list and you'll understand why Paul concludes by saying, "Against such things there is no law." We won't need law to rein us in when the Holy Spirit is producing His life-transforming fruit in us. So if you and I are going to live victorious Christian lives, it occurs to me that we'd better get all of the Holy Ghost we can get. Better yet, allow the Holy Ghost to get all of us He can get!

In verses 24–25, Paul gives us two ways the Holy Spirit can get more of us. Verse 24 is a reminder instead of a command. If you are a Christian, you have already been crucified with Christ (Romans 6:1–11). Therefore, your flesh was put to death on the cross, and you were raised spiritually to a new way of life. What Paul is saying is that when it comes to this conflict between flesh and Spirit, you are already on the victor's side.

Then he says in Galatians 5:25, "If we live by the Spirit, let us also walk by the Spirit." This connects us back to verse 16, which is where we started. Back in chapter 9 we discussed at length what all is involved in this metaphor of walking, so I won't repeat that here.

I do want to refresh your memory, however, by simply reminding you of the three components of walking. First, walking always implies that you are going somewhere. Watch out for people who spend all their time walking and never move.

Second, walking assumes continuous movement. It means you keep going. If you fall down, you get up and start walking again. Can you imagine how long it would take you to learn to walk if you only practiced on Sunday and then sat around the rest of the week? A lot of Christians do that spiritually and then wonder why they can't seem to stay on their feet.

The third component of walking is dependence, putting your weight down on your legs one leg at a time. Dependence in walking means you are trusting your legs to hold you up. Walking in the Spirit means you are depending on the Holy Spirit to hold you up.

Let me dwell on this one for a minute. You say, "How do I know when I am depending on God?" There's a simple answer: prayer. If you pray in the morning, then the Spirit doesn't hear from you again all day, that means you are depending on Him to get you started, but then leaving Him out the rest of the day.

See, if prayer is an extra, that makes the Holy Spirit an extra. And if the Spirit is an extra, that inner well we talked about above will run dry. Prayer is meant to be like breathing. You cut it off, you die. It's something you do all the time.

You say, "But it's so hard to pray. It's easier just to give up." Well, I grew up with bad asthma, and it was hard to breathe. But I can assure you I didn't give up breathing. In fact, I insisted on it! My bronchial tubes would be blocked, and I would be wheezing and coughing.

But I stayed with it until those tubes were clear and I could breathe.

When sin congests us, it's hard to pray. But we must insist on praying until those tubes get cleared up. Once you have prayed enough formally, you will wind up doing it naturally. Practice makes perfect.

## BRINGING IT HOME

How do we bring all of this home? Consider with me Galatians 6:7–9:

> Do not be deceived, God is not mocked; for whatever a man sows, this he will also reap. For the one who sows to his own flesh shall from the flesh reap corruption, but the one who sows to the Spirit shall from the Spirit reap eternal life. And let us not lose heart in doing good, for in due time we shall reap if we do not grow weary.

Paul says if you want to understand the spiritual life, look at farming. The principle is simple. What you plant is what you get back. If you sow to the flesh, if you feed the flesh, the flesh will grow and produce fleshly deeds. If you sow to the Spirit, you will reap the fruit of the Spirit.

The Greek word translated "mocked" means to thumb your nose at something. Don't thumb your nose at God, Paul says, because He will always have the last word.

How do you thumb your nose at God? By thinking you can wade around in the cesspool of the flesh without slipping and going under. If you are a drunkard today, it is because you have developed a habit of drinking. You are not a drunkard because you took one sip. It was that second sip, and third, and fourth, and so on, that got you hooked. Now drink controls you.

What you sow is what you reap. So if your life is marked by a conspicuous absence of spiritual fruit, it's because there has been an absence of sowing to the Spirit. But when you sow the right seed, you get the right result.

In fact, the beautiful thing about sowing to the Spirit is that you always get back more than you put in. When you sow a corn seed, you don't get just one ear. You get a stalk with many ears. What you sow is an investment that comes back many times.

So, do you want the Holy Spirit's brand of love, joy, peace, and so on? Then don't grow weary of sowing righteousness, of walking by the Spirit, because when the harvest comes "in due time," you'll reap a whole basketful of ripe, luscious spiritual fruit.

So how do we experience the Spirit's fruit? Many of us have sown bad things even as Christians. We have developed damaging habits or attitudes or addictions. Some of us are in our second or third marriages because of what we have sown.

Well, you may not be able to change what you have already reaped, but you can plow up your field! You may have some bad things in the ground even now, but the Holy Spirit knows how to plow that field and turn over the soil so you can sow new seeds in the same soil.

See, as long as you're still here, you are a candidate for a fresh new spiritual harvest. When you come to the Lord in repentance and submission, the Holy Spirit will get out His plow and turn over that old soil of your heart until it is fresh and moist and ready for some new seed. Even if you have sown bad seeds, God is offering you a chance for a different harvest. The Spirit can plow that ground, and who knows? God may have the greatest crop of spiritual fruit you've ever seen waiting for you next harvest time.

# EXPERIENCING THE SPIRIT'S FRUIT

**I**f you want to experience the Spirit's fruit, walk by the Spirit. That is, every time your flesh wants to do that which is selfish and ungodly, call on the Spirit of God to help you at that moment. Don't depend on the prayer you prayed last night. Ask the Spirit at that moment for His power to give you victory right then and there. When you see the Spirit kick in, you will never be the same:

1. We seem to keep coming back to the importance of prayer. I don't have any easy formulas to help you develop a potent and consistent prayer life except what I said before: Practice makes perfect. Ask God to help you approach prayer the way you do breathing. Insist on it!

2. Was there something on the list of fleshly deeds in Galatians 5:19–21 that really hit home with you? Or was your "pet" sin not listed? Either way, take that sin to God in prayer, stating it by name and asking the Holy Spirit to make you so sensitive to it that you react just thinking about doing it. Also, ask the Spirit to show you if there's something you are doing without even being conscious of it.

3. Go through the list of the fruit of the Spirit in Galatians 5:22–23, and chances are that one of these qualities will leap out at you as something you need in a special way right now. Take your need for that fruit to the Holy Spirit in prayer, telling Him how much you want to see Him produce it in your life. Then be ready for Him to deal with whatever He needs to in order to prepare the soil of your heart for that fruit.

4. For a lot of Christians, the biggest challenge is simply not to "lose heart in doing good." Are you growing weary in the process of planting the seed? Take a few minutes to sit under a shade tree and meditate on the harvest waiting for you. Read Revelation 21–22 and thank God that the harvest will be far greater in value than any effort we make in plowing and sowing!

# CHAPTER FOURTEEN

# EXPERIENCING THE SPIRIT'S INTERCESSION

I have been in enough foreign countries to know that if you don't know somebody who lives there, you are going to be in trouble, because there are a lot of folks who will take advantage of you and steer you the wrong way if they know you're new to the territory.

When it comes to functioning in the spiritual realm, we need someone who has been living there for a while. Somebody who understands the terrain and can speak the language. Somebody who can point us in the direction we need to go and help us find the things we need. Somebody who can intercede, who can approach another person and make an appeal on our behalf. We need an intercessor.

We need that kind of spiritual help because as believers in Jesus Christ we are living in a world that is utterly foreign to our human nature. It's a world unlike anything the natural mind can see or understand. It's foreign terrain, and we need a guide. Paul calls this realm "the heavenly places" (Ephesians 1:3; 2:6).

We have such a Guide in the Person of the Holy Spirit. He not only knows the realm, He knows the King of the realm. The Spirit intercedes on our behalf in the very presence of God the Father, so in this chapter I want to help you know how you can experience the Spirit's intercessory ministry. Romans 8:26 is a key verse here: "In the same way the Spirit also helps our weakness; for we do not know how to pray as we should, but the Spirit Himself intercedes for us with groanings too deep for words."

## OUR NEED FOR THE
## SPIRIT'S INTERCESSION

This is good news. How many of us have said, "I don't know what to say when I pray"? We all have. How many of us have ever been confused about this issue of talking to God? Same vote. Well, here is the help we need, and it's not just a book of instructions. It's a Person, the Helper Himself, the Holy Spirit.

The Holy Spirit helps us in prayer. He is God's agent of communication. We've already talked about why we need help in the spiritual realm as a whole. But everything I said above is doubly true when it comes to prayer.

### An Unfamiliar Language

If the world of the Spirit is a foreign realm to our fleshly minds, prayer is the unfamiliar language of that realm. When you're in a place you have never been before, among people whose language you don't speak, somebody needs to intercede for you.

Paul says we need help in our prayer lives because we are weak. There are plenty of reasons for this. Some of us are in circumstantial weakness. Things are not going very well and we don't know what to do, where to turn, what decision to make. We are frustrated and tired and need somebody who understands the territory to show us the way.

Others of us are in moral weakness. There are sins in our lives that we desperately need and want to get rid of. Yet they hang around like flies around raw meat. Every time we shoo these sins away, they keep swarming back. We need someone who knows the terrain of righteousness and can help us.

Still other believers are physically weak. Their bodies are not working like they need and want them to work. The fatigue and frustration of coming to grips with physical suffering and all that it involves has left these people weak. They need someone who can help them navigate their confusing terrain.

Whatever your need, God has Someone for you. It is the Holy Spirit's job to make sure that what you need and where you are get properly communicated to God. Paul says we don't know how to pray. That's obvious because we don't pray. We are so messed up in our weakness that coming before God is a job.

We aren't very adept at communicating with God, and the effort is a struggle. But the good news of Romans 8:26 is that when you don't know how to construct your prayer, when you don't know how to say it, when you don't even know what to say, the Holy Spirit steps in.

The Spirit has the ability to take your cares and needs and hurts and confusion and so clarify, correct, and focus them that by the time they leave you and get to heaven, they have been fixed. So don't worry that you pray poorly. Worry that you don't pray at all.

I say that because Romans 8:26 assumes that we do pray. Not knowing how to pray is a lot different from giving up and not praying. We have no excuse for not praying, although there may be reasons for not praying well. Perhaps we have never learned to pray. Perhaps we have not practiced the discipline of prayer. Maybe we don't understand enough of the Word to pray biblically and accurately.

But whatever our prayer problem, the Holy Spirit's job is to help us by interceding for us. So you never have to worry that you didn't get your prayer just right. By the time the Holy Spirit takes it and gets it to the throne of God, that thing is cooking, because the Spirit's job is to carry it to God properly.

### Learning the Language

Now if you want to learn a foreign language, the best way to do so is not in a classroom. The best way to learn it is by hanging out in an environment where people speak it. It's amazing how many Christians say they want to pray but don't hang out in a prayer environment.

If you don't want to hang out in the environment, if you don't want to be around people who know the language, you don't really want to learn that language. The reason this is critical for prayer is that prayer is God's "walkie-talkie" system of communication.

So if there is no prayer, there is no divine communication taking place. If there is no divine communication taking place, you have not given the Spirit anything to work with. And, if you have not given the Spirit anything to work with, then you won't hear back from God on the issue you are facing.

But as you pray, the Holy Spirit is there to interpret your prayer and clarify the meaning. That way, by the time your prayer arrives at the foot of the Father, the One who grants the request, that prayer has been corrected, fixed up, chopped off, and realigned so that, often, what you said does not look anything like what finally gets delivered in heaven.

Your prayer needed Holy Ghost reshaping. What you said needed a lot of help. When you prayed, you did not have all the information you needed. When you prayed, you did not understand all the related things that were going to happen down the line.

But the Holy Spirit added all the needed data to it so that it was ready for the Father to receive it. What happened was that your few-second prayer turned into a five-page petition because the Holy Spirit clarified it, fixed it up, and corrected it, bringing it into conformity with God's will.

Now you can see why I said Romans 8:26 is a good news verse. To have such a dynamic prayer life available to you and not to use it doesn't make any sense. Paul doesn't say the Spirit will pray for you if you don't want to bother praying for yourself. We must give the Spirit something to interpret by praying. If not, we will live unassisted, defeated Christian lives. The Spirit is there to help us in our weakness, not in our absence.

### The Need to Pray

We have an orchestra at our church. I could listen to those skilled musicians play all day long. But I am unskilled musically. I could listen to our orchestra play every day for a year and still be unskilled, because nobody learns to play an instrument by listening to people play instruments. People learn to play instruments by playing them.

My point is this: Don't worry about the fact that you can't call down fire from heaven yet in your prayers. Don't fret that you can't change the structure of things yet in your prayers. Make sure you are learning to pray; make sure you have decided and determined that communication with God is top priority for you.

If you really want to see some changes take place in your life, link up with the Holy Spirit in prayer. The apostle Jude tells us to "[build] yourselves up on your most holy faith; praying in the Holy Spirit" (v. 20). Prayer builds you up. Prayer keeps your love for God hot. Prayer can keep you hanging in there when you want to quit.

Now if prayer is this powerful and you were the Devil, what would you do? Anything you could to keep people from praying. That's exactly what Satan does. He keeps us from coming face-to-face with God so that the Holy Spirit has nothing to grab hold of and deliver to the Father.

Then we don't experience the building up that occurs through "praying in the Holy Spirit," which means praying in the environment or realm of the Spirit. That's exactly where the Spirit's intercession is experienced, so let's find out what the terrain looks like and how to get there.

## THE NATURE OF THE
## SPIRIT'S INTERCESSION

Paul gives us a look into the nature of the Holy Spirit's intercession in verses 26b–27 of Romans 8:

But the Spirit Himself intercedes for us with groanings too deep for words; and He who searches the hearts knows what the mind of the Spirit is, because He intercedes for the saints according to the will of God.

Imagine the Holy Spirit engaged so deeply in prayer on your behalf that He enters into yearnings and groanings that cannot be expressed in words. This is not some type of heavenly language here. Paul is talking about the deep, quiet, inaudible prayer groanings of the Spirit.

## The Spirit's Groanings

Now we all know what it is to feel something so deeply that we groan under the burden of it. That's the concept here, and it permeates all of creation. Back up in verse 22 of Romans 8, Paul says, "We know that the whole creation groans and suffers the pains of childbirth together until now."

The whole creation groans and aches like a woman in childbirth, Paul says. A woman in labor groans as the baby serves notice on her that the nine months are up and he or she is ready to be born. But for that to occur, there must be a period of groaning as the contractions begin and pain sets in.

So the groaning is both good and bad news. The bad news is, it's going to hurt. The good news is, the hurt is worthwhile because it's going to produce something good. The good news always outweighs the bad. Jesus Himself said that after her child is born, a mother forgets the pain because of her joy at this new life (John 16:21). The product of the groan is greater than the pain of the groan.

The Bible says the entire universe groans under the curse of sin that expresses itself in things such as hurricanes and tornadoes and earthquakes. Those are not just random happenings in nature. They are "labor pains" as the creation groans to be delivered from the chaos into which sin has plunged it.

Now don't misunderstand. Paul is not talking about some kind of modern-day "mother earth" theology in which the earth is invested with a spirit and a soul and all of that. He's saying that even the unthinking natural creation feels the curse of sin and longs to be delivered from it because this is not what God created it for.

So the upheaval and violence of the created world is unnatural and will someday be reversed when the curse of sin is lifted. In other words, nature groans in expectation of something better ahead that will replace the groaning with joy. In this way, the groanings of nature illustrate the Holy Spirit's groanings for us in prayer.

Nature definitely groaned at our house the morning we had to "funeralize" two of my son's three pet rabbits. The third one had disappeared. I had heard our dog barking in the middle of the night, but if you know my dog you realize this is a meaningless exercise.

I mean, if you want to rob me, go ahead. My dog is not going to stop you. So when he woke me up with his continued barking, I did wonder for a minute what was going on. I thought I heard a noise, but it was so faint I didn't pay any attention. I just turned over and went back to sleep.

But when we went to feed the rabbits the next day, two were dead in the cage and the third was missing. Evidently, raccoons had gotten into the cage during the night and attacked the rabbits. There was evidence of a tremendous struggle as the rabbits were clawed to death.

The Bible declares that this kind of violence is part of the curse. Animals preying on other animals is not the way God created the world, and it's not the way things will be in the new creation. When the labor pains are over and the new birth comes, then according to Isaiah 11:6–9:

> The wolf will dwell with the lamb, and the leopard will lie down with the kid, and the calf and the young lion and the fatling together; and a little boy will lead them. Also the cow and the bear will graze; their young will lie down together; and the lion will eat straw like the ox. And the nursing child will play by the hole of the cobra, and the weaned child will put his hand on the viper's den. They will not hurt or destroy in all My holy mountain, for the earth will be full of the knowledge of the Lord as the waters cover the sea.

When this creation gets its new birth, when God sets up His kingdom, there will be no more animals preying on each other or hurting people. There will be no more earthquakes or hurricanes or other destructive acts in nature, because the groaning will have produced a new birth.

### Interpreting Our Groanings

But the natural world is not the only part of creation that's groaning. "And not only this, but also we ourselves, having the first fruits of the Spirit, even we ourselves groan within ourselves, waiting eagerly for our adoption as sons, the redemption of our body" (Romans 8:23).

Why do we have to go through the pains of life? Because we have been affected by the sin that has cursed our environment and cursed us as well. So we groan when our bodies don't work the way they should. We groan when our families don't turn out like they should. We groan at our own sin and failure.

Paul groaned when he cried out, "Wretched man that I am! Who will set me free from the body of this death?" (Romans 7:24). One reason God allows His children to experience pain at death is to cause them to want to leave earth and enter eternity (8:24–25). God wants us to desire heaven more than earth, eternity more than time. So He permits us to groan.

Creation groans, the people of God groan, and the Holy Spirit groans. What's the connection? Creation groans to be relieved from the curse of sin. We groan because of sin's effects upon us. The Spirit groans in prayer in order to identify with our groanings, deliver them to God, and deliver to us from God what we need to be sustained in a world that produces pain.

In other words, the Holy Spirit identifies with our pain, clarifies that pain, and communicates it to the Father in a way we could never do ourselves. Then the Spirit brings out of that pain the will of God for us, "because He intercedes for the saints according to the will of God" (Romans 8:27b).

So the greater the groans, the closer we are to some kind of divine intervention and deliverance, either in time or eternity, or both. When we are experiencing the pains of life that produce groaning that cannot be uttered, that means God is sending something down the life canal. It's time to keep our eyes open for the new life and victory God is about to deliver.

### Linking Up in Prayer

Now what does this say about prayer? The Holy Spirit only links with your prayer when it is tied to your heart, when it is tied to that which groans. If you just say a prayer because it's bedtime or mealtime, if your prayers never get deep enough to enter Spirit territory, you aren't experiencing the Holy Spirit's intercession.

That's why you can say nothing and be engaged in intense prayer, or say something and not really be praying at all. You can say, "Now I lay me down to sleep," or "Thank You, Lord, for this food I am about to receive," without anything happening to you internally. The Spirit resonates with your groans. He doesn't just groan with your words.

Prayer has to come from within to be valid. Prayer is not valid just because words fall from our lips. The Lord said of Israel, "This people draw near with their words and honor Me with their lip service, but they remove their hearts far from Me" (Isaiah 29:13). Prayer must be rooted in who you are inside.

See, if God did not allow us to groan, we would never pray. We might say prayer words, but we would never pray from within.

One of the purposes of pain is to draw us to God. You appreciate the sun a lot more after a day of bad weather. When every day is good, you assume every day is supposed to be good and you take things for granted.

God is the most taken-for-granted Person in the universe. That's not the way it is supposed to be, so to keep us from becoming complacent or self-sufficient, God allows us to groan under the weight of our sin and weaknesses. Then we're ready to seek His face.

Before we turn to our last point, let me make an observation about intercession. We saw at the beginning of the chapter that it means to approach or appeal to some-one on behalf of another. And we learned that the Spirit's intercession means He communicates what is coming from our hearts. That's so important because in our weakness we don't even know how to pray at times.

Now for us to reach this level of intensity in prayer, two things need to be included in our prayer lives that very few of us use regularly. I'm talking about the Word of God and the discipline of meditation.

See, when you groan about something, you are think-ing about it. You are feeling it. It's experiential. Your mind is in gear. Some of us can pray and keep our minds in neutral because we just say the same thing over and over again. That's not what God wants. He wants to hear from us from deep down within so that the Holy Spirit can take those desires and do something with them.

But for that to happen, there must first be the regular intake of God's Word. If you are not praying based on God's Word, then you are praying out of His will. The only way you can pray biblically is to immerse yourself in the Bible. God must speak to you before you are ready to speak with Him.

Once you have taken in the Scripture, meditation needs to begin. This is the process of thinking something through, musing on it, simmering it the way a good cook simmers a dish until the flavor penetrates all the way through.

If you skip meditation, you are just blurting out words to God. David said, "I remember Thee on my bed, I medi-tate on Thee in the night watches" (Psalm 63:6). To medi-tate is to think deeply about who God is and where you are and what you need Him to do. God does not want us trying to communicate with Him without any thought of Him. To include God in your thoughts is part of the groan-ing process.

## THE RESULTS OF THE
## SPIRIT'S INTERCESSION

Did you notice where we have arrived in our study of Romans 8? We're at verse 28: "And we know that God causes all things to work together for good to those who love God, to those who are called according to His purpose."

You say, "Tony, I didn't realize Romans 8:28 is set in the context of the Holy Spirit's intercession." Believe it. You can't get to verse 28 without going through verses 26–27. In fact, notice that this verse begins with a conjunction: "And." Verse 28 is very closely connected with verse 27.

### The Divine Blueprint

What does this mean? Well, it means that the people on whose behalf God is working all things together for good are the same people on whose behalf the Holy Spirit is interceding according to God's will. And these are the same people whose prayers the Spirit interprets with deep groanings (v. 26) as He prays according to God's will. The net result is bringing us into the experience of God's will.

So the Spirit is interpreting, redirecting, and reshaping our groanings in light of God's plan. He's following the divine blueprint, not just haphazardly bringing our requests before God. So you only get the Spirit's help when you are on God's program. You only get to enjoy what God is doing when God is free through the Spirit to take what you express and align it with His plan.

When you look at your world, it may seem chaotic and confusing. But once the Holy Spirit lifts you above your circumstances, you can see how God is aligning everything for your good according to His will. It's the difference between driving through farm country and seeing it from an airplane. From up high, things look orderly.

What we as Christians need to do is take a flight. We need to allow the Spirit to take us to another level—the vantage point of God's will. He can take any mess of circumstances, blend them in His divine pots and pans, and come out with a nice meal. But you only get to experience and enjoy the meal if the Spirit is interceding for you with the Father. And He only does that if you're praying from the heart.

## Conformed to Christ

So if God's will is the plan by which He is ordering our lives, then what is God's ultimate will or purpose for us? Paul answers that in Romans 8:29. God wants us "to become conformed to the image of His Son, that He might be the firstborn among many brethren."

God's optimum goal is to conform us to the character of Christ, and God is so passionate about this that He will stop at nothing to achieve it. So He is always answering prayer according to His will (1 John 5:14). Many times we don't pray because we don't think anything is happening. But with God, something is always happening. He is always working.

You say, "But I don't see anything." Well, when you plant a seed in the ground, you don't come out the next day and complain, "I don't see the plant." Does that mean nothing is happening below the surface?

Of course not. Necessary things are happening so that you can see the plant when you are supposed to see it. Don't ever think nothing is happening just because you haven't seen it happen yet. It's just not harvest time. God is either moving to answer your request as you prayed it, or He is changing and reshaping the request to conform to His will.

## According to God's Will

Someone might object, "Wait a minute. If I had wanted something different, I would have asked for something different." If that's the way you view prayer, you need a review of Romans 8. Prayer works "according to the will of God" (v. 27). That's because we are called "according to His purpose" (v. 28) that we might be conformed to "the image of His Son" (v. 29).

God is not in the business of being anybody's Santa Claus. He is not up in heaven saying, "Oh, you asked for that, didn't you? Let Me run and get it." Or, "You want Me to do this? Let Me run and do it for you."

No, God only does what is in His will. So if what you are asking is God's will, the Spirit is interceding for it on your behalf, and God is doing something even though you haven't seen the answer yet. But if you are asking outside of God's will, the Spirit has to change your request because it is illegitimate. But to change your request, the Spirit has to change you, and sometimes that can make you groan.

So God is always doing something. He is either doing what you ask, or doing what He wants done by changing you so you will want what He wants. But there is no time when God is not doing something with regard to our prayers. It's like a puzzle. One piece of a puzzle by itself doesn't look like much, but plug it into the whole puzzle and you have a pretty picture.

### Being Devoted to Prayer

So what's the best way to experience the intercession of the Holy Spirit? Colossians 4:2 says, "Devote yourselves to prayer." That means it should be abnormal not to pray. Is that the way it is in your life? If you pray abnormally, don't be surprised if you hear from God abnormally. If you pray every now and then, you are going to hear from God every now and then. Paul says prayer should be so important that not to pray is the exception.

But we have it backwards, because prayer interrupts our regular schedule. It should be that *not* praying interrupts our schedule, but we basically view prayer as something that intrudes into our day. If we were to give prayer the importance God gives it, we would see prayer as our normal routine and the other stuff we do as interruptions to prayer.

### TWO EXAMPLES OF INTERCESSION

I want to close with two examples that continue to remind me of the power of intercessory prayer. They're not earth-shaking events, but they meant a lot to my family. The first happened one weekend as our older son worked at a Christian camp a couple of hours' drive away.

He called me and said, "Dad, we've got a problem." He was leading a group on a horseback ride when his keys fell out of his pocket on the trail. We're talking about hundreds and hundreds of acres here. "We're going out to look for them tomorrow."

I wasn't happy about this because it would either cost a hundred bucks for a locksmith to come and open the car, or it would require me to make a two-hour drive to the camp.

So my son and his friends got up the next morning to look for his keys, and he said, "Let's pray." They reminded God that He knew where those keys were, and they asked Him to show them where the keys were. Then they took off. Now what made it even harder was that the color of the pouch the keys were in was the same color as the leaves that had fallen to the ground.

But they started looking anyway, and before long my son said he felt impressed to go look in a certain spot. For some reason he didn't go check out that spot, but one of the friends he had prayed with did go over there. And as he was walking over the spot, he kicked the keys. Despite the huge area, despite the similarity in color between the key pouch and the leaves, they found the keys.

Now was that chance, or was it the Spirit of God groaning? I think I know why the Spirit answered that prayer. First, He heard my groanings. Then He heard my son's groanings about what was going to happen to him if he didn't find those keys! Seriously, this is an example of what happens when our groanings line up with the Spirit's groanings.

The second story is one I told my readers in an earlier book. It concerns a vacation our family took to the Grand Canyon some years ago. This one is indelibly imprinted on my mind.

I had forgotten to make reservations at the other end. If you've been to the Grand Canyon, you know there are only three hotels in the whole place. If you miss out on those, it's an hour to an hour and a half to the next hotel. So there we were at midnight with no reservation, and all the hotels were full.

I was frustrated and agitated. I had been driving all day. I didn't smell very sweet, and neither did the people who were with me. The family had been in the van for a long time, and it was not a very pleasant sight. And now we had to drive an hour and a half back the other way.

Well, we went back to one of the hotels where the clerk had told me they had already turned away twenty people that night. Our plan was to wash up in the rest room and try to get something to eat. We sat down and my daughter said, "Dad, we haven't prayed." Now I know I am a pastor, but I did not want to hear that at that moment.

So I said to my daughter, "You pray." I did not want to pray. I wanted something practical!

She prayed, "Lord, we know that You are in charge. We don't have a hotel room, but You can give us a hotel room. In Jesus' name. Amen." When she finished, I got back to the practical issue of who was going to drive all the way back that night.

I will never forget what happened next. As we were eating, the clerk came through the dining room. He stopped at our table, and he said, "Aren't you one of the families that was just looking for a room?"

I said, "Yes."

He said, "It's the oddest thing. A family just said they had an emergency and had to leave. None of the other twenty people who were here before you are anywhere to be found. Do you still want the room?"

I will never forget that incident because it was nothing short of the Holy Spirit hearing our groanings.

Let me ask you a question I often ask myself. With the third Person of the Trinity making Himself available to us as our Intercessor, why don't we pray more than we do? Why do we wait until we're in trouble to pray? Why don't we pray that God will keep us out of the messes we get into?

With the Holy Spirit there to interpret our deepest longings, we should be bringing everything to God in prayer. With the Spirit's intercession available to us twenty-four hours a day, we should be starting and continuing our day in prayer instead of cramming it in the last five minutes before bed.

You get the idea. What are your most heartfelt needs and requests? What are the things that keep you awake at night, the requests you would give anything to see God answer? Take them to Him in prayer. The Spirit will do a wonderful job of presenting them to the Father!

# EXPERIENCING THE SPIRIT'S INTERCESSION

**E**ven when we don't know what to say, we have a Helper who understands our groanings and will interpret them to the Father. We may be in a foreign realm when it comes to prayer, but we have a Guide who knows the language of the realm. Let's call on Him:

1. As is true for almost all the spiritual benefits God has for us, our sense of need determines how serious we will be about making the most of His blessings. That's true for intercession. The Spirit is ready to carry your deepest groanings to the Father, but you must engage Him in heartfelt prayer. How much do you long to experience the Holy Spirit's ministry of intercession on your behalf? That's how much you will experience it.

2. Take a close look at your prayer list. Any needs or situations there that seem beyond any hope of solution or supply? Those things are great candidates for intensive, Spirit-assisted prayer. Don't give up on the tough ones. It's just when you run out of answers and even words that the Spirit takes over.

3. Have you ever felt the pain of your sin and lack of conformity to Christ so deeply that your spirit groaned in its grief? You're on the right track, because if the Holy Spirit can bring you to feel about your sin the way He feels about your sin, He'll do some amazing things with you. Now don't get proud about your brokenness. Just ask the Spirit to keep you sensitive.

4. Do you really want God's will and Christ's image to be worked out in your life? Better make sure before you seek the Spirit's intercession, because these things are what He's after for you.

# CHAPTER FIFTEEN

# EXPERIENCING THE SPIRIT'S GUIDANCE

**W**hen you open a road map to plan the route of your vacation or some other trip, it quickly becomes obvious that there are multiple ways to get to your destination. The map shows all the possibilities because the mapmaker has access to the big picture. He knows all the major highways, state roads, farm roads, and side roads.

You may already know how to get where you're going, but a map reminds you that the route you know is only one of many possible routes. When you leave, you don't have the big picture in front of you unless you have a map.

The Christian life is like that. God is leading you from Point A to Point B, but He has the big picture in front of Him and He knows all the roads that can take you there. The problem is that you can't see the big picture, and more often than not, God doesn't issue detailed maps. So it's easy to get confused, even lost, when you're trying to get to Point B, because there are many ways to get there.

Being able to determine the Holy Spirit's leading as we navigate through life's choices and decisions is a challenge for all of us. Every sincere Christian wants to find God's will, to know that He is guiding in the decisions we make. So let's talk about how He guides us.

## SEEKING THE SPIRIT'S GUIDANCE

This matter of the Spirit's guidance is so important that people try a number of ways to discover it. Some look for miracles. They say, "God, if this is Your will, then do this miracle to let me know it's really You leading me." The problem here is that if the miracle does not happen, these people are left wondering if they missed God's will.

Some people resort to magic or luck. Judging from the growth of a palm reader's business near our church in Dallas, things are booming on that front. Other people who don't want to spend money for a palm reader just pick up the newspaper and read their horoscopes.

Still others are more pragmatic than that. They divide the sheet of paper in half, putting the pros for a decision on one side and the cons on the other. If the pros outweigh the cons, it's a go. If the cons outweigh the pros, it's a no-go. But many who choose the pros over the cons find out later they were conned when they made the decision.

Then there are those who count on their emotions. *How do I feel about it? Does it feel right?* The problem is that feelings are very fluid. You can feel good about it today and then tomorrow wonder why you ever did it. Sadly, for a lot of people, marriage is an example of that kind of decision. After the initial excitement is gone, they wonder, "Why did I do this?"

So the question is, How do I know when God is leading me? How do I determine the voice of God? Well, I would like to suggest that spiritual guidance occurs when there has been a wedding between the objective revelation of Scripture and the subjective witness of the Holy Spirit—the witness of the Holy Spirit to our individual human spirits.

This definition reflects my belief that there are two extremes in the Christian community today. To go to either extreme is to miss the truth of the Spirit's guidance.

One extreme says just to read the Word. Now don't misunderstand. It is certainly not extreme to read the Bible. But anybody who has ever read the Bible knows that it does not give all the specifics for your life. It does not say whether you should accept the job with IBM or Xerox. It does not say whether Bill or Butch or Mary or Martha is the one you should marry.

What the Word does is give you certain specifics and a multiplicity of principles. So if you have the objective Word without any subjective verification, you are left with a lot of questions.

The other extreme is to look for subjective verification without an objective revelation. Then you get people counting anything they do as from God because they feel good about doing it, regardless of what the Bible says. That becomes a faulty witness, like when your house alarm goes off and there is no burglar.

## THE SPIRIT AND THE WORD

There is no question that God wants to guide His people through the Holy Spirit. We already know from our study of 1 Corinthians 2 that the Holy Spirit searches the "depths" of God and reveals these things to us because the Spirit knows what God the Father wants (vv. 9–10).

The result of the Spirit's searching is that when there is no solution in sight, He reveals to the believer things that the eyes cannot see. He reveals solutions that the ears have not heard, and when you can't reason your way out of a situation, He unveils answers that have not entered into the heart of man. It is this revealing work of the Spirit to the believer that is experiential in nature.

### Objective and Subjective

The Spirit does this in a unique way, "combining spiritual thought with spiritual words" (1 Corinthians 2:13), which I believe refers to the objective and subjective combination that must happen for spiritual guidance to take place. When the Holy Spirit connects with the human spirit, there is an illumination to the mind concerning the plan of God. This is because "the spirit of man is the lamp of the Lord" (Proverbs 20:27). God uses the spirit to illuminate His will to the believer.

It is possible for us to be so Bible-centered that we miss the Spirit. Don't get me wrong: God expects His people to be Bible-centered. The Bible is the final authority to govern the church. But if your Bible-centeredness has not led you into a spiritual sensitivity, then the Bible will be to you as words on a page with little meaning for the heart. God is after your heart. The role of the Spirit is to lead His children into the will of God.

Notice how the Spirit and the Word are blended together in another familiar passage, John 14:16–17. Even though we quoted this passage in an earlier chapter, it's important enough to give it again here:

> I will ask the Father, and He will give you another Helper, that He may be with you forever; that is the Spirit of truth, whom the world cannot receive, because it does not behold Him or know Him, but you know Him because He abides with you, and will be in you.

Here Jesus promises that the Holy Spirit will take up the leadership role Jesus had among His followers when He was on earth. Then in John 16:13, Jesus says that the Spirit's role will be to guide the believer in the light of God's truth to accomplish God's will.

That means something real important. That is, the Holy Spirit does not come up with independent ideas. He does not speak on His own. He is telling you what God wants. So the only way the Spirit of God is ever going to lead you anywhere is if you are willing to do the will of God.

Now if you go to the Holy Spirit and say, "Show me the way," but there is a question mark about whether you are going to go in the way He shows you, you can be assured that He will not guide you. The Spirit is not going to reveal God's will to you so you can debate whether you want to obey it.

Therefore, there must be a predisposition in your mind to obey the will of God once it has been revealed. If that is not there, then you are not a candidate to be guided by the Spirit, even though He is ready to be your Guide.

If you go on a guided tour and then decide you want to do your own thing, you are going to be in conflict with the guide. The guide is there to lead you on his tour, not to help you do your own tour. If you want the guidance of the Holy Spirit, you must be willing to go where the Holy Spirit is taking you.

## God Does Speak

The Bible is clear that God speaks to His people. As we have just seen, He speaks objectively through the Word and subjectively through the Spirit. Consider once more the experience of Peter in Acts 10:10–16. He had a dream, but the dream was not talking to him; the Spirit was. An experience means nothing unless there is spiritual instruction. Peter had a dream, but he heard the voice of God.

We also mentioned Acts 16:6–10 in the previous chapter, where the Spirit forbade Paul and Barnabas to go into Asia. Here was an action of the Holy Spirit, who speaks to the whole church.

Now many evangelicals tend to dismiss these examples. "Well, that was unique to the book of Acts. The Spirit talked to them because it was an unusual time. It was start-up time for the church. The church needed to hear the voice of God."

But that does not hold up, because in the book of Revelation, the risen Jesus says repeatedly, "He who has an ear, let him hear what the Spirit says to the churches" (2:7, 11, 17). But He means more than just reading the text, because the problem was the churches were not hearing what the Spirit was saying, even though they were reading the text.

It is possible to read the Bible and not hear the voice of the Spirit. I think this is why Paul says that when you pray, you ought to "pray at all times in the Spirit" (Ephesians 6:18). If we're not careful, we can pray words with no spiritual reality behind them.

So God speaks to His people. He speaks objectively, which means this is what God expects no matter what you feel or think about it, and whether you have a subjective witness or not. If it is in the Word of God, it is automatically of the Spirit. God also speaks subjectively to us through the Holy Spirit's witness within.

## HOW THE SPIRIT GUIDES

That leads to a very important question. How does the Holy Spirit guide us? How do I know when I am hearing His voice guiding me? See, this is important once you get outside of Scripture, because guidance is not automatic in that case.

So assuming that I am not looking to violate the clear precepts and principles of Scripture, how do I know when I am hearing the guiding voice of the Holy Spirit? Well, I believe the Bible tells us in Romans 8.

### The Spirit's Witness

In Romans 8:14, Paul says, "For all who are being led by the Spirit of God, these are sons of God." What does the Spirit do? He leads God's children.

Now look at verse 16: "The Spirit Himself bears witness with our spirit that we are children of God." If you have the assurance that you are saved, it's because you have heard the voice of the Spirit. If you just think you are saved or hope you are saved, that is not good enough. I want to know that I know that I am saved, and God wants me to know it too (1 John 5:13). The way a person knows, Paul says, is by the witness of the Spirit.

So if you know what it is like to receive the assurance that you are saved, then you know what it is like to hear the Holy Spirit. If you have never had that experience, it could be you are not saved or that the scar tissue of your soul is blocking the voice of the Spirit.

The witness of the Spirit is the inner confirmation in your spirit of His direction. One way you know you are experiencing the Spirit's guidance is that He confirms to your human spirit that you are doing the will of God.

What is true of your salvation is also true of Holy Spirit guidance in other areas of life. If you are not building up and feeding your soul, then you have no way to hear the Spirit's voice. You will have to count on your body to lead you. You know you're in trouble when that happens.

Now if you live your life body first, then you are going to focus on satisfying physical appetites. This is the reason so many Christians never get to hear the Spirit's voice. When it comes to spiritual guidance, the body is the least important part of our makeup. It is just the vehicle that is going to take you to the will of God, not reveal to you the will of God.

Why is the body of least importance? Because it is the one part of us that will not make the trip to heaven. God is so disgusted with the effect of sin on these bodies that He is going to discard them and give all of us brand-new ones.

So if you live from the outside in, body first, your focus is going to be off. But if you live your life spirit first, then you are going to focus on what 1 Peter 3:4 calls "the hidden person of the heart."

### Access to Your Spirit

This means if you want to hear the Spirit's voice, He has to have access to your spirit. If there is no spiritual development in your spirit, there will be no understanding in your soul. And if there is no understanding in your soul, there will be no direction for your body. If you are not hearing anything in your spirit, your body does not know which way to go because your soul does not know which way to think.

Just as a parent gives a child his nature, so God has given you His nature. You are a new creation in Christ. You are brand-new in your spirit, and you are a temple of the Holy Spirit. So when He guides you, what He does through your human spirit is stamp on your soul an uncompromising confidence that this is what God wants you to do.

When you have that Spirit confidence, you don't care what the circumstances are. You don't care how many people say you can't do it. You don't care how many people say it has never been done before. When the Spirit has spoken to you, you have that inner confidence that you are in God's will.

That's why, if you have a problem in your life that you want God to lead you out of, yet you don't connect with the Spirit, you are no different from nonbelievers. A nonbeliever can get better by learning to think differently or by taking a twelve-step program. But he cannot hear the voice of God. He cannot get spiritual direction, because he doesn't have God's Holy Spirit directing his human spirit.

Have you ever answered the phone when the TV is on loud and the kids are making a lot of noise? You say, "Be quiet in there! I am trying to talk on the phone and I can't hear." That's not because the person on the other line is not talking. The reason you can't hear is that your environment has a dominating influence over you. The Holy Spirit has been trying to talk to some of us for years, but we keep hanging out in this loud room where we are continually distracted by the external. We are no longer able to hear the voice of God internally.

When the Holy Spirit takes up His residence within you (1 Corinthians 3:16; 6:19), He does His talking inside of you, in your spirit, either confirming or convincing or convicting. He gives you a tenacious assurance of God's will for you. He tells you what God wants.

In Romans 9:1, Paul says, "I am telling the truth in Christ, I am not lying, my conscience bearing me witness in the Holy Spirit." Here we see Paul's subjective confirmation of the truth because the conscience is internal. His conscience now having been sanctified by the Holy Spirit, Paul was convinced he was speaking truth because He had that inner confirmation.

That is why you don't try to force other believers to conform to your standards (Romans 14:1–13). The Holy

Spirit may be telling them something different in their spirits than He is telling you. This is a very freeing thing. As long as we are both within the boundaries of Scripture, don't try to make what the Holy Ghost is telling you work for me, because God leads people differently.

We must give people the right to hear the voice of God for themselves in the application of the truth of Scripture to their personal context. Thus Paul can write, "Let each man be fully convinced in his own mind" (Romans 14:5).

### Trying to Disconnect You

Satan does not want your spirit to get connected with the Holy Spirit. Why? Because he can handle your body. He'll let you have all the New Year's resolutions you want. And to some degree he has already messed up your soul.

But Satan knows that he can't mess with your spirit. That's out of his realm because you have been made brand-new in your spirit. So Satan tries to cut off your communication with the Holy Spirit. He tries to distract you so you won't hear the guiding voice of the Spirit.

### Applying the Word

So how does the Spirit lead us? Objectively, by the Word of God. If the Word has spoken, you don't have to listen to your spirit for a different message. The Holy Spirit will never contradict the Word He inspired (2 Peter 1:20–21). The only thing your human spirit will tell you once you hear the Word is how to implement God's truth in your life.

But He also leads us subjectively in the application of the Word. Have you ever heard someone say, "God gave me a verse"? That person finds an application of the verse to his life even though the verse itself may have been written about Moses or Abraham or someone else.

How does this Christian know that this verse can be applied this way in his life, when another Christian who is in the same situation may not be led to that verse? I believe the answer is the internal witness of the Spirit. He applies different verses to different Christians in different ways at different times.

If you sit down with the Bible without the influence of the Spirit, you won't truly grasp the meaning of the passage or how to apply the specific biblical text to your life. So the Spirit leads us by His objective revelation and His subjective confirmation. If we can get those two concepts down, we can begin to experience the Spirit's guidance in the practical decisions of life so that we accomplish God's will for us.

## THE GOAL OF THE SPIRIT'S GUIDANCE

The overarching goal of the Holy Spirit's guidance is to help us discover and do the will of God. To help us better understand God's will, let me give you what I call the three tiers of the will of God.

The first tier is God's sovereign will. This is the will by which God mysteriously and majestically manages all the details of the universe. I say mysteriously because we have no absolute knowledge of much of God's sovereign will as it unfolds in history.

We don't always know why He allows the events of time and eternity to unfold as they do. Deuteronomy 29:29 says, "The secret things belong to the Lord our God." Paul writes that God's ways are "past finding out" (Romans 11:33 KJV).

God's sovereign will often leaves us asking why with no answer, because He "works all things after the counsel of His will" (Ephesians 1:11). He does not feel the need to explain all His actions to us, just as parents do not try to explain all their actions to their children. As Sovereign of the universe, God takes that prerogative.

God also has a moral will, which He has clearly revealed to us. God's moral will is the Scripture. Scripture gives us the specifics out of God's sovereign will that He definitely wants us to know.

You may guess about God's sovereign will, but there is no guessing about His moral will because it has been written down. That's why the Bible says do this, don't do that, go here, don't go there, and so on. God's moral will is clearly recorded in His Word.

The third tier of God's will is His individual will for each of His children. This is where the problem comes because it involves what God wants us to do in a particular situation, decision, relationship, career choice, etc. Since God's sovereign will is often hidden and the Bible doesn't tell us which job to take or where to live or which person to marry, we need His individual guidance.

That is where our experience of the Spirit of God comes in. He works from the inside out. Jesus promised in John 7:37–39 that there would come out of our innermost being a well of water. John says, "This He spoke of the Spirit" (v. 39).

Jesus was saying that you would have a reservoir called the Holy Spirit inside your human spirit. When you hear the voice of the Spirit in your human spirit, and that is transferred to your soul (intellect, emotion, and will) so it can be executed by your body, then you begin to live out the will of God.

To experience the Spirit's guidance, you must be committed to all three tiers of God's will. That is, you must say, "Lord, not my will, but Thine be done, because You are sovereign. I will search the Scriptures to know the parts of Your will that You have revealed to me. But I am also going to depend on You for guidance in my individual choices in life."

The reason you must ultimately trust the sovereign will of God is that you don't see all the facts. You never get all the details. It's like the man who was stuck behind a big truck on a two-lane highway and wanted to get around it.

But every time he came out into the other lane to see if he could pass the truck, a car was coming the other way. He would have to dart back into his lane. Then he would try it again, only to meet another oncoming car and have to swerve back into his lane.

As he was going through this futile process, a helicopter flew over and something dawned on him. "If I could only see what the pilot of that helicopter can see," he said to himself, "I wouldn't have to guess when to pass. I would be able to see the whole highway."

When we make decisions, we are like the man in that car. We can't see down the road very far. We can't see around the next curve to know whether another car is heading our way. But the Holy Spirit is in the helicopter. He sees the whole road.

So when you make a decision and He blocks it, as happened to Paul in Acts 16, you have to trust that He sees something in the road ahead that you can't see. God's sovereign will must superintend your individual choices.

## THE CHANNELS OF
## THE SPIRIT'S GUIDANCE

Now let me show you how the Holy Spirit intertwines these three aspects or tiers of God's will as He communicates with our spirits and gives us spiritual guidance.

### Through the Word

First, the Spirit guides us through the Scriptures by clarifying and communicating to us God's moral will. The Bible is sufficient because it gives all believers everywhere the underlying principles God wants them to predicate their decisions on. So don't tell me the Spirit has ever led you to do anything that contradicts the Word of God.

A believer once tried that on me. This person was getting ready to marry a non-Christian, a clear violation of Scripture. But this particular believer tried to argue that this case was an exception. "The Holy Spirit told me I was to marry this person."

No, the Spirit didn't say that. He has never told anybody to go against God's plainly revealed moral will, which says, "Do not be bound together with unbelievers" (2 Corinthians 6:14).

So God's moral will is clear, but in some cases God's moral will is also flexible. Here's what I mean. In 1 Corinthians 10, Paul is advising the believers about what to do if an unbeliever invites them over for dinner:

If one of the unbelievers invites you, and you wish to go, eat anything that is set before you, without asking questions for conscience' sake. But if anyone should say to you, "This is meat sacrificed to idols," do not eat it, for the sake of the one who informed you, and for conscience' sake. (vv. 27–28)

Paul says if somebody invites you to a dinner party and you want to go, feel free to go. It's up to you. But if an issue comes up that may hurt another believer or wound your own conscience, then back off. Not hurting another brother or wounding your own conscience is more important than your freedom.

The principle here is, when you are operating in God's moral will, He gives you a lot of room for preferences in His individual will for you based on your personal desires. Paul says go to the party if you want to go. God's will in that case is that you choose. Paul even tells the Christian widow who is contemplating marriage to marry whomever she wants, "only in the Lord" (1 Corinthians 7:39).

God's moral will gives the parameters. As long as you are within those parameters, He gives you a degree of freedom in your choices. So you don't have to get up tomorrow morning and say, "Lord, do You want me to wear the blue suit or the green suit today?" When you go to buy a car, and you're looking at two possible purchases that are equal in cost and don't overextend your budget, I don't think you have to agonize in prayer over whether you should buy the Honda or the Toyota.

When you are functioning within the context of God's moral will, you don't have to worry about whether you are within His sovereign will. God is concerned that we are in His sovereign will, but He has not revealed every detail of His sovereign will in His moral will. He has given us precepts and principles to guide us. So your first concern should be that you are operating within the context of His moral will.

### Through the Inner Witness

Now there are times within the moral will of God that our general choices do matter. In other words, it does not matter whether I wear the blue suit or the green suit tomorrow. But it matters very much whether I choose to take a loved one off life support. It matters whether I submit to a risky operation or try to live with my condition or illness as it is.

Decisions such as these are far different from choosing my suit for the day or deciding which color car to buy. There are decisions in your individual will that are not covered by God's moral will. For these, you need the Holy Spirit's more specific guidance. Some decisions are easy. But others demand the leading of the Spirit—especially when there are kingdom implications involved.

Many Christians differ at this point. Some hold that as long as we are operating within God's moral will, we have total freedom in our decisions. But others argue that the Spirit gives specific directives to believers that go beyond what is recorded in Scripture.

My contention is that one of the Spirit's major roles is to provide us with specific guidance in the details of life. The reason we don't always think about it is that we are much more conscious of, and more concerned about, some details than others.

Here's an example of what I mean. You may go to buy a new car without worrying about the Spirit's guidance, figuring God doesn't care which brand of car you buy. But if your new car were to explode just after you left the dealership and you were injured, you would suddenly be very concerned about that detail of life. Why? Because you would be wondering why God allowed you to purchase that particular car knowing it was defective and you were going to be hurt.

In other words, the explosion changed the significance of that detail in terms of whether it was worth asking the Spirit for guidance. It seems fruitless to ask the Spirit for guidance and then not expect it even in life's details.

The real question is how the Spirit's guidance comes. Those who reject individual guidance say you cannot equate impressions and hunches with the Spirit's voice. They argue that much that goes under the heading of spiritual guidance ("The Lord led me to . . .") is badly mis-guided and dangerous mysticism.

However, we don't need to throw the baby out with the bath water. I believe we experience the Spirit's guid-ance when there is a compelling inner conviction about a decision that is within the scope of God's moral will, be that decision large or small. The Spirit is guiding when my heart is gripped and stirred to make a certain decision or move in a particular direction. It is just that Christians differ in the degree to which they require or desire the Spirit's guidance, based on the value they place on the decision.

Even in the Old Testament, we see God guiding His people through the Spirit's work of stirring their hearts as well as through His objective revelation. In the building of the tabernacle, God filled Bezalel and Oholiab with His Spirit so that they might oversee the construction process (Exodus 31:1–6; 35:30–31; 36:1).

With God's objective command came the Spirit's presence, which produced the subjective stirring of the heart which, in turn, validated both the will and the empowering of God. This was true not just for these two men, but for the rest of the people too (Exodus 35:21–22, 26, 29; 36:1–2).

God also stirred the human spirit of King Cyrus and the Jews to build the temple, in keeping with the revela-tion He had given through the prophets (Ezra 1:1, 5; Hag-gai 1:14). In these cases God's objective revelation worked in concert with the Holy Spirit's subjective activity in the human spirit to bring people into conformity with His will.

It is this same experiential work of the Spirit that Paul speaks about for the church when he tells the Corin-thians that they are living letters, having been trans-formed by the Holy Spirit on the inside (2 Corinthians 3:1–3).

I am not in the ministry today simply because I chose this career path out of ten different options. I didn't look over the choices and say, "The ministry looks good. I think I'll try it." No, I am in the ministry today because I was called. I was called by a compelling, inner conviction I could not shake, the witness of the Spirit within my spirit.

Now there is no verse that says, "Tony Evans, go into the ministry." But one day I was reading Paul the apostle's testimony of his obligation to proclaim the gospel of the Lord Jesus Christ (Romans 1:13–16). Those words jumped off the page and gripped my spirit. Paul's words became my words because the Spirit of God applied a moral principle to my personal decision.

If the Holy Spirit does not provide a specific inner conviction or stirring of the heart regarding a matter, then He can speak through your personal preference. Sometimes He speaks louder than at other times. The greater the kingdom implications of the decision, the louder He speaks—which is why He is screaming in the book of Acts.

So I agree that we must be careful of excesses, mystical extremes, and false theologies that make Scripture the servant of personal feelings, inner voices, visions, and dreams. But I also believe we must avoid the other extreme of being so pedantic that people can recite biblical facts with little or no life-pulsating experience of the Holy Spirit.

Another reason you need the Word of God is that it is the only thing that can distinguish between what is coming from you and what is coming from God. Have you ever asked, "Lord, is this You talking to me, or this me talking to me?"

That's why Hebrews 4:12 is so vital. As I said in an earlier chapter, the Word can split the "unsplittable" soul and spirit. It can clarify what is coming from your humanness, which is the soul, and what is coming from God, which is the Holy Spirit. That's why you want to muse and meditate on Scripture so the Spirit can clarify it to you.

Since God's Word can separate soul from spirit, if you are confused about which way you ought to go on an issue that demands specific guidance, you want the Word. Perhaps you have been in church when the Word was preached, and it separated soul and spirit. You came in not knowing what you should do. You left saying, "Now I know what to do."

What happened was that the Spirit of God grabbed your human spirit and told your soul, "This is the way we are going." The Spirit can use the Word to do that. That's why you don't want to spend all your time listening to the world, because the world will tell the soul to boss the spirit. You want the spirit to boss the soul.

You say, "Well, I don't experience that kind of Spirit guidance." It's not God's fault. Remember, you have the anointing (1 John 2:20, 27), the teaching and illuminating ministry of the Holy Spirit.

We have already discussed illumination, but since the various ministries of the Spirit overlap and blend together in actual experience, I want you to see that the Spirit's illumination can provide His guidance. This is really what happened to me when I read Paul's words about the sense of compulsion he had to preach the gospel.

As I read that text, something in my heart said, "Bing! That's it, that's it!" It was the Holy Spirit turning on the light in my heart.

I remember trying to explain the gospel to a man one day. He heard me. He could repeat back what I was saying, but it wasn't connecting. I knew he was interested, however, so we went over it again. Still no response.

But about the fourth time we went over the gospel, the light came on. He did not have to say a word. I saw it on his face. The Spirit witnessed to his heart, and now he was ready to receive the gospel. And what the Holy Spirit did to all of us when we were converted He continues to do. He keeps turning the light on. This is why you want to meditate on the Word until the light comes on, until there is that unshakable inner conviction that the Holy Spirit is speaking to you.

### Through Prayer

The Holy Spirit also guides us through prayer. I believe many Christians think prayer is a waste of time. Now you don't want to tell anybody that, because it will make you look bad. But I know that many of God's people think prayer is a waste of time.

How do I know that? Because they don't pray. They say, "I prayed for a while, and nothing happened," so they give up. But James 1:5 reminds us, "If any of you lacks wisdom, let him ask of God, who gives to all men generously and without reproach, and it will be given to him."

That's a pretty awesome promise. God promises to give us wisdom, which is skill in living, if we will ask Him for it. Wisdom is basically the ability to make right choices, so it has to do with guidance. James says we must ask God for it.

You see, many of us don't experience the Spirit's guidance because we never get around to praying. If prayer is low on your spiritual program, if you are too busy to pray, then I can guarantee you that you will know little of the guidance of the Holy Spirit.

I applied this principle as I was preparing this manuscript. I prayed, "Lord, I need to make this principle clear. I need wisdom to explain this. Help me." As I was sitting there praying in dependence on the Holy Spirit and looking around the room, the light came on as I noticed the antenna on the little television that sits in the kitchen. "Bing! That's it, that's it!"

You see, that little television is not hooked up to the cable outside. It has rabbit ears for reception. So when you turn it on, there is often a lot of static. There is a picture and there are words, but you can't get the message clearly. It's not coming through.

It doesn't matter how much I mess with the cable outside. It's not going to help clarify the picture on this television, because it isn't hooked up to the cable. The issue is what is happening inside this set. When I move the antenna to just the right spot, everything is clarified.

Do you see where I'm going with this? Prayer is your antenna to God. When you get on God's wavelength, He clarifies the picture. You say, "But I have not seen Him do anything yet."

That's because you are looking for what He is doing outside, rather than what He is saying inside. What God does in prayer is remove the static from the line so He can clarify what He is telling you in your heart. Then you can see the picture clearly.

To put it another way, the Spirit begins to conform your thinking and desires to God's will. Paul calls this the renewing of the mind (Romans 12:2). We are often looking for God to do something externally when He is actually working within us, stirring us to move in a certain direction. This stirring is the experience of the Spirit's guidance.

If you have been praying and yet God is silent, let me give you some good news. Whenever God is silent over an extended period of time, it is generally because He has a big one coming through the pipe.

You can see an example of this in John 11. Martha was upset because Jesus stayed away while her brother Lazarus got worse and worse and finally died. Martha was saying to Jesus, "How could You stay away so long when You knew that Lazarus was sick?" Well, Jesus had good news for Martha. Because He is "the resurrection and the life" (v. 25), Lazarus came alive again that day even though he was dead. Jesus was silent because He had a big one coming through the pipe. Maybe you have not heard from God for the same reason.

## Through Circumstances

The Holy Spirit also guides through circumstances— but let me clarify something. Circumstances are to *confirm* the Spirit's inner witness, not *determine* it.

Here is where a lot of Christians get off track. They say, "This door opened, so it must be the will of God." Well, sometimes doors close in the will of God. That's why spiritual guidance must always start from the inside out. If you are not starting with the Spirit and moving out through the body, you are often going to misinterpret the message of outward circumstances.

See, we generally label only our good experiences as the will of God. If something negative happens, that can't be His will. But when a person has the inner witness of the Spirit, it doesn't matter how negative the circumstances are.

If it were not for the inner witness and unshakable conviction of the Spirit that I was called to the ministry of Oak Cliff Bible Fellowship, I would not be the pastor there now. I would have quit a long time ago. There were some rough times during those first years, some real headaches.

More than once Lois and I said, "We don't have to take this." Circumstances said it was time to go. But I could not let the negative circumstances overrule the inner witness. I could not make my decision from the outside in, but from the inside out. Circumstances only validate and confirm the witness.

Moses ran into this problem of circumstances. After he went to Pharaoh with God's message, Pharaoh responded by making it harder on the Israelites. So Moses said to God, "O Lord, why hast Thou brought harm to this people? Why didst Thou ever send me? Ever since I came to Pharaoh to speak in Thy name, he has done harm to this people; and Thou hast not delivered Thy people at all" (Exodus 5:22–23).

Have you ever felt like that? You feel that God has told you to do something, yet everything that happens seems to fight against the very thing He told you to do. In Exodus 6:12, Moses goes on to complain that no one is listening to him. He is saying, "Lord, what in the world is going on here?"

By now, if Moses had been listening to his circumstances, he would have quit. But he hung in there, and God answered in a mighty way:

> Then the Lord said to Moses, "See, I make you as God to Pharaoh, and your brother Aaron shall be your prophet. You shall speak all that I command you, and your brother Aaron shall speak to Pharaoh that he let the sons of Israel go out of his land. But I will harden Pharaoh's heart that I may multiply My signs and My wonders in the land of Egypt. When Pharaoh will not listen to you, then I will lay My hand on Egypt, and bring out My hosts, My people the sons of Israel, from the land of Egypt by great judgments. And the Egyptians shall know that I am the Lord, when I stretch out my hand on Egypt and bring out the sons of Israel from their midst." (Exodus 7:1–5)

God was telling Moses, "I have to make the circumstances negative in order to come out with My will in the end. When I get through with this deal, Moses, everybody is going to know that I am God. Pharaoh is going to know that I am God. Pharaoh's horses are going to know that I am God. Israel is going to know that I am God. Moses, stick with what I told you. Don't let the circumstances take you in the other direction."

### Through the Church

The Holy Spirit also guides through the church. That is why He made you part of a body that is vitally interconnected. If you are not a dynamic member of a Bible-believing church, you will miss a large element of the Spirit's guidance. One of the things God uses to guide us is the other members of the body. You will not be guided properly if you are not plugged into the body of Christ through a local fellowship.

The great church council of Acts 15 is a classic example of the Spirit revealing His will to the church as a body. We have already looked at this passage in some detail, so I won't go over it again except to remind you how often you read the phrase "it seemed good" to someone (vv. 22, 25, 28, 34).

God brings people into your life who love the Lord and whose spirit witnesses with your spirit. That's why a church needs to seek unity and move with one accord.

Our church elder board wrestled with whether we should build the sanctuary or the Christian education building first. We had all kinds of different ideas and held meeting after meeting. Yet we could not resolve the issue until one day, a few months later, it just "seemed good" to all of us to build the sanctuary first. It all fell together. We were of one accord.

Well, when things seem good and the witness is validated by other believers, that is the work of the Holy Spirit, according to verse 28 of Acts 15.

## GETTING READY TO HEAR THE SPIRIT

That leads to one final question. What must you do to position yourself to experience the Holy Spirit's guidance? Let me sum it up by pointing you to Acts 13:1–2. While these prophets and teachers were "ministering to the Lord," the Holy Spirit spoke a word of clear guidance (v. 2). He speaks most clearly when you are ministering to the Lord.

What do I mean by that? The more intimate your relationship with Christ, the clearer you will hear the voice of the Spirit. If you have only a Sunday relationship with Christ, don't expect to hear the Spirit on Monday. But if you have a daily relationship with Christ, you have an ongoing experience of the Spirit's guidance. You can't be an Easter Christian. You can't just cry out to God in a crisis. Intimacy with Christ is the key. Hebrews 1:1 tells us that the God who spoke at various times and in various ways to guide His people has now spoken to us through His Son. In other words, the Holy Spirit guides us through our relationship with Jesus Christ and His Word. "If you abide in Me, and My words abide in you, ask whatever you wish, and it shall be done for you," Jesus said (John 15:7).

Why? Because you have a relationship with Him. Therefore, you can hear the voice of the Holy Spirit. How do you get yourself ready for the Spirit's guidance? First Thessalonians 5:16–22 sums it up clearly. Look at the imperatives: "Rejoice always" (v. 16); "Pray without ceasing" (v. 17); "In everything give thanks" (v. 18); "Do not quench the Spirit" (v. 19); "Do not despise prophetic utterances" (v. 20); "Abstain from every form of evil" (v. 22).

When you do that, what's the result? You become sanctified from the inside out: spirit, soul, and body (v. 23). When you commit yourself wholly to the Lord, you get the inner conviction of the Spirit. When you hear that conviction, don't change because the going gets tough. God may promise you something now but may not deliver it until years from now.

Why? He wants you to know early so He can prepare you for it when it comes. God told Abraham he was going to have a son many years before Isaac arrived. Noah knew a storm was coming 120 years before a drop of rain ever fell. God wanted Noah to live his life in light of His word, so that when the flood came Noah would be ready for it.

When we live in intimacy with Christ, we experience the Holy Spirit's power and guidance. I think of Paul and Silas locked in a Philippian jail at midnight (Acts 16). Their circumstances were bad, but what did they do? They didn't complain or question God. They began having a worship service in prison. Paul struck up a hymn. They entered into praise and adoration. They entered into worship.

All of a sudden, the Spirit of God sent an earthquake (v. 26). The cell started to shake. The doors flew open. Paul and Silas even led the jailer and his family to the Lord. They were ministering to the Lord, which put them in a great position to hear from the Spirit. We can experience that same power as we minister to the Lord.

# EXPERIENCING THE SPIRIT'S GUIDANCE

I hope this chapter has helped to take some of the confusion out of the subject of the Holy Spirit's guidance. The bottom line is this: The Spirit does guide God's people, so if you are a child of God, you are a candidate for the Spirit's guidance. For a lot of us, the problem is removing the obstacles that keep us from hearing the Spirit's voice. Here are a few "obstacle removers" that may help you:

1. Even though people love to look for mysterious signs and happenings and all of that for spiritual guidance, it's amazing how often our study of this subject keeps bringing us back to the Bible. Are you soaking your spirit in the Scriptures? If not, don't expect God to write you a message in the clouds. Get in the Word, and you'll be in touch with the Holy Spirit.

2. Circumstances will always be a struggle for us because they are always there and always highly visible. That's why it is so important that you understand the *confirming*, not the *determining*, nature of circumstances. Are you up against something that seems to go against what God wants you to do? Before you turn around and head the other way, devote some special time in prayer to this thing. Ask God to show you specifically how to handle your problem.

3. If prayer is your "antenna" to tune you in to the guiding voice of God through the Holy Spirit, guess what you should be doing a lot of? Now I know this isn't the first time you've been admonished to pray. But I'm thinking particularly of an almost lost art in prayer: the discipline of listening. Next time you pray, try beginning with total, focused silence. It may help to open your Bible and let your mind muse on Scripture as you seek the face of God.

4. That formula I gave you from 1 Thessalonians 5 isn't just for special occasions or for "super saints." It's the will of God for your life, no matter what your circumstances. Take your spiritual temperature today by asking yourself how well you're doing in these disciplines of the spirit: rejoicing, persistence in prayer, giving thanks, not quenching the Spirit, a willingness to hear God's Word, and keeping yourself from evil.

# CHAPTER SIXTEEN

# EXPERIENCING THE SPIRIT'S GIFTS

**W**e can't talk long about the ministry of the Holy Spirit without coming to the subject of this chapter. Now if it were just a matter of figuring out what gifts the Holy Spirit wanted to give us and then receiving them, our task would be easy.

But few topics generate more confusion, crisis, and criticism than the issue of the Spirit's work in gifting the church. Churches have split over issues such as which of the Spirit's gifts are for today and which, if any, have ceased. Libraries are filled with books written in an attempt to make sense of this thing called the gifts of the Spirit.

Now my purpose in this chapter is not to try to settle the argument. My purpose is to help you experience the reality of a truth the Bible is crystal clear about: The gifts of the Holy Spirit are for every member of Christ's body, the church. That includes you and me.

So let's begin with a basic question: What do we mean by the term *spiritual gifts*? A spiritual gift is a divinely bestowed ability given to every true believer in Jesus Christ in order to serve the church.

The reason the Spirit bestows His gifts on the church is that we are the ones charged with carrying out God's program in this age. When Jesus arose and ascended to heaven, He gave to His management team, the church, those tools necessary to pull off His kingdom work.

Now let's talk about the distinguishing features of a spiritual gift. A spiritual gift is more than a human talent. All of us have talents, things we do well. Some of us are multi-talented. But you don't have to be a Christian to be talented. All of us know very talented sinners. They don't know God but they can do many things well.

When you become a Christian, you bring your talents with you. But they are not the same as spiritual gifts. As we'll see, spiritual gifts are the sovereign choice of the Spirit. A natural talent may be involved in your spiritual gift, but the focus is not on your ability. The one overriding purpose of spiritual gifts is to serve the family of God, to enhance the body of Christ, to move the church forward.

The distinguishing feature of a spiritual gift is the blessing and empowering of God on it when it is used for Him. A person may have a talent for teaching, for example. He or she can organize material well and explain it well so the student benefits from the instruction.

But when a person exercises the spiritual gift of teaching, you receive more than just facts for the mind to store. Your heart is stirred and moved to follow Christ. A person who has the ability to show mercy can make you feel better. But the spiritual gift of showing mercy can so minister to you that in your weakness and your distress you are transformed by the Holy Spirit and you keep on keeping on in spite of circumstances.

In other words, spiritual gifts differ from natural abilities in the results they produce. On the human level, we can usually account for the results based on the ability being used. A good teacher produces good students. But the proper use of spiritual gifts often produces results far beyond anything human ability can account for.

So spiritual gifts are Holy Spirit–empowered abilities given to the members of the body to facilitate the growth, edification, and maturity of the church. There are three basic categories of spiritual gifts. In no special order, they are: serving gifts, such as service itself and showing mercy; speaking gifts, such as teaching and prophecy; and sign gifts, those more demonstrable gifts such as healing, miracles, and tongues that the Spirit of God bestows when He wants to make a "megapoint."

Most of the controversy over spiritual gifts is located in this final category. I don't want to say much about them here, because we'll deal with this area in detail in the next chapter. Suffice it to note here that the sign gifts are not for everybody to exercise in any and every situation.

## SPIRITUAL GIFTS
## AND SPIRITUAL MATURITY

For the rest of the chapter, I want to deal with the four primary New Testament passages that address spiritual gifts. The first of these is 1 Corinthians 12. Let's begin with verses 1–7:

> Now concerning spiritual gifts, brethren, I do not want you to be unaware. You know that when you were pagans, you were led astray to the dumb idols, however you were led. Therefore I make known to you, that no one speaking by the Spirit of God says, "Jesus is accursed"; and no one can say, "Jesus is Lord," except by the Holy Spirit. Now there are varieties of gifts, but the same Spirit. And there are varieties of ministries, and the same Lord. And there are varieties of effects, but the same God who works all things in all persons. But to each one is given the manifestation of the Spirit for the common good.

It's important to note first that there is more said about spiritual gifts in 1 Corinthians 12–14 than in any other place in the Scriptures (we'll see a lot more of this in the next chapter). The reason for this is that the Corinthians had more problems with spiritual gifts than anybody else. Paul had to spend so much time talking to this church about this subject because they were so messed up regarding the gifts.

### No Necessary Correlation

I say that because most people who appeal to 1 Corinthians to defend their position on spiritual gifts appeal to it from the wrong vantage point. They say, "Let's go to 1 Corinthians to learn about spiritual gifts." It would be more accurate to say, "Let's go to 1 Corinthians to find out how to fix the mess we have made of spiritual gifts." The fact is, the church at Corinth had messed up in the area of spiritual gifts.

It wasn't because these believers were lacking in the gifts. Just the opposite. They possessed every gift the church could possess (see 1:7). But despite their giftedness, the Corinthians were so spiritually immature and carnal that Paul said he had to feed them with milk like spiritual babies (see 3:1–3).

The Corinthians were gifted . . . and fleshly, unspiritual, and secular in their thinking. You can have all the spiritual gifts it's possible to have and be as carnal as you ever want to be. There is no necessary correlation between being gifted and being spiritually mature. If there were, the most gifted among us would always be the most mature. But you cannot use giftedness as a criterion of spirituality.

Don't let anybody make you feel less spiritual because you don't have what he or she thinks ought to be your gift. The fact is, that person may have the gift and be less spiritual than you. These Corinthian believers had all the gifts, but they were sorely lacking in the spiritual life.

In almost every chapter of 1 Corinthians, it seems, Paul had to tackle a different crisis, problem, or sin that was operating in the life of this church right alongside the gifts. The apostle had to spend so much time teaching on spiritual gifts because things were a mess.

We'll see below that the other three major references to spiritual gifts are short and to the point. See, when you are right with the Holy Spirit, the gifts take care of themselves. When you are wrong with the Spirit, you have to talk about spiritual gifts all day long.

### The Purpose of the Gifts

All of that is preliminary to our study of 1 Corinthians 12. After introducing his subject in verse 1, Paul reminded the believers of their pagan background and dealt with a situation where false teachers among them were evidently denying Jesus' humanity, denying that He was fully human as well as fully divine (vv. 2–3).

His point is that nothing in the Corinthians' background or in the false teachers' heresies would help them in the matter of discerning the true activity of the Spirit. In other words, here was a church exhibiting the spiritual gifts, yet the people were ignorant ("unaware," v. 1) of their proper use and purpose.

So Paul begins setting the record straight (vv. 4–6). Notice the threefold contrast between "varieties" and "the same." All three Persons of the Trinity are unified in purpose when it comes to spiritual gifts. See, the reason God gifts the church is to mature her so she can pull off His one agenda. God does not gift you and me so we can do our thing. He gifts us so we can do His thing.

What is the one agenda God wants to see accomplished through the use of our spiritual gifts? Paul hints at it all the way through chapter 12 before stating it clearly in the latter verses. So let's see where this chapter takes us.

The first indication of the purpose of spiritual gifts is in verse 7. They are to be used for "the common good" of the body. Gifts are not to make you feel good or advance your personal agenda. They are to flow through you to the benefit of others beyond you.

That's why it's a tragedy if you don't know what your spiritual gift is, if you're not in the process of finding out what it is, or if you're not using your gift in the body. That means the body of Christ is not benefiting from your supernatural endowment. God wants to know, "Who is benefiting from the gift I have given you?"

Too many Christians are like young children with their Christmas gifts. They have their stash, and they do not want their brothers or sisters to touch their gifts. The parents have to spend part of Christmas playing referee because of the children's unwillingness to share a gift.

In most cases, those children added nothing to the purchase of their gifts. They made no contribution to what was under that Christmas tree, yet they hoard their gifts as if they personally bought and paid for them.

If the Spirit's gifts to you are not coming through you for the benefit of others besides you, you get cut off from the blessing God intended for you. If you are a selfish Christian who is not willing to use your gifts for the common good, you lose out.

That's what happened to our kids one Christmas when they were fighting over toys they did not want to share. I took all the toys away from them, and they did not get to play with anything. When God cannot make you a conduit because you insist on being a cul-de-sac, then what He does is limit His blessings to you. His purpose for giving you spiritual gifts is that you might serve the common good, His bigger agenda.

Let me highlight some key phrases in 1 Corinthians 12:8–27 and see if you detect a pattern emerging. Notice "the same Spirit" (vv. 8–9, 11); "one Spirit" (v. 13); "one body" (vv. 12–13, 20); "no division in the body" (v. 25); and "you are Christ's body" (v. 27).

### The Unity of the Body

Do you see the pattern? What God is after in this matter of spiritual gifts is unity in the body of Christ. The analogy of the human body is critical because, although we only have one body, that body is made up of thousands of parts. The reason the body functions so well is that these parts are interconnected, operating on one agenda.

Whenever the parts of your body start operating on conflicting agendas, you are sick. You need a doctor.

Whenever the body of Christ stops functioning as a har-monious whole, it demonstrates that the Spirit's gifts are not being used properly. The Corinthian believers were creating disunity in the body by comparing gifts and say-ing, "I'm more gifted than you." That led to jealousy over who had what gifts. And some were refusing to use their gifts for the benefit of the body.

Again, that's why Paul spent so much time in 1 Corin-thians giving instruction on spiritual gifts. He had to sort out the mess. If you understand this, it will help a lot as we come to the issue of tongues in 1 Corinthians 14 (our next chapter). Most people don't understand that what Paul wrote about the use of tongues was not a compli-ment, but a criticism. He had to correct their doctrine and their practice.

But don't miss the point here. If you are a believer in Jesus Christ, you have a supernatural endowment from the Holy Spirit that will produce supernatural results if you will use it in His power for the common good.

It's great to know that Christ saved you with the pur-pose in mind of using you to minister to His body. The Holy Spirit's gifts are given to all, regardless of ability or education or location. No matter who you are, you can contribute to the growth and maturity of the church. In fact, your gift is needed in your local assembly.

## SPIRITUAL GIFTS
## AND SPIRITUAL LEADERS

Ephesians 4 is another key passage on the subject of spiritual gifts because it brings home the purpose of gifts in such a graphic way:

> But to each one of us grace was given according to the mea-sure of Christ's gift. Therefore it says, "When He ascended on high, He led captive a host of captives, and He gave gifts to men." . . . And He gave some as apostles, and some as prophets, and some as evangelists, and some as pastors and teachers, for the equipping of the saints for the work of ser-vice, to the building up of the body of Christ. (vv. 7–8, 11–12)

Christ has gifted His church to equip the saints for service in order that the body might be built up. Paul refers both to the universal nature of spiritual gifts and to the gifted leaders that Christ has given the church.

## The Role of Gifted Leaders

The job of church leaders is not to do all the ministry, but to equip the saints for ministry by helping them to understand and use their gifts. Nothing can replace the power, impact, and spiritual enrichment and development that occur when the body's giftedness is being used under the authority of the Spirit. In my view, one of the primary reasons for the anemic nature of many churches is the failure of the body to function and the overdependence on paid professionals to do with human talents what God wants to accomplish through the proper exercising of spiritual gifts. When this happens, the whole body grows and the church moves forward. At Oak Cliff Bible Fellowship, we require every member to be in a ministry because we believe that the failure of even one member to serve hampers the common good. It hinders the maturing of the body.

The goal of this service by gifted saints led by gifted leaders is found in Ephesians 4:13–16:

> Until we all attain to the unity of the faith, and of the knowledge of the Son of God, to a mature man, to the measure of the stature which belongs to the fulness of Christ. As a result, we are no longer to be children, tossed here and there by waves, and carried about by every wind of doctrine, by the trickery of men, by craftiness in deceitful scheming; but speaking the truth in love, we are to grow up in all aspects into Him, who is the head, even Christ, from whom the whole body, being fitted and held together by that which every joint supplies, according to the proper working of each individual part, causes the growth of the body for the building up of itself in love.

Someone has said that some Christians are like wheelbarrows. They are no good unless they are pushed.

Other Christians are like kites. You have to keep pulling on the string or they will fly away. Other are like kittens. They are only content to serve when you pet them.

### The Role of Gifted Saints

The reason for this kind of situation is that many Christians do not see the spiritual issue involved in gifts. The Holy Spirit has bestowed His gifts on us because God wants to accomplish His program through us. If we are negating the Spirit's work, the program of God is hampered. One reason the church's impact is not being felt is that too many members of the body have little interest in serving for the common good. So they are not interested in their spiritual gifts.

What they want to know when they come to church is, "What am I going to get out of it?" But that's only half the question. The other half is, "What am I going to put into it?" How is God working through you to strengthen the body? To put it in more personal terms, is your church better because you are in it? If you can't answer that positively, it's time to take a hard look at yourself. Are you looking to accrue the benefits of membership in the body but incur none of the responsibility?

Cancer cells work like that. They want to operate in your body, but on their own terms, for their personal benefit. The result is the deterioration of the body rather than its growth and development.

I hope you see by now that the question is not whether the Holy Spirit has given you any gifts or whether He wants you to use them for the good of the body. The question is how badly you want to experience the gifts He has given you.

### SPIRITUAL GIFTS AND SPIRITUAL SERVICE

The third passage I want to unfold with you is Romans 12:1–8, a classic text in a classic book. In these verses we learn that worship must lead to service, and that service is possible because of the Holy Spirit's gifts.

Verses 1–2 are Paul's great call to total commitment to God, the ultimate act of worship. Then he writes:

> For through the grace given to me I say to every man among you not to think more highly of himself than he ought to think; but to think so as to have sound judgment, as God has allotted to each a measure of faith. For just as we have many members in one body and all the members do not have the same function, so we, who are many, are one body in Christ, and individually members one of another. And since we have gifts that differ according to the grace given to us, let each exercise them accordingly: if prophecy, according to the proportion of his faith; if service, in his serving; or he who teaches, in his teaching; or he who exhorts, in his exhortation; he who gives, with liberality; he who leads, with diligence; he who shows mercy, with cheerfulness.

Notice how Paul moves from the loftiest worship to the most mundane areas of service without any interruption. Worship always comes first. But it is always followed by service. When Jesus was tempted to worship the Devil, He said, "You shall worship the Lord your God, and serve Him only" (Matthew 4:10).

How does this relate to spiritual gifts? Well, you will never know what your gift is if you are sitting around saying, "God, show me my gift so I can get started serving You." You are going to be in the same spot for a long time with that kind of prayer, because God only hits a moving target. If you are not willing to do anything, the Spirit will not show you the gift He has entrusted to you—even though you have His supernatural ability to pull it off.

As he introduces the subject of spiritual gifts, Paul cautions us not to think too highly of ourselves. See, outside the doors of the church, you may have a big name or a big reputation. But when you come to God's house, you are a sinner saved by grace. You may be a rich sinner saved by grace. You may be a professional saved by grace. But we are all equal at the foot of the cross. It is not the church's blessing to have you. It's God's grace that let you in.

That's why there are no big "I's" and little "you's" in the church. A person may be a corporate executive, yet serve in a more humble position in the church. Thinking with sound judgment means that you look for the area where the Spirit has gifted you as you minister to the body. It may be in the same areas as your natural talent, but then it may not be.

Sound judgment says don't try to force the Spirit's work into a preconceived mold, because He never runs short of options. Be sure to get the point of Romans 12: Worship must always lead to service, and service means exercising spiritual gifts.

## SPIRITUAL GIFTS
## AND SPIRITUAL STEWARDSHIP

Our fourth and final passage is 1 Peter 4:10–11:

> As each one has received a special gift, employ it in serving one another, as good stewards of the manifold grace of God. Whoever speaks, let him speak, as it were, the utterances of God; whoever serves, let him do so as by the strength which God supplies; so that in all things God may be glorified through Jesus Christ, to whom belongs the glory and dominion forever and ever. Amen.

Here's another truth we need to know about the Holy Spirit's gifts. Someday, God is going to ask us whether we opened and used them for His glory.

Notice how Peter ties the concept of the stewardship of our gifts with what we were talking about earlier, the fact that our gifts are for the benefit of others. Peter says clearly we are to use our gifts to "serve one another," which is the definition of being good stewards of those gifts.

We serve one another as good stewards because spiritual gifts are God's gifts. It's God's program. We are to employ our gifts for God's glory as recipients of God's grace so that God's Son might be glorified. You will never be fulfilled in your Christian life until you are serving God using the Spirit's supernatural equipment, His gifts.

## THE IMPORTANCE
## OF SPIRITUAL GIFTS

God has specifically given spiritual gifts so the church can be edified, built up, and spiritually developed (1 Corinthians 12:7). The point, then, is that if spiritual gifts are not dynamically operating in the life of the local church, then the body of Christ is not being built up, regardless of how much the Bible is being preached.

If believers are not serving one another, the spiritual impact that is essential for them to grow will be absent, resulting in stunted spiritual growth, disunity, a lack of love, and spiritual pride (Ephesians 4:11–17).

One has only to look at the anemic nature of so many of our churches today, coupled with the reality that in most places 10 percent of the people are doing 90 percent of the work, to understand what happens when spiritual gifts are not working properly. The church's impact upon its membership, as well as the community it should be serving, is stunted.

Instead of being salt and light in the world, the church becomes satisfied functioning as a weekly Bible study with a few songs mixed in. Worship should always result in service (Matthew 4:10).

Absolutely nothing can replace the power, influence, and impact of a church that is fulfilling God's kingdom agenda through the operation of the gifts of the body. Why? Because that's how the Spirit manifests Himself, and when the Spirit manifests Himself, powerful things happen.

This explains the unique influence of the church in Acts. Evangelism was at an all-time high (2:47; 5:14; 6:3–7). There was no need for welfare (2:44–46; 4:32–35). And racial disunity was overcome by racial harmony (10:17–23, 44–48; 15:1–35). All of this happened because the Holy Spirit took charge, expressing and manifesting Himself through the gifts and service not only of the leaders (4:33; 5:12), but of the whole assembly of believers (8:4).

Whenever this dynamic of the Spirit is absent, the church becomes anemic and our witness is compromised. Members who refuse to serve and thus fail to see the Spirit exercise His power for the benefit of the whole body are cancer in the church, receiving the benefits without incurring any of the responsibility. Unless the gifts of the church are unleashed for the building up of the body, the church will continue to limp along with a marginal influence on our world.

## DISCOVERING YOUR SPIRITUAL GIFTS

It's interesting that nowhere in Scripture are believers urged or exhorted to discover their spiritual gifts. This reality flies in the face of the "gift inventories" being used in many churches today.

Well, if gifts are so vitally important to the functioning of the church, it may seem odd that we are not commanded to discover them. Besides, you may say, "Tony, I thought you said we need to find our gift."

Yes, but the discovery of spiritual gifts flows out of service. Whenever you see God gifting His people, it's because He has given them a task to perform, not vice versa. The problem is that we have a whole generation of Christians who sit, soak, and sour every week waiting for God to reveal their gifts to them before they get busy serving.

These people will never discover their gifts. Remember, spiritual gifts are the manifestation of the Holy Spirit as He ministers to the body. So if there is no ministry, there is no manifestation.

One reason this principle is so often missed is that most studies on spiritual gifts begin and end in the New Testament. They should begin in the Old Testament, where we are first introduced to the manifestation of the Spirit for service.

The call of Moses is a clear example. Moses did not feel that he had the necessary gifts or abilities to lead the Israelites out of Egyptian bondage (Exodus 4:1–13). God's response to Moses' sense of "ungiftedness" was to let him know that the task would be accomplished by God's power (vv. 14–17). But Moses would not experience this power until he obeyed God and went before Pharaoh.

The same was true of the work that Bezalel and Oholiab did on the construction of the tabernacle (Exodus

31:1–6; 35:30–35). The giftedness came as they were being given a specific task to perform. This principle also operated in the lives of Israel's judges, who received the presence of the Spirit as they fulfilled the assignment God had given them (Judges 3:9–10).

One implication of this principle is that when God changes a believer's task, He may also change the gift that believer has, because He always equips us with whatever is necessary to do the job. In other words, if God is clearly pointing out an area of ministry to you, you can't argue, "That's not my gift. Ask Susie." When we see the supernatural presence of the Holy Spirit manifesting Himself through our gifts as we help to build up the body, we will know what it is to truly experience the Spirit.

So the question now is, How do we know what task the Spirit is assigning to us? First, the Spirit stirs our hearts toward fulfilling an area of need. This is what happened in the building of the tabernacle. The people wanted to be involved because their hearts were stirred (Exodus 35:21–22, 26, 29). When you are operating in concert with the Spirit, He brings joy along with the job.

Second, when the Spirit is leading there will be skill in the execution of the task (Exodus 36:1–2, 8).

Third, when the Spirit is leading in the assignment of the task, God's glory will always be manifested through its execution (Exodus 40:34–38; 1 Peter 4:11).

At our church in Dallas, we require all of our members to serve in a ministry. We give them a list of almost one hundred ministries, from which they must select one, since it seems clear from Scripture that God only gives one gift at a time (1 Peter 4:10). As they serve, one of several things happens. Either their spiritual gift begins to emerge, or it becomes clear that they should be in another area of service due to lack of skill or a willing heart or effectiveness in their present service.

This much is clear. Failing to serve for the common good of the body will greatly limit a believer's experience of the life and power of the Holy Spirit. Conversely, as we serve others we allow the Spirit to unveil Himself in new and exciting ways in our lives. When we build up Christ's body, the Spirit builds us up. Ask God to direct you to the service He has for you, and He will give you the gift you need to fulfill it.

## SOME FINAL OBSERVATIONS
## ON SPIRITUAL GIFTS

In none of the four passages we studied will you find a comprehensive list of the spiritual gifts. Why? Because giving you a "shopping list" of gifts is not the point. The point is to get us right with the Spirit of God, because when we are right with the Spirit, His gifts will find us. We will not have to find them. They will track us down.

Maybe sharing my experience will help you see how it can happen. My gift is that of teaching. It is the ability to expound the Word of God in such a way that people understand and are motivated to respond to the proclamation.

Now as a kid growing up, I couldn't speak very well. I had to take special speech classes in school. I would stutter and have trouble even getting a sound to come out. But when God saved me, something happened to my tongue. My stammering tongue smoothed out.

I can recall as a high school student stammering to get a word out. But when I went to witness to somebody, that all changed. Somehow, something supernatural took over. I was using a gift that I did not possess in my normal speech because the Spirit was gifting me for His purpose.

The Holy Spirit has a gift for every believer, and the way you know it is a gift is that it is benefiting somebody else in the body of Christ. As I said above, God saved you to be a conduit of His blessings, not a cul-de-sac.

And since the Holy Spirit gives His gifts "just as He wills" (1 Corinthians 12:11), you don't need to go gift-hunting. Now you may be saying, "Wait a minute, Tony. Didn't you just tell me to get busy serving God as a great way to discover and develop my spiritual gift?"

Yes I did, but that's a long way from what I'm talking about here. Let me illustrate what I mean by comparing it to a single Christian who is earnestly seeking a godly mate. There's nothing wrong with that person praying for a mate and keeping watch, as it were, for candidates to come along.

But Paul tells the single Christian in 1 Corinthians 7 not to seek a mate. What he means is, don't let the search for a mate become such a consuming thing that it takes your focus off your devotion to the Lord. If that happens, the goal can become getting married at any cost, and the real purpose of Christian marriage goes by the boards.

It's the same with spiritual gifts. If you become so obsessed with possessing a certain gift that you start chasing after it, the real purpose for desiring the gift can get lost. So instead of going gift-hunting, go "Spirit-hunting" as you seek to live in tune with Him.

What about other people who know you well? Other people can help you discover your gift, and often they recognize your gift before you do. But other people can't dictate what your gift should be, because the Spirit is the sovereign Giver of the gifts.

Remember the need to distinguish gifts from talents, because only spiritual gifts bring the internal joy of the Spirit and the external benefits to others in the body. Talent only says you have a good singing voice or whatever. A spiritual gift says others are closer to God because of what the Spirit has supernaturally empowered you to do.

Now I know there is a raging argument over which of the Spirit's gifts are meant to be temporary and which are ongoing. Frankly, I think that argument is a waste of time. We don't have to spend our time talking about which gifts worked yesterday and which gifts will work tomorrow.

See, if your church is a Spirit-led church, when the Spirit needs to call forth any gift, He can call it forth. If somebody who speaks only Spanish walks into our church in Dallas, he will not understand the gospel because I preach in English.

But if someone in our church who has never spoken Spanish before were suddenly to begin explaining the gospel to this visitor in fluent Spanish, that would be the New Testament gift of tongues. The gospel would be interpreted so the person would understand it.

Can the Spirit do that if He desires? Of course! The issue is, is it biblical? Is it operating according to God's standards? Is it enhancing the body? These are always the questions.

Let me ask you a final question. What are you doing with the gift or gifts the Holy Spirit has graced your life with? Are you using them for the benefit of the body, or have you neglected them? Have you appropriated them for your own benefit? Once you see spiritual gifts in their true light, as sovereign and gracious bestowals of the Holy Spirit, you'll never want to mishandle them or take them for granted again.

The story is told of the boy who did his household chores and left his mother this note: "For cleaning my room, $5.00. For washing the dishes, $3.00. For raking the leaves, $10.00. Total: $18.00. You owe me, Mom."

The mother read the note while the boy was at school and put eighteen dollars on the table. With it she left her own note: "For bearing you nine months in the womb, throwing up for three months, no charge. For cooking your breakfast every day, no charge. For washing and ironing your clothes, no charge. For staying up all night when you were sick, no charge. Total: grace."

When the boy read that note, he ran to his mother and asked, "What more can I do to let you know I am grateful?"

Our salvation cost a lot, but it was no charge to us. In grace, God has given us eternity. In grace, He has given us forgiveness. In grace, He has done more for us than we could ever do for ourselves.

One thing you can do to show your gratitude is to pray, "Holy Spirit, as I serve the family of God, show me how You have gifted me. Reveal to me what supernatural endowment You have given me that I can use for the common good of my brothers and sisters in the family of God." He'll answer that prayer every time!

# EXPERIENCING THE SPIRIT'S GIFTS

Spiritual gifts—or, we should say, the Spirit's gifts—are another of His wonderful provisions that enable us to pull off the Christian life. Anything the Holy Spirit has to give me, I want to receive. Don't you? Here are some ideas I hope will help you experience all that the Spirit has for you:

1. Are you waiting for the Holy Spirit to drop your gift in your lap before you get around to serving God? As I said before, you'll be sitting there a long time. If you don't know where to begin serving and finding your gift, ask your pastor what the needs are at your church. The Holy Spirit can use openings like these to reveal His plan to you.

2. Spiritually mature people whom you trust and who know you well can be a good source of encouragement and counsel as you seek the Spirit's place for you. If you feel the need, seek out the help of several godly people whose wisdom and spiritual maturity are evident to you.

3. Have you benefited in any way from the ministry of Spirit-gifted and Spirit-directed leaders? Why not tell them so, beginning with your pastor? I heard somewhere that pastors need encouragement too.

4. Several hints in Romans 12:8 help answer the question, "How will I know when I have found my gift?" This is not ironclad, but verse 8 pictures people exercising their gifts with great enthusiasm and joy. One way to validate your gift is to ask yourself, What service brings me the greatest joy? What area of service makes my heart cheerful just thinking about it? What really gets me excited about serving the Lord? When the answers to these questions are combined with the fact that other believers are being helped by your service, you most likely are operating in the realm of your gift.

# CHAPTER SEVENTEEN

# EXPERIENCING THE SPIRIT'S LANGUAGE

I suppose nothing related to the Holy Spirit is more controversial today than the issue of speaking in tongues. It has split churches, families, and friendships. It has created all manner of confusion. Yet it is clearly something the Bible deals with, and it is a facet of the Spirit's ministry. So we must deal with it if our study of the Spirit is to be complete.

There are at least two good reasons that you need to know what the Bible teaches on this subject. The first is for your own understanding of how the gift of tongues relates to your spiritual life. The second is so you will be able to give a biblical reason for the view you hold. It is one thing to agree or disagree with a teaching. It's another thing altogether to know why you believe what you do.

## TWO BASIC APPROACHES

So let's tackle this intriguing and difficult topic, because if we approach it in the right manner, God the Holy

Spirit has some good things to teach us. There are two basic approaches to the issue of tongues, which I will call the charismatic and the noncharismatic because of the popular use of these words.

Our primary biblical focus will once again be on 1 Corinthians 12–14, which makes this study a good follow-up to our previous discussion on spiritual gifts. This study is actually an extension of the previous chapter, because of course tongues is listed among the gifts of the Spirit.

Without meaning to oversimplify, the charismatic approach to tongues speaking understands Paul's purpose in 1 Corinthians 12–14 to be that of encouraging the practice and explaining how the gift of tongues is to work in the church.

We certainly want to understand how the Holy Spirit designed His gift of tongues to work. My problem with the charismatic view is that it tends to make the gift a universal experience that every believer needs to have if he or she wants to be spiritually mature. That view is based, I believe, on a deficient understanding of Paul's purpose in 1 Corinthians 12–14.

My problem with the strong conservative noncharismatic position that tongues are not for today is that it boxes God into a narrow theological framework that He is not allowed to break out of. It is also, in my view, exegetically indefensible.

The approach I will seek to explain and defend is that the gift of tongues, while a legitimate experience, is not meant to be a universal experience and that, if we understand 1 Corinthians 12–14 properly, we will see that Paul was rebuking, correcting, and restricting the Corinthians' use of this gift.

In previous chapters we have already set the stage for part of this argument. From time to time we have "dropped by" the church at Corinth and found it to be an assembly riddled with moral and spiritual problems. I don't need to review those here.

Suffice it to say that, as I mentioned in chapter 16, the first letter to the Corinthians was not written to compliment this church. It was written to castigate this church for its many errant attitudes and practices that did not reflect biblical Christianity. That purpose didn't change when Paul came to chapter 12 and began his discussion of spiritual gifts. The Corinthian assembly was in dire need of correction here too.

## CORRECTION CONCERNING GIFTS

Among other problems, this chapter indicates that some of the believers at Corinth were allowing their gifts to go to their heads. They were feeling more important than others because they had the more spectacular gifts. So the big shots made the others feel less important, like a foot on the body of Christ instead of a hand or eye (1 Corinthians 12:15).

There was also a scramble for the "showy" gifts. Corinth was a happening place. Everybody wanted to be in on the act at Corinth Bible Fellowship. So Paul had to remind them that God had given different gifts to different believers. The whole church couldn't be on the stage together (vv. 28–30). There was "a still more excellent way" they were neglecting: love (v. 31).

Now we can see how chapter 13 fits into the flow of Paul's thought. This is called the great love chapter, and that's true. But it's a stinging rebuke to the Corinthians' lack of love in the use of their spiritual gifts. The message of 1 Corinthians 13 is that unless the motive for the exercise of your gifts is love for your fellow believers, you're just making noise.

These people were using their gifts for self-aggrandizement. But the "more excellent way" of love demands that we exercise our spiritual gifts to benefit the rest of the body and not to show off who we are (1 Corinthians 12:7).

Notice how Paul links chapters 13 and 14. Chapter 13 ends, "the greatest of these is love" (v. 13). Chapter 14 opens with the exhortation, "Pursue love" (v. 1). So the subject is still love as the more excellent way.

This context is important as we come to Paul's detailed discussion of the gift of tongues. The thing we need to keep in mind is that Paul is saying what you need to run after is love, not this or that spiritual gift. There is no command in the Bible to go after a certain gift. But there are plenty of commands in the Bible to love your brothers and sisters.

There is no command in the Bible to show off your skills or gifts, but there are plenty of commands to love your neighbor. So Paul says if you want to be a "show-time" kind of Christian, show your love for the family of God, not what you can do with whatever gifts the Spirit of God has given you.

Yet spiritual gifts are important. Paul didn't hesitate to tell the Corinthians, "Earnestly desire the greater gifts" (1 Corinthians 12:31). Then he told them, "Desire earnestly spiritual gifts" (14:1). In 14:2, then, he began a discussion of a gift that was literally tearing the church apart: the gift of tongues. It was causing chaos in the body.

As I said above, chapter 14 was not written to expand the use of this gift, but to restrict it, because the Corinthians were using the gift to show off, not as an expression of love. Unless you set 1 Corinthians 14 in its immediate context and in the context of the entire book, you may wind up arguing the very opposite of the point Paul is making.

He is not saying that everybody should speak in tongues. He is saying to the church at Corinth, "You have too many people speaking in tongues." This is the very opposite of the emphasis given to tongues today, as evidenced by the question, "Have you received the gift yet?"

That's not the issue. The issue is whether what you have is what you are supposed to have.

### SEVEN CRUCIAL ISSUES

So let's get to the biblical text to see what God's Word says. I want to deal with this subject by raising and attempting to answer seven issues or questions that come out of 1 Corinthians 14 and several related passages.

### The Issue of Definition

The first thing we need to do is define the Greek word *glōssa*, translated "tongue" in 1 Corinthians 14:2. We saw earlier in our study that this word means "language." One controversy is, Does this mean human languages such as English, French, or Spanish, or does Paul have in mind some sort of heavenly language?

Many people who speak in tongues speak in syllables unrelated to any known human language. They will tell you they are speaking a heavenly language. But does the Bible support such a view? Well, let's check the evidence, beginning where the New Testament gift of tongues began, on the Day of Pentecost.

We have examined the early verses of Acts 2 on several occasions already, so I won't repeat them here. Just note that the "tongues as of fire" (v. 3) is the word *glōssa*. In fact, every appearance of the word *tongue* in Acts, 1 Corinthians, and the rest of the New Testament, whether singular or plural, is a translation of this word.

The only exception is 1 Corinthians 14:21, where "strange tongues" is simply a compound of *glōssa*. What's more, in every reference outside of the discussion of the gift of tongues, the meaning of the word is clearly human languages or dialects.

So we should not be surprised that on Pentecost, when the gift of tongues was first exercised, each of the Jews assembled in Jerusalem heard the message of God "in his own language" (Acts 2:6). The Greek word for "language" in Acts 2:6, 8 is *dialektos*, from which we get our English word "dialect." It means human languages, not ecstatic utterances. Clearly, the tongues spoken on the Day of Pentecost were human languages. Luke even listed them (vv. 9–11). The purpose was to get the message of Jesus Christ out to the world, because Jerusalem was filled with people from every corner of the earth.

The experience of tongues was repeated twice more in the book of Acts, in 10:46 and 19:6, as the Holy Spirit continued to bring different groups together to form the body of Christ. In neither case are we given any reason to believe that these were anything other than human languages that could be interpreted by someone who knew the language or had the gift of interpretation.

These last two occasions happened among the Gentiles, with tongues serving as a witness to the apostles that the speakers were now full members of the body of Christ along with their Jewish brethren.

The point is that what happened to these people was an extension of the gift of tongues at Pentecost. And we know that the tongues spoken at Pentecost were known human languages. The word *unknown* in the King James Version of 1 Corinthians 14:2, 4, 14, 19, and 27 is an unfortunate addition by the translators and is not a part of the original text.

So the gift of tongues is the supernatural ability to speak in a human language that was previously unknown to the speaker. Let's go back to 1 Corinthians 14 and plug that definition in to see what we come up with. In verse 10, Paul says, "There are perhaps, a great many kinds of languages *in the world*, and no kind is without meaning" (italics added). He's talking about human languages.

Look at verse 21: "In the Law it is written, 'By men of strange tongues and by the lips of strangers I will speak to this people, and even so they will not listen to Me,' says the Lord." Paul quotes Isaiah 28:11, which prophesied a time when the Jews would hear a foreign language, the language of the Assyrians. The Assyrians would conquer the Jews and take them to a strange land to live among a people whose language they did not know.

Paul uses this prophecy in 1 Corinthians 14:22 to show that tongues were a sign to cause the Jews to listen to the message of Christ, which is what happened at Pentecost. Both Isaiah's prophecy and Paul's use of it have known human languages in view.

This raises the question of what Paul means by his reference to the "tongues . . . of angels" in 1 Corinthians 13:1, since this verse is a primary verse where people get the idea of a heavenly language. The argument is that this verse distinguishes between human speech and angel speech. Let me make two observations.

First, whenever angels speak in the Bible, they speak human languages. There is no reference in all of the Bible of a heavenly angelic dialect. Whenever angels speak, they speak in the language of the people with whom they are communicating.

Second, in order for us to identify an angelic language we would have had to hear angels speak. How can one claim a language is heavenly otherwise?

Third, what Paul is doing here is using hyperbole, that is, exaggerated speech. He says that if you do not have love, you become a "noisy gong or a clanging symbol" (v. 1). He talks in verse 2 about knowing all mysteries and all knowledge. Now we realize that is impossible. Neither Paul nor nobody else can know everything. Only God knows everything. Paul didn't remove any mountains by his faith either (v. 2b).

Paul is speaking in exaggerated ways to emphasize his point. So when he speaks about the language of angels, he is using hyperbole to drive home his point that exercising gifts without love is a waste of time. This passage does not contradict our definition of a tongue as a human language that was previously unknown to the speaker.

### The Issue of Order

Now let me deal with the issue of order. Remember, our thesis is that Paul's purpose in writing about tongues is not to encourage the expansion of the gift, but to restrict it. Look at several key verses in 1 Corinthians 14:

> What is the outcome then, brethren? When you assemble, each one has a psalm, has a teaching, has a revelation, has a tongue, has an interpretation. Let all things be done for edification. . . . For God is not a God of confusion but of peace, as in all the churches of the saints. Let the women keep silent in the churches; for they are not permitted to speak, but let them subject themselves, just as the Law also says. And if they desire to learn anything, let them ask their own husbands at home; for it is improper for a woman to speak in church. . . . But let all things be done properly and in an orderly manner. (vv. 26, 33–35, 40)

The problem here is that the church at Corinth was confusion incorporated. Paul was not saying that it was improper for a woman to minister or improper for women to be involved in the life of the church. Evidently, the women Paul was referring to had usurped the authority of their husbands so that the result was spiritual confusion. They were using the church service to display their rebellion against their husbands' spiritual authority. So here was one area of confusion and chaos.

Another problem was that the services were apparently conducted in chaos. Somebody would be preaching the Word, and somebody else would break out in a song or a word of revelation or speak in tongues. Their argument was, "The Holy Spirit led me to do it."

It's hard to argue with a person when he tells you, "It's the Holy Spirit." How do you know whether it is the Spirit or not? Well, according to Paul, if it is of the Spirit, it's going to be orderly. If it produces chaos and confusion, it is not the work of the Holy Spirit.

Was the church at Corinth orderly? No, it was more like the rhythm section of a kindergarten band. How bad was it? Verses 6–9 of chapter 14 give us an idea. Paul says that tongues are of little use if no one knows for sure what is being said.

He uses his famous example of musical instruments to make the point. If the bugle gives an uncertain sound, the troops won't know whether to attack, retreat, or fall in for roll call. In the same way, if the use of tongues does not produce edification, the speaker might as well be talking into the air.

What does this tell us about the gift of tongues? It reinforces the point made earlier that if the manifestation of tongues is truly a work of the Holy Spirit, it will occur under clearly defined and restricted conditions. To try to get everyone in a service or even in a congregation to speak in tongues violates the apostle's instructions here.

### The Issue of Priority

A third issue we need to tackle is that of priority. Those who want to make tongues a universal gift often argue this way. If you want to be really spiritual, you need to speak in tongues. Translation: If you don't speak in tongues, you won't reach "super-Christian" status. You will just be an average sort of Christian.

Is the gift of tongues a priority experience for every believer? Well, if you go back to 1 Corinthians 12:28, you will see that in Paul's ranking, the gift of tongues is at the bottom of the list. Then he asks this question in verse 30: "All do not speak with tongues, do they?"

Here is more evidence that the gift of tongues is not for every believer. Now in 1 Corinthians 14:5, Paul does say, "I wish that you all spoke in tongues." Does this contradict what we just read? No, Paul is expressing a wish, just like he said in 1 Corinthians 7:7 that he wished everyone was celibate like him. He didn't expect everyone to be celibate. Neither did he expect every believer to speak in tongues.

We've already seen the church's priority in 1 Corinthians 14:1: "Pursue love." In 14:5-6, Paul says that prophesying is a much more profitable gift to pursue than tongues. Prophesying is the proclamation of God's Word in a known language. What the church should desire most is the ministry of the revelation of God through His Word. "One who prophesies speaks to men for edification and exhortation and consolation" (v. 3).

Now suppose I got up in church one Sunday morning and began preaching in French or German. The sanctuary would soon empty out because my message would be meaningless to all but a few of the people. In fact, if it were in French or German it would be meaningless to me, because I don't know those languages!

Paul says that unless what you say in the church has meaning for the body, it is of no benefit. But the people who want everyone to use this heavenly language are propagating meaningless speech. It is empty of content.

Now follow what Paul says in 1 Corinthians 14:18-19. It's important to see that Paul did not denigrate or dismiss the gift of tongues. As a gift of the Holy Spirit, tongues was a gift that Paul himself exercised. When Paul used the gift of tongues, he did so outside the church for evangelistic purposes or inside the church on a very limited basis for those who needed to be edified in their own human dialect. He realized that the exercise of prophecy, the proclamation of divine revelation in a known language, was more beneficial to the entire body.

The apostle states this dramatically in verse 19: "In the church I desire to speak five words with my mind, that I may instruct others also, rather than ten thousand words in a tongue." Can you imagine someone preaching a five-word sermon? I couldn't do it, and I doubt if Paul could either. But that's how much more valuable prophecy is in this setting than tongues.

Whenever the gift of tongues is emphasized in the church, it's out of place, because that has to do with another language. The Lord knows that most of us have all we can do to understand and apply His Word as we receive it in our native language. Someone who isn't following God in English isn't going to follow Him in another language.

So the priority for the church is clear: the communication of the Word of God. In fact, Paul goes on to say in 1 Corinthians 14:20 that he hopes the Corinthians will mature in their thinking beyond their current infatuation with tongues.

Let me say it again. Paul is not saying prophecy is good, tongues is bad. Not at all. In verse 39 he sums up his argument by saying, "Therefore, my brethren, desire earnestly to prophesy, and do not forbid to speak in tongues."

Now this is where I depart from many of my conservative friends who say, "Tongues was strictly a temporary gift to help get the church started. It was no longer needed after those early formative days and ceased as a viable gift."

I can't say that because Paul says, "Don't forbid the use of this gift." I believe the gift of tongues is still a viable gift, but it is not to be our priority focus. Notice that Paul nowhere says, "Insist on the exercise of tongues." No, he permits it. So I don't deny the validity of the gift of tongues, but neither do I promote its use. That's the Holy Spirit's sovereign choice.

### The Issue of Purpose

Here's a fourth issue we need to think about. Why did the Holy Spirit give the gift of tongues in the first place? We have already read the answer in 1 Corinthians 14:21–22, where Paul quotes Isaiah 28:11 and then says, "So then tongues are for a sign, not to those who believe, but to unbelievers" (v. 22).

We saw how this sign aspect was fulfilled on the Day of Pentecost. And in the previous chapter, I gave an example of what a legitimate use of tongues in the church would look like today. You may want to review that. It would be the same basic phenomenon as Pentecost: that is, someone supernaturally endowed by the Holy Spirit to speak in a language he or she did not previously understand, so that another person or persons who did speak the language would understand the message of God's Word.

So the gift of tongues is a sign to unbelievers. But this gift has another purpose that relates to the body of Christ. Paul refers to it several times in the opening five verses of 1 Corinthians 14. That purpose is edification.

You can see how much of a bottom-line issue this is in verse 5, where Paul says that tongues should not be occurring in the church unless someone is there to interpret what is said, "so that the church may receive edifying." Later in verse 26, Paul strengthens the exhortation when he says, "Let all things be done for edification."

The word *edify* means to build up, so we can conclude that anything that does not build up the church is illegitimate. The gift of tongues is given by the Holy Spirit to edify the assembled body of believers. Now here's why this is important. Stay with me because we are entering controversial ground.

Let me state my premise and then defend it. The gift of tongues was not given just for your personal spiritual benefit. See, there are people in the church today who are eager to instruct you in the techniques of speaking in tongues. I call them "tongues trainers."

These people will show you how to connect syllables and phrases in such a way that soon you are repeating them faster and faster until finally, things are coming out of your mouth that you don't even recognize or understand. You will then be congratulated and told you are now speaking in a heavenly language or a "prayer language" you can use for your private edification and blessing as well as for the church.

The point of all this is to give you something for your personal spiritual enhancement. Now I'm not saying we don't need all the help we can get when it comes to our personal prayer and devotional lives, and if such an experience and mode of communication benefits you personally and privately, fine. The issue, however, is whether such a view of tongues is consistent with biblical teaching on the meaning of the gift of tongues, particularly within the context of the gathered body.

I don't believe it is, because the consistent teaching of Scripture is that the gift of tongues is designed to build somebody else up, not to make us feel better. In fact, we saw in the previous chapter that all of the Spirit's gifts are for the benefit of others, not to make the gifted person feel special or more spiritual.

Verses 2 and 4 of 1 Corinthians 14 are difficult verses that throw a lot of people off in this regard:

> For one who speaks in a tongue does not speak to men, but to God; for no one understands, but in his spirit he speaks mysteries. . . . One who speaks in a tongue edifies himself; but one who prophesies edifies the church.

Those who seek to promote the gift of tongues often quote these two verses about the private use of tongues. But what they fail to see is that these verses are criticisms of the Corinthians' practice of tongues, not compliments.

In verse 2, Paul is saying the reason a tongues speaker is speaking only to God is that nobody else in the assembly knows what in the world he is talking about, unless someone interprets (v. 5). He makes the same basic point in verse 4: The only person being ministered to is the person speaking in tongues. That violates the principle that spiritual gifts are given for the "common good" (1 Corinthians 12:7). It also disregards the principle of love, which "does not seek its own" (13:5).

Now I don't think Paul is necessarily forbidding privately praying in your own way. The idea is that if you go in your closet and speak in some private tongue and it blesses you and ministers to God, that's fine because you are by yourself. You can do whatever you want to by yourself that ministers to you and ministers to God, because you and He are the only two who are listening.

God can understand any language, even languages that aren't languages. He also understands "the language of silence," manifested in "groanings that cannot be uttered" because they are too deep for words (Romans 8:26). I am saying, however, that this is not the biblical gift of tongues; it is simply your own private communication code with God.

But when it comes to the church, the goal is to edify the body—not simply to edify oneself. So if we can't all get in on it, something is wrong with your practice of the gift of tongues.

Singing is a good illustration of what I'm talking about. As a body of believers, we sing to God that we might worship and adore Him as well as bless one another (Ephesians 5:19). You don't come to church to sing just to make yourself feel better. By lifting up your voice with the other members of the body, you are contributing to the ministry of encouragement and strength that sacred music provides for God's people.

So the issue isn't whether you feel like singing on any given Sunday. If you refuse to lend your voice to the praise of God in the assembly, you are refusing to serve your brothers and sisters. You are cheating the body. Your singing is for the benefit of others. All things in the church are to be done for edification.

So it is with the gift of tongues and all the spiritual gifts. If you do what you do only for yourself, the Holy Spirit will not honor that. If He sees that you are not using the gift He gave you to serve and benefit others in the body of Christ, He is going to stop blessing you with the effective use of that gift. The Spirit of God does not honor selfish Christians.

### The Issue of Procedure

Next we come to the issue of procedure. Remember, Paul is restricting the use of the gift, not encouraging it.

For churches that are speaking in tongues, 1 Corinthians 14:27 offers the acid test: "If any one speaks in a tongue, it should be by two or at the most three, and each in turn, and let one interpret."

So when you hear about church services where everybody is speaking or singing or praying in tongues at the same time, those services have failed the test of verse 27. Paul plainly says that the exercise of the gift should be limited to two speakers, or maybe three on holidays and special occasions.

But there's more here than the number of tongues speakers permitted. Each one is to speak "in turn." That means one at a time, not all at once. Why? Because the issue isn't the speaker. It's the body. The body can't receive edification if there's chaos. Paul also limits the tongues speaking by saying that someone must be present to interpret.

A man once got up in our church and began speaking in a so-called tongue. I wasn't preaching, which would have made it illegitimate because prophecy is greater. As he spoke, I thought, *Is the Lord doing something?* I had to allow for that possibility, so I let him finish since it was not disruptive.

Then I waited for an interpretation that would edify the body, because no one had understood what he was saying. There was no interpretation, so I had to get up and say, "What you just experienced was illegitimate."

Now that did not make the speaker feel good, but I was under obligation to deal with the experience from a biblical frame of reference. I had a whole congregation of people wondering what was going on. The point is, when a person speaks in tongues in the church, he is not speaking to himself. He is speaking to the body, so there must be an interpreter.

Otherwise, the people involved are like foreigners to each other (1 Corinthians 14:11). If there is no interpreter, mum's the word (v. 28). Let all things be done for edification.

## The Issue of Pride

Paul addressed the issue of pride very forthrightly in 1 Corinthians 14:36–38:

> Was it from you that the word of God first went forth? Or has it come to you only? If any one thinks he is a prophet or spiritual, let him recognize that the things which I write to you are the Lord's commandment. But if any one does not recognize this, he is not recognized.

Paul, you are so hard. But he was saying, "Listen, I got this from the Lord. It doesn't matter what you think or what you have experienced. If it does not match what has come from the Lord, it's wrong. And if you don't agree, it's because you are not really as spiritual as you think you are."

A lot of Christians are being made to feel less spiritual by other Christians because the latter group has had an experience the former did not have. But we have learned by now that the Holy Spirit does not give His gifts to elevate some believers over others, or to cause believers to compare experiences to see who is the more spiritual.

Since the Spirit's endowments are given by His sovereign choice, how can I feel superior to another believer because of the gifts I may have? Whenever someone tries to give you the idea that he or she is privy to some spiritual secret that only a select few know about, you know something's wrong somewhere.

Look at verses 14–15 of 1 Corinthians 14:

> If I pray in a tongue, my spirit prays, but my mind is unfruitful. What is the outcome then? I shall pray with the spirit and I shall pray with the mind also; I shall sing with the spirit and I shall sing with the mind also.

God does not expect your body to be in church while your mind is still home in bed. You worship God not only with your spirit and with your emotions, but with your mind.

If I preach and you don't understand it because your mind did not comprehend it, either I did not do a good job or you did not get enough sleep. When you sing, God doesn't want you just to mouth words like "To God be the glory, great things he has done." He wants you to think about what you are singing to Him.

God wants your mind in gear while you are worshiping Him. If any portion of your worship causes you to disengage your mind, there's something wrong with it. If your ideas of what constitutes true worship are at variance with what the Bible teaches, you need to get your ideas fixed, not be proud of them.

### The Issue of Permanence

The final issue concerning the gift of tongues that I want to deal with is that of permanence:

> Love never fails; but if there are gifts of prophecy, they will be done away; if there are tongues, they will cease; if there is knowledge, it will be done away. For we know in part, and we prophesy in part; but when the perfect comes, the partial will be done away. When I was a child, I used to speak as a child, think as a child, reason as a child; when I became a man, I did away with childish things. For now we see in a mirror dimly, but then face to face; now I know in part, but then I shall know fully just as I also have been fully known. (1 Corinthians 13:8–12)

Now hold on to your seat. Paul says there will come a time when the gift of tongues will cease. He describes that time in verse 10 as "when the perfect comes." There are two prevailing views of what Paul means by this phrase.

The first view says that what Paul has in mind here is the completion of the Scriptures. In other words, in the early days of the church before the church had God's completed revelation, miraculous gifts like tongues were necessary. But now that we have the completed canon of

God's Word, the need for spectacular gifts has ceased. In this view, the gift of tongues has already ceased.

But the charismatic community argues that the *perfect* that Paul is referring to is the Perfect One, the Lord Jesus. The argument here is that until Jesus comes back, the gift of tongues is valid and remains operative.

I would like to propose a third view of this text that I believe better fits the context of this passage of Scripture. When Paul uses the word *perfect* (the Greek word *teleios*), he usually means "mature, complete," referring to the spiritual development process. This is clearly the case in his use of the word in 1 and 2 Corinthians (1 Corinthians 2:6; 14:20; 2 Corinthians 7:1). You can also see this in Colossians 1:28, where Paul says the goal of his ministry is to "present every man complete in Christ." Paul wanted to see every Christian become a spiritually mature believer.

Therefore, I believe the "perfect" of 1 Corinthians 13:10 is consistent with Paul's normative usage of the term, namely, the maturing process in relationship to the completed Scriptures, not just a reference to the existence of the completed Bible.

So here is what I believe Paul is saying about the gift of tongues. Tongues are basically for the immature. When you become mature, you will not need to see and hear continuous miraculous signs to sustain and build your faith.

This view also fits the immediate context of 1 Corinthians 13, where Paul makes the contrast between childhood and becoming a man (v. 11). The most obvious way to understand Paul's distinction is to see it as a contrast between immaturity (child) and maturity (man). The difference between the two is knowledge that leads to spiritual perceptiveness, which I believe explains Paul's distinction in verse 12 between seeing in a mirror dimly and the greater spiritual understanding "face to face."

In other words, the more mature you are, the closer you are to Christ. To get closer to Christ, you need to know His Word. And the closer you are to Christ, the more your relationship to Him determines your spiritual clarity and the less you will need to depend on miraculous gifts to become mature.

This view also fits well with the spiritual condition of the Corinthian church. As I said in the previous chapter, these believers were spiritually immature, even carnal (1 Corinthians 3:1–3), and in desperate need of spiritual growth. Yet of all the New Testament churches, this church was the most dependent on the gift of tongues. I contend that it was this immaturity that explains the dominance of the gift of tongues in Corinth. It also explains why Paul did not address the issue of the gift of tongues in letters to other New Testament churches that were maturing.

Now I know what you're going to ask. "Wait a minute, Tony. First Corinthians 13:8 also says that prophecy and knowledge will stop when the perfect comes. You're not singling out tongues, are you?" No, I believe that the specific gifts of prophecy and knowledge will also cease when the perfect comes.

Prophecy refers to the oral communication and prediction of God's truth. Knowledge is the special understanding of these prophecies. These gifts were crucial when there was no complete written Word to edify the church. I believe Paul's point is that when a church matures because of its response to God's truth as deposited in Scripture, these gifts are not needed for believers to hear God's voice or know His mind. Why? Because spiritual maturity enables believers to hear the voice of God for themselves from the Word since they now possess the mind of Christ revealed in Scripture (1 Corinthians 2:15–16).

John calls this "the anointing" (1 John 2:20, 27). When believers mature because of their response to the Word, tongues will cease to be actively demonstrated. The form of the Greek verbs used in 1 Corinthians 13:8 indicates that tongues will "cease" (this verb is in the middle voice) or discontinue in, by, and of themselves. The voice of the verb translated "done away," used with prophecy and knowledge, indicates that God will make them inoperative.

Now I am not saying that God cannot give the more miraculous and exotic experiences to accomplish His unique purpose for a specific time as a private, non-normative manifestation. On the contrary, God does use these miraculous experiences to validate His message and messengers as He deems necessary to do so. However, when believers become mature in the Word, there is a decreasing need for the church to depend on these exotic gifts for its effective functioning and walk with God. The nonexotic gifts will be more than sufficient.

See, a baby needs a miracle every day. He needs his mother to swoop down and use her giftedness to put food in his mouth and dress him because he is too immature to do it himself. But if mama is still putting food in his mouth and dressing him when he is twenty-one years old, we have a fundamental problem.

When you are mature, you don't need the things you needed when you were immature. The same is true for a church. Go back to 1 Corinthians 14:20: "Brethren, do not be children in your thinking; yet in evil be babes, but in your thinking be mature." Paul is saying to the church at Corinth, "You're immature. You are acting like babies" (see also 3:1–3).

People who go around saying, "You have to speak in tongues to be spiritual," are immature. When the perfect comes, when the process of maturity sets in, you don't need God to do the miraculous for you the same way it was needed when you were immature.

See, Christians who are always running around looking for miraculous manifestations through the gift of others to enable them to hear from God rather than as an outgrowth of their own walk with God simply have not grown up yet spiritually. It's interesting that when a person first gets saved, God often does a miracle or two in that person's life. A marriage may be miraculously saved and turned around. A specific prayer is answered, a sickness gets healed, a job or money comes in out of nowhere.

But let's say that new Christian does very little over the next ten years to nourish and grow his miraculously restored marriage. Can he expect God to keep doing miracles to rescue his marriage when he is not growing and maturing as he should?

Or to put it another way, can a ten-year-old boy expect to just sit in a high chair and wait for his mother to spoon-feed him? No, after ten years he ought to be able to pick up a spoon and feed himself. Maturity automatically changes the nature of the relationship.

So while God may have miraculously given you a job when you were first saved, today He expects you to go job hunting. When you grow up as a Christian you don't need special revelatory signs to keep you going.

Paul says in 13:12 that we are now looking in a mirror dimly, but someday we will see face-to-face. Most people think this means when we see Jesus in heaven. But I don't think that's what Paul has in mind. The Bible says that Moses spoke face-to-face with God here on earth. Moses knew God so intimately that God spoke to him like two friends having a conversation.

You know what happens to your bathroom mirror when the shower is on. The steam from the hot water covers the glass and dims your vision. But when you turn off the water and wipe the mirror, you can see clearly because the obstruction has been removed.

When you draw close to Jesus Christ and remove the steamy obstruction of worldliness and sin, you come before Him face-to-face. When you look into His face and He looks into your face, then you will say you don't need the miraculous revelatory gifts of others anymore because of your face-to-face relationship with the miraculous One.

But when you don't see Jesus face-to-face, you have to turn to something or someone else to solve your problems and meet your needs. When you don't see Jesus face-to-face, you have to go to one conference after another, one meeting after another, seeking one experience after another.

But when you see Jesus face-to-face, when you grow up in Him, He is your conference center, your meeting, and your experience. Jesus will be your victory, your sufficiency. You may still get a miracle, but then it's a bonus.

# EXPERIENCING THE SPIRIT'S LANGUAGE

I hope you got the point I've been trying to make throughout this chapter: Don't look for the gift of tongues—or any gift, for that matter. Look for Jesus Christ, because when you see Him face-to-face, you will have all you need:

1. Perhaps you're like a lot of Christians who feel a little nervous and uneasy when the subject of tongues is mentioned. But since tongues is a gift of the Spirit, we need to deal with what the Bible says about it. If this is the first time you've ever really tackled this issue biblically, ask the Holy Spirit to illumine your mind to His truth.

2. You may belong to another group of Christians—those who have been made to feel a little less "with it" spiritually because they have not had a certain spiritual experience. If that's your feeling, you need to thank the Lord for the spiritual gift or gifts His Holy Spirit has chosen to give you and not allow either yourself or others to play the comparison game.

3. First Corinthians 13 is a great corrective to many of the spiritual excesses to which we humans are prone. If you want to do a checkup on the quality of your spiritual life, lay it alongside this chapter—but be careful, because the Spirit may want to do a powerful work of grace in you!

4. Is there an area of your life where you are sort of limping along, hoping that God will somehow pull off a miracle to fix things? Then let me say in love that you need to wake up and start doing what you know God wants you to do. The Spirit will give you the power, but He won't move your feet for you.

# CHAPTER EIGHTEEN

# EXPERIENCING THE SPIRIT'S SURPRISES

During the first week of October 1995, our church in Dallas dedicated its new worship center with a week-long series of meetings.

One of our guest speakers for the week was my good friend Dr. Joseph Stowell, president of the Moody Bible Institute in Chicago. Dr. Stowell brought a great message, but what was interesting was that he started out by saying he didn't apologize for the biblical text he was going to use, because he didn't believe God gave it to us for just one week out of the year.

Dr. Stowell's text that night was Matthew 1, the Christmas story of Jesus' birth. I like what he said, because I want to use Matthew 1 as the basis for our final study in this book on the Holy Spirit, and I don't want to apologize either!

## THE SPIRIT'S GREATEST SURPRISE

I have read the Christmas story in Matthew a thousand times, and you probably have too. But as I was reading it again for this chapter, I was reminded in a new way that the events of Jesus' birth were instigated and orchestrated by the Holy Spirit.

Matthew began his account by cutting right to the heart of the story: Mary was "with child by the Holy Spirit" (v. 18). This stupendous, never-before-heard-of and never-to-be-repeated fact was confirmed to Joseph by an angel in verse 20. Mary's conception was "of the Holy Spirit."

The greatest miracle in history was the result of the Holy Spirit's activity. I am sure we would agree that a pregnant virgin is indeed a miracle. Miracles do happen, and the reason is that God the Holy Spirit is real and is at work in the world. Whenever the Spirit shows up, the miraculous is possible.

So in the final chapter of this section on the Spirit's provisions, I want to consider with you how we can experience the miracles, or what I call the surprises, of the Holy Spirit. Now let me say right off I am not talking about presuming on God or demanding something from Him because you named it and claimed it. Nor am I speaking of the gift of miracles.

That's the kind of thing I addressed in chapter 17 when we talked about those who are always running after the miraculous and needing a miracle a day to prop up their faith. The danger of saying that is that someone may conclude, "Oh, I get it, Tony. You don't believe in the miraculous. You don't think Christians should expect anything from God but the ordinary."

If that is the impression you got from the previous chapter, it's a false one. We serve the God of the extraordinary. The Holy Spirit has unlimited power, but He exercises it according to His timetable and agenda, not ours. And He wants us to seek Him, not just His goodies.

That's the basic difference between what I was talking about in the last chapter and the stuff we're going to talk about in this one. But let there be no question that I believe in the miraculous.

In fact, one of my concerns for the body of Christ is that when you look at the great God we serve, it's a tragedy that so many of us live such predictable lives. We operate by a predictable theology that allows no room for the Holy Spirit's surprises. Too many of us would be hard put to remember the last time the Holy Spirit did anything out of the ordinary for us.

That's tragic because the Holy Spirit's presence guarantees that we are not limited to the ordinary or the natural. I got happy as I was reading the Christmas story because I realized again that the same Holy Spirit who conceived a child in the womb of a virgin is living in you and me. The Holy Spirit is a miraculous Person, and He always changes the equation because nothing is impossible with God.

So let's see what God's Word has to say about the miracles of the Spirit. I need to begin by defining my terms. A miracle is the action of God that interrupts the normal course of events and produces a powerful and/or unusual result that would not have occurred otherwise. I call them the Spirit's surprises because a miracle is out of the ordinary. It is God's surprising power at work.

I recently saw a good example of God's miracle power at work in our fellowship through a couple who were told by the doctor that they could not have children. They adopted a baby, only to find out two days after the adoption that the wife was pregnant. I know many other Christian couples could give similar testimony. It looks like the Holy Spirit is still in the business of doing miracles in the womb when it fits God's purposes!

That was certainly the case with Mary and Joseph. Of course her problem was not the inability to conceive. She was a virgin. There was no human possibility of conception, so her child would not come through the normal course of events. Mary's life would be infused with power from above, the power of the Holy Spirit. When you have the Holy Spirit, you have the Person behind the miraculous activity that breaks the norm.

## THE REASONS FOR MIRACLES

I said above that the Holy Spirit doesn't do miracles on demand. His miracles are always purposeful—according to *His* purpose. The Spirit of God never does a miracle just to show off, or because He is in a miracle-working mood. From God's vantage point, miracles are always well calculated.

### Gospel Opportunities

One reason for miracles is to open a greater opportunity for the gospel of Jesus Christ. Miracles can be used to open people's ears to the gospel. The angel told Joseph concerning Jesus' birth: "She will bear a Son; and you shall call His name Jesus, for it is He who will save His people from their sins" (Matthew 1:21).

The Holy Spirit conceived a baby in the virgin's womb because a Savior was needed to pay for our sins. So God performed the miracle of the Virgin Birth to accomplish His purposes in bringing about mankind's salvation.

Many of the miracles Jesus and the apostles performed in the New Testament, such as the healing of the blind man in John 9, opened hearts to the gospel and in many cases resulted in great numbers coming to the Lord. The miracle of Pentecost is a classic example of this purpose for miracles.

### Bringing Christ Glory

Another reason the Holy Spirit does miracles is to bring greater glory to Jesus Christ.

One of the great problems with people who want "a miracle a day" is that what they want is often unrelated to God's glory. They only want the miracle for themselves. That explains why Jesus was so upset when He healed the ten lepers and only one came back to praise and glorify Him (Luke 17:11–19).

Jesus asked, "Were there not ten cleansed? But the nine—where are they?" (v. 17). The other nine took their miracle and ran. They did not have time to bring God glory. Our priorities are badly misplaced when God gets shoved into the background. The Spirit interrupts the normal course of events with a miracle when God's glory can be enhanced.

That's why it is important that we live for the glory of God. The more glory God can get through you, the more miracles He can do for you and through you. Watch out for people who invite you to their church meeting so you can see a miracle. What they ought to be inviting you to do is live for the glory of God.

If you live for the glory of God, you are a candidate for a miracle—because His own glory is what God is after too. In the book of Acts, the apostles were doing one miracle after another. Read Acts 3:12–13 carefully and you'll see that God was getting all the glory. Acts 4:21 underscores this by telling us that when the people saw these miracles taking place, they glorified God too.

Matthew 15:29–31 gives us another beautiful picture of this purpose being fulfilled. Great multitudes of sick folk were brought to Jesus, and He healed them all. Verse 31 says, "The multitude marveled as they saw the dumb speaking, the crippled restored, and the lame walking, and the blind seeing; and they glorified the God of Israel."

## To Fulfill God's Plan

The Holy Spirit also performs miracles to fulfill God's sovereign plan. We can see this in Matthew 1:22–23:

> Now all this took place that what was spoken by the Lord through the prophet might be fulfilled, saying, "Behold, the virgin shall be with child, and shall bear a Son, and they shall call His name Immanuel," which translated means, "God with us."

Jesus was the fulfillment of God's divine plan. Mary was part of a miracle that occurred to help fulfill the plan God had determined from eternity past and had prophesied many centuries earlier in the Old Testament. The Holy Spirit does miracles to achieve God's program.

So let me say again that when you are interested in the proclamation of the gospel, living for the glory of God, and committed to the plan of God, you are a great candidate for a miracle. Mary's pregnancy was part of God's greater plan. To the degree that we are in God's plan, the Holy Spirit is free to bring Him glory and transform the souls of people through His miraculous activity in our lives.

## THE PREREQUISITE FOR MIRACLES

The simplest way I can state this is to say that the prerequisite for miracles is faith.

Now some of my conservative, noncharismatic friends will point to those cases where people are told the reason they weren't healed or whatever is that they didn't have enough faith.

I know some people use this argument to explain why their prayers or laying on of hands or other miracle-seeking ministry didn't work. So let me say that I am not talking about using faith as an excuse for a miracle that did *not* happen. I'm talking about biblical faith as a necessary ingredient for a miracle *to* happen. God does not produce miracles merely because we have faith; but He also does not usually perform miracles in the absence of faith.

Luke's version of the Christmas story illustrates what I mean. Mary's relative Elizabeth, and Elizabeth's husband, Zacharias, were godly people who were very old, barren, and well beyond childbearing years. Yet an angel appeared to Zacharias in the course of his priestly duties and announced that Elizabeth was going to have a son (Luke 1:13). We are talking miracle here.

Now Zack knew his physical condition and Elizabeth's, so he questioned the angel's word—whereupon he learned that he was speaking to Gabriel, who had come straight from the presence of God (vv. 18–19). What's more, because Zacharias did not believe in the Holy Spirit's ability to do a miracle in Elizabeth's body, he got to spend the entire pregnancy in silence (v. 20).

In other words, Zack's lack of faith disqualified him from the full enjoyment of participating in the miraculous activity of God. Zacharias's response did not change what God planned to do, but it sure changed his enjoyment of what God planned to do.

What a contrast when we come to Mary later in Luke 1. When she asked the angel, "How can this be, since I am a virgin?" (v. 34), this was not an expression of doubt like Zacharias's question. Mary knew it was impossible for her to get pregnant. Besides, the angel hadn't yet told her how all of this would come about.

But notice that when Mary is told this will be accomplished by the Holy Spirit (Luke 1:35), and that "nothing will be impossible with God" (v. 37), her immediate response is a declaration of submissive faith: "Behold, the bondslave of the Lord; be it done to me according to your word" (v. 38).

Mary believed the Word of God over and against her physical circumstances. She did not know how, but she did know who. When you and I are properly related to God, we don't have to know how God is going to do what He wants to do. We just have to know that it is God who is going to do it.

See, too many of us are always trying to figure God out. But God has already made it clear that He is "unfigureoutable." I know that's not normally a word, but it is here.

God is "unfigureoutable." That is, He does not always make clear the methodology He will use when the Holy Spirit performs His miraculous activity through His people to accomplish God's glory and program.

Mary's question was, "How is this possible?" When the angel answered, "The Holy Ghost is going to do this," her response was not, "I don't believe that. This has never happened before. I want a doctor to substantiate it." She did not ask for any of that. She simply said, "Holy Ghost? That's all I need to know."

When the Holy Ghost is involved, God is not necessarily going to use a method you are familiar with. He is not necessarily going to use a normal means. So stop trying to figure out how God is going to do everything and be content with this knowledge: "Holy Ghost? That's all I need to know."

Consider three more examples of how people's faith became the prerequisite for a miracle. They are all in Matthew 9, a remarkable display of Jesus' power. Notice what He said in each case:

Jesus seeing their faith said to the paralytic, "Take courage, My son, your sins are forgiven. . . . Rise, take up your bed, and go home." (vv. 2, 6)

"Daughter, take courage; your faith has made you well." (v. 22)

Then He touched their eyes, saying, "Be it done to you according to your faith." (v. 29)

Why don't more of us see supernatural intervention like this? We don't expect it. We do not believe that the God for whom nothing is impossible can work out our meager situation.

Now again, we're not talking about naming and claiming miracles from God. So let me separate faith from presumption once more. Presumption says God must do it because we say so. Really? God doesn't have to do anything. We presume upon Him when we take that approach.

Now let me move quickly to head off what may be another false assumption you could draw from what I just said. That is, to avoid presumption we should never ask God boldly for what we need if we believe it is within His will to grant it. You'll never hear me say that.

Look again at the examples I just cited in Matthew 9. In each case, the people involved approached Jesus with great boldness. We know from Mark 2:2–5 that the paralytic's friends took the roof off the house to get to Jesus. The woman pursued Him in a crowd and grabbed His robe. And Mark 10:46–52 says one of the blind men, Bartimaeus, yelled his head off for a miracle.

No, faith does not have to be timid. Faith says God can do it. That's His ability. But faith also says God does *the thing I am believing Him to do*. Do you see the difference? I say this because we have a generation of Christians whose theology is unrelated to life. They go around saying God can do anything, but they cannot point to anything God is doing for them.

It's because their theology is in the abstract. They have heard it preached somewhere that God can do anything, but they have never said, "God, I believe that You are great enough to do something for me. Whether You choose to act is Your prerogative, but I am believing You and counting on You."

Jesus did not do many miracles in His hometown "because of their unbelief" (Matthew 13:58). Could it be that we are missing out on many of the things the Holy Spirit wants to do for us because of our lack of faith?

You say, "How can I know when I am trusting God?" When you act on what He says even when you can't figure out how He is going to do it. You know you are trusting God by where your feet are taking you. Trust goes beyond a feeling.

Faith is Peter stepping out on the water and not just theologizing about God's ability to keep Him afloat. He could have stayed in the boat and said, "I know He's able to keep me from drowning. I know He can make a way. I know that He can hold me up."

That's faith theologizing, but that's not a working faith (James 2:14). Faith is stepping out on the water. It's believing that God not only *can*, but that if it pleases Him to do so He *will*. You know you are trusting by the way you are walking and not by the theology discussions you are having.

We know Joseph had faith because after he heard from the angel he took Mary as his wife (Matthew 1:24). Before this, he was getting ready to divorce her quietly so he would not hurt her reputation or his integrity.

But when Joseph heard from heaven, he said, "I believe God so completely that I am going to go through with this marriage." Joseph believed God, and he acted on it. So did Mary. In her Magnificat (Luke 1:46–55), Mary glorified God for this miraculous thing that was going to happen to her.

The prerequisite for the Holy Spirit's surprises is always faith. You must not only believe that He can, you must believe that He does. Then the only question is, "Will He at this time for you?"

Now I wouldn't be honest with you if I did not tell you that a miracle may not happen to you. Unless somebody tells you that, you are not getting the whole story. Miracles are God's prerogative. Our job is to live by faith and get ourselves in a position where the Holy Spirit is free to work His miraculous power in our lives.

## THE PREPARATION FOR MIRACLES

There ought to be more miraculous testimonies coming out of the body of Christ about what the Holy Spirit is doing among us. I don't necessarily mean big miracles. For some of us, it would be a miracle to get a good night's sleep, because we are overwhelmed by life's circumstances. Whatever the need, I am convinced that the miraculous will be involved when the Holy Spirit is at work, but we have to get prepared.

How do you prepare yourself for the Spirit to do the miraculous? There's an important clue in Matthew 1:19 and Luke 1:28. Joseph and Mary were candidates for miracles because they were righteous people. The Holy Spirit was free to do His Holy Spirit thing because their passion was living for God.

If you and I are to be candidates for the Holy Spirit's miracles, then living for God and pleasing Him must become the passion of our lives. I don't mean we have to be perfect. I mean that when we mess up, we fix it up as soon as possible so that we are in line with God. The drive of Joseph's and Mary's lives was honoring God in their attitudes and their actions. They had a passion for holiness.

That means if you need a miracle, the way to get it is not to go miracle-hunting—any more than the way to receive a spiritual gift is to go gift-hunting. Instead, put this principle down in your book: Passion for Jesus Christ is the key to miracles by the Holy Spirit.

The way to engage the Holy Spirit's miracle power is not to go miracle-hunting, or even Holy-Ghost-hunting. The way to engage the Spirit's power is to develop a passion for Jesus Christ. There is a direct correlation between the fervor with which you pursue your walk with Christ and the power you experience from the Holy Spirit.

What happens to so many of us as Christians is that we lose our passion for Christ. When we lose that, we lose our access to the power of the Holy Spirit. Remember that one of our foundational passages for this book is John 16:14, where we read that the Holy Spirit's task—and His passion—is to glorify Jesus Christ.

So if Satan wants to keep you from experiencing the power of the Spirit, all he has to do is lower the flame on your "Christ burner." All Satan has to do is cool your passion for Christ, and the loss of power will follow.

One reason new Christians often see a lot of miracles is that they are newly fallen in love with Jesus Christ, and the presence of the Holy Spirit rides on the back of that passion. If you want to see the Spirit's miraculous intervention in your life, then you must pursue a passion for Jesus Christ.

Let me tell you what a passion for Christ is not. It is not simply academic knowledge of the Bible. At Oak Cliff Bible Fellowship, we love the Bible. We preach it and teach it and try to enforce it. We do everything we can to honor the Word. But it is possible to know the Book and not know the Lord. It is possible to know theology and be spiritually cold inside.

Knowing the Bible is necessary to having a passion for the Lord, but knowing the Bible is not *equal* to a passion for the Lord. Our problem is not loving the Bible too much. Our problem is loving Christ too little. You can read the Bible every day without a passion for Christ.

Now I know that *passion* is an emotionally charged word. I chose it on purpose. God does not want our limp, lifeless religious activity. You can go to church fifty-two Sundays and fifty-two Wednesday nights a year and still be as cold as a doorknob on a winter day.

The Holy Spirit wants to cultivate within us a warm, throbbing passion for Jesus Christ. That's why Romans 6:17 talks about obeying the Lord from the heart, not merely as an exercise in external religious activity.

Now let me tell you something about passion. Anybody who has loved anybody else passionately knows that passion left uncultivated will die. Some of our marriages can testify to this truth. Passion that is not cultivated will die.

Two people can start out a marriage being passionately in love. But if that passion is neglected and dies,
something happens to their relationship. They may still
be doing married-people types of things. He may still go
to work and bring the money home. She may still cook
and clean. But a husband and wife can do all these things
without any passion.

That's because passion is not cultivated simply by
performance. It is cultivated by performance that has relationship as its goal. You can go to work and bring the
money home simply because it's a job and you know if
you don't pay the bills, you will have no place to stay.

If you want Holy Ghost power and Holy Ghost miracles, you must develop Jesus Christ passion, which means
you do the right things with the right goal in mind. I can't
tell you how many wives and husbands have sat before
me in my office and the husband says, "Hey, look. I do
this, this, and this."

The wife responds, "But that's not what I need."

That is a very informative statement. That wife is
saying, "What you are doing is OK, but what you are doing is not touching where my heart is aching. It's not cultivating my passion."

The same thing can happen in your relationship with
Christ. The power of the Holy Spirit is tied to a passion for
Jesus Christ. You can see a fascinating example of this
principle in reverse in Acts 19:13–16, where the seven
sons of Sceva tried to cast out demons by the power Paul
used.

They saw Paul casting out demons by the power of
God and they said, "This is good. Let's try a little of this
hocus-pocus." They tried to cast out a demon, but the demon said, "I know Jesus and I know Paul. But who are
you?" And the demon-possessed man clobbered all seven
of them.

What did Paul say? "That I may know [Christ], and
the power of His resurrection" (Philippians 3:10). Paul
was ready to forget everything else to know Christ (see
3:13). Unless the goal of your life is to know Christ, any-

thing else you do is like the husband whose efforts are OK but aren't touching his wife's heart.

In Acts 4:13–14, the Bible says that it was apparent to everyone in the Sanhedrin that the apostles had been with Jesus. They couldn't argue with the miraculous power that had been displayed through Peter and John, because the man the apostles had healed was standing there with them. The apostles' passion for Jesus had produced the miraculous.

One woman put it to her husband this way: "I would rather have you stop working two jobs, lose our house, move back to one car and an apartment, and yet have each other, than to have you work two jobs, have a house and two cars, and extra money, and yet not have each other."

## THREE CLOSING SUGGESTIONS

That's the idea. The Holy Spirit would rather see us have less performance and more passion than more performance and less passion. So let me close this chapter and the book by giving you three suggestions to help you regain or sustain your passion for Jesus Christ and thus become a candidate for the Holy Spirit's surprises.

### Time in God's Presence

First, set aside regular time for meditation in God's Word and in His presence. I did not say just read your Bible and pray. In fact, one of the signs that we are losing our passion is that all of our prayers start to sound the same.

We saw above that routine sets in when passion leaves. When you have passion, you make a way where there is no way. You come up with new ideas when you have passion. The key thing here is meditation, which we discussed in detail earlier. It's taking time to roll God's truth around in your mind, let it sink in.

When David said, "Lord, show me marvelous things in Your Law," he was not just saying, "Help me understand the Bible." He was saying, "Let me see You in Your

Word." When you sit down with your Bible or pray, God is asking you to meet with Him.

Remember we said earlier that the Holy Spirit is our Guide into a whole new realm, the spiritual realm. It is when we are in touch with the Spirit that He begins to reshape and re-create our lives and develop in us a passion for Christ. That's why, if you are trying to get a married couple to rekindle their passion for one another, you have to get them talking to one another.

I have a friend who has a cup of coffee with the Lord every morning. He sits down with his coffee and opens his Bible because the Bible is reflective of the mind of Christ, and so Christ is sitting at the table with him and they talk.

But you say, "That's just a one-way conversation." No, once you add the dynamic of meditation, you have initiated a two-way conversation. The Holy Spirit is now free to roll the truth of God through your mind. God talks to you.

### Dealing with Sin

A second way to rekindle your passions is by addressing sin forthrightly and completely. You must address sin, because when you sin against another person with whom you are in relationship, fellowship and communication are broken.

When you confess your sins and trust the blood of Jesus to forgive you and cleanse you of all unrighteousness, you are saying, "Lord Jesus, I did this and I confess it because I don't want anything to break our relationship. So I am trusting Your blood to wash me and restore our relationship." We have also talked about confession at length elsewhere, so I just want to mention and underscore it here.

### Confidence in Christ

A third means of restoring passion is to remember what we discussed above. Our confidence must be in Christ and not in our performance. Many of us believe that because we are doing the right things, Christ is happy. The Holy Spirit is satisfied.

No, it's a little trickier than that. You need to do the right things, to be sure. But you cannot *trust* your doing of the right things to give you a passionate relationship with Christ. Do you see the difference? Many of us are guilty of trusting what we do instead of trusting Christ to take the right things and make a relationship out of them.

We need to pray, "Lord Jesus, I am trusting You to bring us close together. I am trusting You to take my Bible study, my prayer, my obedience, my church membership, my ministry involvement, and all the other right things I am doing and turn those into something You can use that we might have a relationship."

Remember Jesus' good friends, Martha and Mary? In Luke 10:38–42, Martha was busy serving and getting upset at Mary because Mary spent her time in Jesus' presence instead of helping out in the kitchen. Jesus gently rebuked Martha and said that what Mary had could not be taken away from her. What Mary had was a passion for Christ. You can't let anyone take away your passion time with Christ.

Now this is interesting because of the scene that unfolds later when Lazarus, the brother of Mary and Martha, dies. When Jesus arrived, Martha ran up to Him and said, "Lord, if You had been here, my brother would not have died" (John 11:21).

Jesus responded, "I am the resurrection and the life" (v. 25). A few minutes later, Mary ran up to Jesus and said exactly the same thing that Martha had said (v. 32). Only this time, Jesus wept in response (v. 35).

What a contrast. Martha spoke to Jesus and got solid theology in response. Mary said the same thing and Jesus wept with her in her grief. Jesus listens to people He is related to.

Martha was a good woman, but she did not have Mary's passionate relationship with Jesus. Martha got theology. Mary got a miracle, because Jesus asked to be taken to the grave, and He raised Lazarus (vv. 34, 43).

The greatest church I know of in America is the Brooklyn Tabernacle in New York City. A lot has been written and broadcast about this church in recent years, but let me tell you the secret to this church's power. The secret is not on Sunday morning. The secret to the Spirit-empowered ministry of the Brooklyn Tabernacle is its Tuesday night prayer meetings, which begin at 7:00 P.M.

By 5:30 Tuesday evening, there is a line of people wrapping around the block. They are waiting to get into the prayer meeting. The church has to keep people at bay because of the number of those who want to come into the presence of God to hear from Him.

No wonder hardly a week goes by at Brooklyn Tabernacle without somebody testifying about a miracle the Holy Spirit did: a wayward child comes home, a marriage is restored, someone the doctors have given up on is healed. Every week there seems to be a new miracle because every Tuesday night there is concentrated, passionate prayer.

The secret to the ministry of Brooklyn Tabernacle is not its program; it's the members' passion to love and serve God and to be in His presence. Jesus Himself described it as loving the Lord with all of your heart and soul and mind, and loving your neighbor as yourself (Matthew 22:37–39).

Jesus Christ looks at passion like this and says to the Holy Spirit, "Let's do some miracles." I want to experience every legitimate blessing the Holy Spirit has for me. How about you?

# EXPERIENCING THE SPIRIT'S SURPRISES

**W**e've covered a lot of ground in these eighteen chapters. We've talked about a powerful Person, the Holy Spirit. So it seems appropriate that we close by preparing our hearts for Him to do whatever He wants to do in and through us:

1. Our study of Matthew 1 and Luke 1, texts usually set aside until Christmas, reminds me of something we can forget pretty easily: Since *all* Scripture is God-breathed and profitable, we can't afford to overlook or "pigeonhole" any portion if we want to know the whole counsel of God.

2. Has your spiritual life become thoroughly predictable? I'm not saying you need to seek some kind of off-the-wall experience, but you also can't afford to put the Holy Spirit in your theological box and refuse to allow Him to surprise you. He is sovereign, and you can't limit Him to the ordinary.

3. Are you a person of faith? I don't mean have you put your faith in Christ. I'm talking about the expectancy of faith that says, "Lord, I do believe. Help my unbelief." This is the flip side of the attitude that says the Holy Spirit can't do anything that doesn't fit within my comfort zone. Ask God to help you exercise the kind of faith that gets the Holy Spirit excited.

4. What surprise, what miracle, do you need the Holy Spirit to do for you? Cultivate your passion for the Savior, and you will experience the power of the Holy Spirit!

# EPILOGUE

I have attempted in these pages to focus our attention on the wonder of the Holy Spirit's work in bringing us into a life-changing experience with God. I have argued that it is our relationship with the Spirit that will determine how real, vibrant, and powerful our Christian life turns out to be.

There is no preacher, teacher, miracle worker, or writer who can substitute for the role of the Spirit in the life of a believer and the ministry of a local church. It is precisely because the Spirit has either been marginalized or made into a "celebrity" that the essence of His work is so often missed.

Why are there so many defeated Christians, so many dead churches, and so many believers whose lives and witness have been wrecked by things such as moral failure, divorce, or financial scandal? It cannot be attributed simply to the wickedness of the world, because the One who is in us is greater than the one who is in the world (1 John 4:4).

It is my conviction that we have lost the centrality of the Spirit's work of bringing God's people into an experiential encounter with Him. Until this is fixed, nothing else we do will matter. Like the missing battery in a car, the absence of the Spirit's life in our lives makes the rest of the "parts" of the car irrelevant. No battery, no power; no power, no forward progress.

With all the churches and supporting Christian ministries available to us today, how can we be failing so miserably to turn our world upside down for Christ? Answer: the absence of a meaningful relationship with the Holy Spirit. Until His power is unleashed, everything else we do will be empty and fruitless. Until and unless the words of the prophet Zechariah become the model of our hearts and the modus operandi of our lives, that it is "Not by might nor by power, but by My Spirit, says the Lord of hosts" (4:6), we will not discover or experience the glory of what it means to be children of the living God.

It is my hope and prayer that God will ignite in us a passion for a relationship with His Spirit that is so deep and intense that we will suffer any inconvenience, endure any trial, and face any challenge to make sure that we cultivate and experience an intimate walk with Him.

# INDEX OF SCRIPTURE

# INDEX OF SUBJECTS